W9-AEV-978

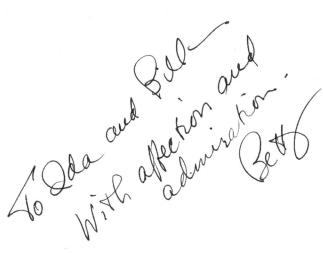
To Ida and Bill —
With affection and
admiration.
Betty

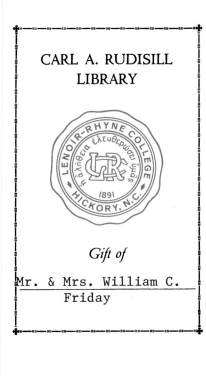

Beyond the Traditional Family

Betty Polisar Reigot is a professional writer whose research interests encompass the physical and natural sciences and their relationship to human behavior, culture, and communication. She received her Bachelor of Arts degree from Smith College and continued graduate studies in psychology and statistics, physiology, research techniques, animal communication, the nature of communication, and orality and literacy. She has authored nonfiction books for children for the past 17 years and has taught and lectured at North Carolina county school conferences (1989–1990), Herricks School District, Long Island, NY (1984–1985), Fordham University (1984), Teachers College, Columbia University (1983), and New York City public schools (1979–1985). Her experience includes coordinating proposals and grants with heads of the Departments of Sociology, Psychology, and Education at Hofstra and Adelphi Universities and New York State University at Stony Brook as the Deputy Director of the Institute for Research and Evaluation, Inc., Hempstead, New York (1970–1973). Prior to that, she was assistant to the Executive Vice President of *The New York Times* (1966–1971). Her current memberships include The NY Academy of Sciences; Authors Guild; Directors Council, National Humanities Center, RTP, NC; Arts Center and Womens Center in Chapel Hill, North Carolina.

Rita K. Spina, PhD, has had 25 years of professional experience as Director of the Psychological Evaluation and Research Center and Assistant Professor at Hofstra University, Chair of School Psychology in the Kings Park Schools, New York, and as a private clinician working with families and couples. She holds a Diplomate in Administrative Psychology and a PhD in School Community Psychology. Dr. Spina presently resides in North Carolina, where she participates as a member of the Board of Directors of the Chatham Coalition for Adolescent Health, and is President of The Home Care Connection, an innovative community organization delivering health-related services. She is also a creative structural artist, mother, and grandmother.

Beyond the Traditional Family

Voices of Diversity

Betty Polisar Reigot

Rita K. Spina, PhD

SPRINGER PUBLISHING COMPANY

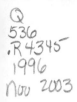
Springer Publishing Company, Inc.
536 Broadway
New York, NY 10012-3955

Cover design by Tom Yabut
Production Editor: Joyce Noulas

96 97 98 99 00 / 5 4 3 2 1

Library of Congress Cataloging-in-Publication Data

Reigot, Betty Polisar.
    Beyond the traditional family : voices of diversity / Betty
Polisar Reigot, Rita K. Spina.
        p. cm.
    Includes bibliographical references and index.
    ISBN 0-8261-9030-8
    1. Family—United States. 2. Family—United States—Case studies.
3. Parents—United States—Interviews. I. Spina, Rita K.
II. Title.
HQ536.R4345   1995
306.85'0973—dc20   95-31402
                                                                    CIP

Printed in the United States of America

For my mother and father, Pauline and Joseph-Marco.

BPR

For Larry, whose script for living became the foundation of
our family
and
For Susan, David, Beth, and Nancy, who live out the model.

RKS

Contents

Preface

I met Rita Spina in 1963—we were both white, middle-class, college-educated Americans in our mid-thirties and about to be divorced. We now realize we had divorced more than our spouses. We had separated from long-held and long-endured traditions of marriage and family.

It was difficult to break marital vows as we did. Questions of economics, what the neighbors would think, whether things would get better so that the family could stay together, and other worries had been inhibiting factors for breaking up our families.

Society was not friendly to divorced women then. Banks and merchants gave credit grudgingly, if at all. We were regarded sometimes with pity, sometimes with disdain, and, too often, with condescension. But there was no time for dwelling on such attitudes. Supporting and taking care of ourselves and our children consumed all our attention.

But by getting out, Rita and I hoped we would be able to preserve our vision of what family was meant to be. We didn't give up a dream; we were searching to realize it. That we each subsequently approached an ideal in our second marriages was our good fortune.

During that period of our lives, Rita pursued a career in psychology, taught and trained other psychologists at Hofstra University, worked within the local school system, and maintained a clinical practice. Meanwhile, I slowly made my way, first as an assistant in the executive branch of *The New York Times*, then as a copy editor for a small firm, then editor, and finally as a non-fiction writer in the fields of the natural and physical sciences.

After many years in our separate worlds, we renewed our

earlier friendship when we moved to nearby towns. We realized that we still had similar concerns, such as the nature of human beings, the complexities of modern life, and what life would be like for our children and our children's children.

We, who had been raised in the typical family of our generation and regretfully abandoned its entrenched precepts, found ourselves yet again living through changes in family life. That struck a resonant chord.

Although, for many, the desire for family appears to be as strong as ever, the context in which this can be achieved is new in human history. Technological advances in physiology and other life sciences make procreation a possibility for those men and women who want children but are unable to conceive. Until recently, they were obliged to accept the unhappy consequences of reproductive fluctuations, or individual deficits, or simply caprices of nature. The average person had rather fixed ideas about having a child based on two concepts: what we knew about human reproduction, and what we believed would meet with society's approval. Ethical and religious considerations have governed our mores for centuries and have been anything but capricious. In today's world, new domestic configurations and attitudes about family are emerging.

We were drawn to the recognition that ever-increasing numbers of people make the decision to have at least one child, even though their life-styles fall outside conventional patterns. As this remarkable century nears its close, an evolutionary change is underway at an accelerated pace. For Rita and me, these were compelling reasons to explore what is going on. We had no idea what we might find.

Acknowledgments

Many helped us along the way. Timothy Carey, MD, physician and friend, introduced us to the infertility clinic at the University of North Carolina Medical School; Shirley Hanson, RN, PhD, author and leader in family nursing, saw the need for such a book, as did Challie O'Neal, RN, and Sharon Belcher, RN, who conduct workshops for expectant parents; Susan Leslie, MSW, informed us about adoption agency policies in the greater New York area; Beth Kaplan Westbrook, PsyD, Cara Rosenthal, Jill Block, MSW, Jan Greenblatt, PhD, John Lass, and Diane Turner all uncovered interviewees in various parts of the United States.

David Frankstone, Esq., ascertained the legal grounds for quoting our oral historians and insuring their anonymity; Isadore Rossman, MD, PhD, offered insightful contextual suggestions; Jonathan Polisar offered general reader reaction that steered us away from dry academic accounts. Many colleagues and friends read portions of the manuscript, commented thoughtfully and candidly, and urged us to push ahead. Larry Spina frequently capped our lengthy but exhilarating working hours with culinary treats, and his support was constant. He is missed.

Paula Schwartz, EdD, helped greatly in keeping the diverse strands of this work separated and then appropriately combined to explicate the main theme we were attempting.

We were fortunate to have the competence and patience of Evie Ward who transcribed lengthy audiotapes of the interviews. Harriet Martin made the preparation of the manuscript infinitely easier through her literacy on and off the computer.

We are especially indebted to Herb Bailey, former director of the Princeton University Press, for his advice on the structure and logic of the book. He and his wife, Betty, added an important element of enthusiasm to our efforts to reveal a subject initially as unfamiliar to them as it was to us. Their steady interest in our work spirited us along to the book's completion.

Working with Bill Tucker, our editor, was a pleasure. His belief that this book fit into a much larger picture of ongoing changes in family life, his critical judgment, and his gentle yet convincing approach to the handling of the multiple subjects easily spanned generational views.

Last, but foremost, we wish to honor the major contributors to this book: the parents. We are grateful for the time they gave us and for the opportunity to have a close and most intimate view of how and why they chose to create a family that fit their life-styles, values, and deep-rooted desires. We wish them continued joy in their parenting efforts, good luck, and greater recognition of their courage.

Introduction

1

This is a book by and about men and women who have elected to have children even though their situations fall outside the traditional definition of family.

When the authors were growing up, custom dictated that a man and a woman marry first, live together, and then have children. If there were other members of the household, they were usually related by blood or by marriage. This was the traditional family we were each born into approximately 65 years ago. At the time, there were almost 123 million people in the United States of which there were 18.4 million families consisting of a husband and wife and one or more children under 21 years of age (U.S. Bureau of the Census, 1930).

By 1963, we discovered we were also members of a newly sprouting population in the United States—The Divorced. There were approximately 45 million families then. Out of all marriages reported in 1960, 2.2% ended in divorce (U.S. Bureau of the Census, 1960). In 30 years, that rate more than doubled (U.S. Bureau of the Census, 1994).

In time, we each remarried. Remarrying placed us and our husbands among the couples who found themselves to be step-parents in recombinant families. A new category of family was beginning to swell. By 1980, there were close to 4 million step-families. Within 10 years, that number increased to over 5 million (U.S. Bureau of the Census, 1990).

Over the course of only a few decades, departures from the prototypical family unit have gone increasing distances. The

1

old social definition of the family no longer implies a particular kind of biologic, economic, or gender context. Parenting roles have broken through many traditional barriers. The variations have become far more complex than the original theme.

Since the 1960s, assorted modes of living reflect the changes taking place. By 1980, the U.S. Bureau of Census officially stopped defining the "Head of Household" as the husband (Rix, 1990). In the 1990 Census under Household and Family Composition, there was a new category: "Unmarried Partner Households" which includes almost 3.2 million persons, of which approximately 3 million are male and female partners, 81 thousand are both male, and 64 thousand are both female (U.S. Bureau of the Census, 1990). In 1993, there were over 3.5 million unmarried couples of which about 35% were unmarried couples with children (National Center for Health Statistics, 1994; Tauber, 1991; U.S. Bureau of the Census, 1993).

There have been innumberable articles in professional and popular magazines, frequent pieces in newspapers, and much commentary on radio and television concerning the development of alternative family situations. A number of books by behavioral scientists present and evaluate certain of the nontraditional parents whose numbers are growing. Some examine the large number of single women who choose to have a child without a permanent, intimate, or even any relationship with the father of the child. Several books recognize and encourage the emotional involvement of fathers in the development of their children. Gays and lesbians who do not wish to be denied the experience of parenting, grandparents who have assumed the role of primary caretakers, parents contending with HIV-positive children, and parents who achieve parenthood via in vitro fertilization have all been written about and talked about. Many of us now know people in at least one of these categories.

To date, there appears to be nothing in the literature that groups the variety of present-day alternative families within one volume. Society is presently confronted with a major paradigm shift in the social history of the human race. The personal stories offered here represent a significant development in the evolution of human behavior and of that closest of relationships—parent and child.

The decision to have a child in a situation other than the traditional family setting is regarded with alarm by many people in this country. Fears and doubts about the future of the family leave many confused and anxious. Forsaking so fundamental a structure erodes established convictions that span important human concerns and activities—education, religion, sexuality, the arts, and politics among others—sapping the inherent strengths of our culture and our society. Mutual benefits historically derived from the interaction of the individual, the family, and society are at risk.

This view was expressed by a Vice President of the United States who publicly deplored the erosion of family values by citing a character in a television sitcom who was scripted to elect to have a child out of wedlock.

Individualism is an American trait that is difficult at times to balance with the cooperative needs of the larger community. There are those who are challenged and exhilarated by the range of new possibilities. These people are not averse to breaking through a wall of hypocrisy to establish who they are, what they want, and what makes a family. Some have found ways to politicize their personal beliefs. Others have simply devised a method to get what they want, and do so because it is possible.

Sperm donors, techniques of artificial insemination, infertility clinicians, and social and educational services that offer the chance for better lives to adolescent mothers and their offspring are some of the available resources which now flourish and make possible what recently was not. Greater psychological and emotional freedom permit the individual to challenge the strong opposition to breaking away from the time-honored tradition of the creation of a family.

The diversity of personalities and situations presented in the oral histories that follow seems to render more remarkable the common threads that bind these interviews and these people together: the desire, indeed the need, to have a child; to experience the mutual love and dependency between parent or caregiver and child; to delight in watching a live, highly complex organism that you love, grow and develop; to know that you and this other human being whom you chose to incorporate into your life are connected throughout your lives for better or worse. Universal and intimate, these experiences transcend not only traditional family structures but the various forms non-traditional families take as well. This is why we chose to present these different oral histories all together.

Having a child is for many the ultimate bond with another—a deep-felt wish, a human impulse, even a fierce desire for parenthood. Many will have this one way or another. New kinds of domestic relationships are springing up in different parts of the country. This became the initial focus of our undertaking.

At the start of our collaboration, we first contacted professionals who might inform us as well as lead us to those with stories to tell. We spoke with doctors in charge of infertility clinics, nurses who counsel expectant mothers and fathers, personnel from adoption agencies, psychologists, social workers, and lawyers. And we spoke with others who knew somebody who knew somebody.

In little time we were introduced to interviewees. What they said breathed life into our project, propelling it along and changing our initial curiosity into an absorbing adventure, expanding our views.

Who are these people? Why have they done this? How is it working for them? Any adults committed to and involved in the daily responsibilities of raising a child and living in a newly configured household were likely candidates for these inquiries. Each told his or her story with extraordinary candor, recounting authentic personal experiences to two interested strangers.

Some are married; some are not. Some are single and male; many are single and female; and some are homosexual. Some biological mothers and fathers are included because of their special situations. There are also those who have adopted children under unusual circumstances. And there are some who have turned to in vitro fertilization and artificial insemination when sexual intercourse was unproductive or desirable partners were unobtainable. Some who were once traditional parents are now full-time substitute parents to their grandchildren.

Observing individual waves does not reveal the impact of a sea change which runs deep, profoundly stirs the waters, and is capable of reconfiguring the landscape. When different groups emerge from the sea of humanity and crash against tradition, they are collectively capable of altering the structure of family life.

Our book is divided into sections comprised of oral histories which reflect various lifestyles. Each category is introduced by an overview. Our interviews, of course, are not offered as a scientific sample, but rather as illustrative of some of the developments in family life in this country. Names and locations have been changed to preserve anonymity. In all other respects the stories have been left to tell themselves.

A caring, loving start in life that enables a child to reach his or her fullest potential is probably the most important gift one human being can try to give another. The rewards are usually reciprocal and are, indirectly, perhaps the most meaningful gifts individuals can bestow on society. Although it may be difficult to define what constitutes a family today, it is easy to see that the parents who speak to us in this book have given much thought to their individual values and priorities. They work hard to create a sense of family for themselves and the children in their lives.

Hear them speak.

PART I

Single Mothers by Choice

Does the female anatomy govern an essentially womanly desire to have a child—and must that event be wrapped in the traditional family package regarded by many as the only true manifestation of "family values?" It is a major question which ultimately affects men as well as women, and maybe children most of all.

Not every woman subscribes to an imperative that she must bear children. Nevertheless, those with strong maternal drives arrive at the decision to mother a child for various reasons and in various ways.

Young women, both hetero- and homosexual, feel empowered by the growing equality between men and women. That, plus feminism and a yearning to be independent impelled many to pursue careers after schooling. Many found out that in realizing one ambition time was robbing them of their bodies' ability to realize another dream—to have a child. The determination to have the experience of giving birth while it still may be possible often takes on a primal urgency. Technology and attitude combine to make the father, albeit not the sperm, superfluous. A few women simply choose to go it alone because they prefer the exclusivity of bonding with a child without having to be concerned about the other parent. Other women do so because they have not found a compatible spouse.

The choices for bringing this deeply embedded wish to frui-
tion include engaging an accommodating male friend, lover,
or husband on his way out of the marriage, or artificial insemination either with sperm from a known donor or an
anonymous one from a sperm bank. Adoption is another major option.

Nineteen percent of all women in the United States over 18
were reported unmarried in 1990 (U.S. Bureau of the Census,
1990). As of 1992, almost one out of four single women 18
years of age and over, had children (U.S. Bureau of the Census, 1993). The Census Bureau did not isolate the number of
these women who were single mothers by choice.

Single mothers have entered the American family scene and
while there are still—and probably always will be—millions
who miss the absence of a father's continuing presence in the
family configuration, thousands of women are now having
and raising a child without him.

Marjorie

2

Marjorie is married and lives in a big house in Maryland. During the interview, her daughter was attending school, and her husband, a writer, was in his study we were told, though occasionally there were noises in the kitchen beyond view. The walls and halls are lined with books. Pictures and photographs add to the atmosphere of warmth and comfort in an amply and tastefully furnished home. Marjorie is 40 years old, has soft brown hair and eyes to match. She wears glasses and a hearing aid, is gentle in manner and pretty.

When I was 9 years old I fell in love with two 4-year olds who didn't live far from us. They were twin boys of friends of my parents. Their mother would let me come and take them to the playground and babysit them—not late at night, just short outings. They were darling. That was the first I remember of consciously looking forward to having kids. For many years I was sure I wanted twins.

My mom was my example of a motherly woman. It wasn't traditional motherliness in the sense that all she did was be a homemaker and focus on my brother and me. She was a teacher—retired now—and child-oriented. Her career was centered on children in general. If she'd been a lawyer or something like that it wouldn't have been the same kind of example.

I was in my late teens when the feminist movement was beginnning in the mid-sixties. I figured I'd have some sort of career and also be a parent. I wanted both, partly because my generation was raised to think of having a larger life than only in the home, and partly through my mother's example of a career woman. I hoped to fall in love with someone and follow the traditional family route. Being non-traditional was never my goal. The circumstances of my life happened to work out that way. I didn't want to rush into having children but it was something I always saw for myself. The only consideration was to have them before it became impossible.

I married just out of college and was divorced when I was 28. I had been an immature child who became an immature young adult after a very rocky teenagehood. My parents were always concerned because I had married someone with a severe depression problem. But in that year of my divorce, with counseling, I considered myself to have radically changed and I think my parents recognized the change in me. I had become an adult and took responsibility for myself.

I was absolutely determined not to get involved with any man who needed a nurse or a mother. I wanted an equal. It was shocking to find out how many alcoholic, neurotic, and baby men there are in the world. I figured maybe I'm one of those people who meets someone when they're in their late forties or fifties and has an older kind of relationship. That would be okay.

Having lived alone for a long time, I had basically come to terms with my aloneness in the universe, which is, I think, what everyone struggles with. I knew I wanted a relationship but I didn't feel desperate. I believe it's wrong to have a child without at least some self-scrutiny, so that you're as sure as you can be that you're not doing it for the wrong reasons—to solve loneliness or have something to love you.

I had 'til my late thirties or even 40 to have a child. So it wasn't like the guillotine was about to drop. It wasn't the biological clock ticking. I put a lot of thought into it and felt I could do it—that I could be a parent, a good parent, even as a single parent. I would still have as a goal finding that relationship, but I wouldn't let not finding it deter me. My parents had respect for me. They recognized that this was not a flighty or irresponsible decision.

So I began to think of going ahead with the idea of having a child. After considering all the different aspects of it, I wasn't fooling myself about the difficulties of being a single parent. I asked myself, "Well, how would I go about it?"

When I was 33, I worked out a plan. I said, "This is what I'll do eventually if things don't work out otherwise." My job was full time at a television station. I saved my money, didn't blow it on foreign travel or anything like that, and I had great maternity coverage and a 6-month leave of absence. I wrote down all the possibilities—the pros and cons of each one. I could sleep with someone and not tell him; or perhaps someone would volunteer; or there is artificial insemination.

I had ethical problems regarding getting pregnant and not telling the person. It felt like stealing and I just wouldn't have done that. Artificial insemination would have been a good choice except for the fact that I couldn't come up with a decent answer for, "Who is Daddy? Who is my father?" It had to be someone I knew so I could say who it was . . . could say this person was a friend for many, many years but wasn't somebody I wanted to marry . . . could say, "I wanted a baby so much and you are the most important thing in the world to me and this person was such a good friend he helped me to have you."

The women at work—older women, traditional types—they approved. It would come up in conversation when we'd go to lunch. They were understanding. So was my mother. As with most women, no matter what their backgrounds, women understand. They understand the urge. It's amazing how nonjudgmental I found women to be.

I felt strongly that, if it wasn't somebody I wanted to marry and be with, I didn't want that person in my life—someone just in the background, a father who isn't really a father. I wanted a kid, but I still hoped to find someone I loved and who would love my child.

I mentioned, theoretically, to my friends, "Would you be

willing, if the understanding was that there would be no role for you, no relationship, would you be willing to basically donate sperm?" Most of them said no. That surprised me. I thought a man might like the idea that some genetic material of his is out there and yet he wouldn't be bothered with the financial responsibility.

By the time all of those thoughts began to jell, I resumed a relationship with someone who had been my first boyfriend. We were able to pick up our friendship over all these years. It was a nice friendship. I asked him my question and he immediately said, "Yes."

I said "Well, you'd better think about it." We both thought about it. A week later he understood all my terms.

I wanted a written contract which I thought would be legal—a document showing that original intent was by agreement and nobody was coerced or lied to. In exchange for no financial support from him and no demands by me or anyone in my family, I had total responsibility. We agreed he couldn't reveal his identity but I could if I chose to. I didn't want some stranger walking up to my child when she is an adult saying, "I'm your father." It turns out the contract would probably never have held up in court because courts do take into consideration parental rights.

The first time we tried I got pregnant. It's amazing! The only regret he voiced at the start was that he liked the idea of a romance resuming and felt that my pregnancy would probably interfere, that I wouldn't be interested in him. I didn't think that was necessarily the case. I wanted us to be friends though I was fairly certain he was not the person I would want to marry.

Shortly into my pregnancy I had a gut reaction that I needed to put some distance between us just in case he should change his mind about not having a parental role. I still had every hope of meeting and falling in love with someone, someone to be the father of my child. I knew I couldn't love anyone who couldn't love my child. I guess I was still holding out for a traditional family structure.

I hate to sound smug but it's amazing how everything I planned worked. If anything, I had planned to have more difficulty—being pregnant, experiencing the little things that are going on with your body, feeling this much joy and not having anyone to share it with. But I had a good network—close friends, women and men, and I'm very close to my parents.

I was a month pregnant when we all met in Boston for Thanksgiving and I told them then. My father is a prominent philanthropist and I felt a little concerned about embarrassing him in any way. I'd go to meetings of his foundation and knew a lot of people. I knew they would ask about me.

My father just said, "If I didn't know how much thought you had put into this and if I didn't trust that you were going to be capable of doing it, of carrying it off, I would have more concerns." I never voiced my concerns to him about his friends and colleagues but he said, "And I want to assure you that in no way would this embarrass me or make me uncomfortable no matter who knows." He's liberal; but he's also straight and narrow. This was the most wonderful reaction. He really came through.

My mom is a free spirit. But when I told her that after all these years I'd actually done it she let out a scream, "Ohhhhhh . . ." but a little later all of the grandmotherly instincts kicked in and she was pretty excited about it.

I wasn't mourning the loss of a husband. I wasn't grieving for a relationship. I guess if you don't have the expectation for something you don't miss it. Having a baby was such a conscious decision and such a wanted, hoped-for thing, and I had so much support.

Two of my friends came when I was about to deliver. They stayed and held my hand through it all. It was long—like a 16-hour delivery. A young student nurse was there who turned out to be very helpful with the breathing. She just did it the whole time so I could copy her. I don't think Lamaze is all that it's cracked up to be.

Thanks to amniocentesis I knew from the time I was 3 months pregnant that I was having a daughter. I don't think I would have been a good parent to a really handicapped child even with a husband. If that were the case, abortion would not have been a problem. I could have chosen not to know the sex but for me that really enriched it. She had her name. I was relating to a little Mara all during my pregnancy. It was great. My mom came the first week and stayed with me, left for a week, and then came back again.

Mara turned out to be an incredibly colicky baby for the first 3 months. She cried from 6 in the morning until 10 at night and would only stop to nurse. Her needs were nonstop. Being alone with her, I was completely available. If I had been married, it would have been a lot harder. I would have felt I wasn't living up to my own expectations of wanting to provide for those that I love. This way I didn't have any split loyalties. I could just be relaxed and have no other pressures. I guess husbands can help, but with a baby that young there's not too much they can do. I mean, all she was was an eating machine.

When Mara was a few weeks old, I began to feel really bad for rejecting her father during the pregnancy. Also, now I was a lot more secure. He had never crossed the line by appearing to be more interested than I wanted him to be. I wanted to have my cake and eat it, too. I figured when Mara would be a pre-teenager she would start asking about her biological father. I didn't want her to look him up and have him say "Get away, kid. I've never heard of you."

So, to protect her from that kind of hurt, I invited him to dinner about once a month, until she was about 10 months. Then he met someone whom he married about 6 months after that. It was clear, once he met someone, that this situation was uncomfortable for him. I am very grateful to him and never want to do anything to make his life uncomfortable.

Going back to work was hard. I would have liked to have been home more with Mara. I arranged for someone who was very loving and warm toward her to come to my house. That eliminated daycare and worrying about the kind of care she was getting. I went to work at a local newspaper where I knew a lot of the people. It was almost like being in a sheltered workshop, a comfortable place to be.

When she was about two and a half, she said, "Where's Daddy?"—not "who" but "where." By the time she was 3, I told her it was a friend of Mommy's. I mean I had to explain to her the facts of life. The answers were satisfactory to her. She never was conscious of being really different from other people.

Everything was fine until she was about 3 years old. I began to realize that she had some developmental delays. About that time, I began to be not quite as great a parent. Being a strong-willed person myself, I was running into a little creature who was developing her own will. You say to yourself, "I'm damping down this child's expression," or "I'm forcing my own will too much." And not quite knowing. I guess that's when parental guilt begins to grow. I was tempted to do everything for her. I should have been more patient and willing to sit there and let her try to do for herself. Even today, I still have to really work on that.

I wouldn't have known if all this was a function of being a single parent until Jim came into our lives. Just having the influence of another person—that's where the relief comes in. You know, when I've blown my stack, yelling, and it's not fair and I should stop, Jim steps in. It's a very good complement.

I felt from the very beginning, before I even had her, that it would be very important that she have men around, be it my father, or close male friends, that she have friendships and relationships with men. I didn't think it was a good thing for a child to be without that.

I understand that women choose men based on the male models they have as children. I don't think I would have been as successful in that. It's a grand idea, but my father lives far away. He has the same deficiencies as a grandfather that he has as a father. He still works and is very career-oriented. He is a very loving father but not there really. Male friends are good up to a point but they're not there that much. So getting that male role model could have been more of a problem than I'd foreseen.

Mara was 4 when Jim and I started seeing each other and things progressed quite rapidly. We'd known each other for a year before we started romantically seeing each other. So within 3 months we decided to get married. Mara was calling him "Dad" within a few weeks—not because I told her to. She just heard her stepbrother doing it.

She was a child ready for a father. I never wanted a "me-and-you-against-the-world" thing with her. I didn't want her to feel that there was just no outside life or potential for it. Still, since she had me and all that attention, Jim and I speculated at first what kind of response she would have to him. But from the very beginning she was just totally welcoming, responded as if she'd known him all her life.

Jim and I fell deeply in love and I'm a demonstrative person, so she saw a lot of hugging and handholding. It's everything I'd hoped for, and didn't expect to find. She just immediately picked up on it, fell right into it, and seemed to love having a father. Jim responded. I mean, he's wonderful with kids. I think it would have been harder for him if she'd had a father who was in the picture, but she was this kid with no father. And Jim had only one child, a son who was now in graduate school. He's never had a daughter. They met each other's needs in a lot of ways, so it turned out well.

After we moved into Jim's house there were some difficulties. Jim works at home and his work environment got shot to pieces having a kid around. She's in school 'til 5 now, so that worked out too.

Any second thoughts I have about my decision to have a child are related more to my quality of parenting. I couldn't foresee how impatient I can be with certain kinds of things, dawdling and stuff like that. I was the most patient of mothers with an infant. I always liked 4-year olds. I taught kindergarten and nursery school before and related to that age. With a baby there is nothing to be impatient about—but once they have a will! I think those are the kinds of regrets any parent has. I might have been this way under any circumstances.

I have so much invested in this one and only child that I adore. I'm just too in her face. I must have kissed her non-stop when she was a baby and a young child. Even now, I feel such a close physical connection with her. Because of her own developmental delays she probably needed someone sort of pushing her out more to try things and here I am enveloping her. Luckily, because of her personality, she's not just attached to my apron strings. She never has had a problem separating from me, yet when I'm there, she sucks her thumb. As soon as I come it's immediate regression.

I'm sure the intensity of this relationship is exaggerated, because she's my only child. I think parents, and mothers in particular, are God in the effect of their influence on their children. I wanted to be a God who created a strong self-image in Mara so she would feel secure and could overcome whatever obstacles there would be from having a single mother. I missed the cue of when to pull back and let the child fly. Jim has saved her in a lot of ways.

My family background is Jewish, but I wasn't raised religiously. I'm an atheist. The moral part is doing something responsibly and not for the wrong reasons.

A year ago Jim adopted Mara. I consider myself phenomenally lucky. I got everything I wanted.

Vera

3

*Vera is 45, single, white, and lives in Seattle with three of her four
sons. Her old house is big with a broad front porch. She explains that
the sandpaper, wood putty, tools and paint littered about are there
because she and the boys are refurbishing the weathered door
frames.*

*The interior is replete with art objects, decorations and mementos
reflecting the culture of Brazil and the American Southwest. In the
kitchen, the refrigerator door is decorated with drawings and greet-
ings for Mother's Day. A family photo album is on the kitchen table.*

I was 40 years old, living in Chattanooga—a nurse/midwife,
on call every other night and every other weekend. I owned
a condominium, had a 280Z sports car, wonderful clothes,
been all over the world, and realized I wasn't happy. I didn't
go to bars. I'm not gay. So those sources of friendships
weren't available to me. I'd go home at night and I'd think,
"What can I do to pass the time until morning, until I go back
to work?" I knew I didn't want to live the rest of my life that
way. I said, "Something has to change." But I didn't know
what.

I had a meeting in California. My roommate was a woman I
had never met before. We stayed up all night talking about
personal things. She and her husband were trying to decide
whether to have a baby.

She said, "I don't know that I want to go through life without seeing it through the eyes of a child." That had never occurred to me. Suddenly I thought I might be missing something.

Two months later, I delivered my sister's second child. It was a snowy night. I had wanted it to be the perfect birth and it was truly wonderful.

While spending a few days at my sister's, I fell in love with her 2-year old. This little one thought his Aunt Vera was great. That added to this new feeling that maybe I was supposed to be a mother. As I traveled back to Chattanooga the thought grew in me.

I mentioned all this to my therapist who didn't respond. But the next week she said to me, "I know a 3-year old boy who needs a mother." That she would consider me made me believe she thinks I'd be okay. Then and there, I decided to become a mother. I had no idea how I would do it. I started to think about the kind of child I wanted.

In my office, directly above the delivery room at the hospital, there is a bed. I figured I could teach a 3-year old to stay there at night while I delivered babies. If the child were to need me, he or she could toddle down the stairs and say, "Where's my Mom?" So that was it. I would adopt a 3-year old.

I went to the state health system that has children for adoption and foster care. I said, "I want to adopt a 3-year old."

They said, "Single people cannot adopt healthy children under the age of 9." This was 1980.

I had two things to think about. Was I ready for a child over 9? Could I adopt a child with some emotional or physical problem under 9? I decided I didn't want either.

I inquired about adopting a 3-year old from a foreign country. I needed a homestudy done by a social worker from a licensed adoption agency in Tennessee.

There was a church-affiliated agency in Knoxville and I contacted one of their social workers. She said if I paid her expenses she would come to Chattanooga and do my homestudy. She stayed with me for 48 hours.

She asked about my family who live in Seattle and what support I would get from them. Did I go to church? I said, "No." But I could drum up something from the past, like "my strong Catholic upbringing." She asked me about discipline. I knew I wasn't supposed to hit children (*laughs*) so I placed my hands, fingers to palm, and said something about "time out" and things like that.

She told me about a group in Brazil that was facilitating adoptions for a fee of $3,000. I had been in the Peace Corps in Brazil. The thought of going back to Rio was wonderful. It didn't dawn on me to question this group's legitimacy. And because this was coming from my social worker, I signed up. They had a contact person in New York. I called her and told her I wanted a 3-year old.

She said, "Send your papers." And I did. I sent my papers and $1,000.

A few months later she called and said, "All we have are newborn babies."

Out of my mouth came, "That would be fine." I didn't think out what being on call every other night might mean with a baby.

"Do you want a boy or a girl?" she asked.

"Is there any difference in the wait?"

"Girls are more popular so you would wait longer for a girl."

"Well, put me down for either, whichever comes first."

She said the wait would be about 6 months. It turned out to be a year. Meanwhile, I decided to buy an old house closer to work.

Right after I put the earnest money down on this house in Chattanooga, I got a call from this woman—a connection in Mississippi—saying they had a baby boy, just born. Did I want him? (*Chuckles*)

"Yes, of course I want him."

"Can you catch the Monday plane to Rio?" It was Wednesday.

I said, "Yes, of course I can."

From that moment, I thought of myself as a mother. It was a whole new thing.

I dash home to get ready. I need a visa, a plane reservation to fly out on Monday, and to make arrangements at work. While tearing around, fed-exing, phoning, and so on, I get a call saying my son is in the hospital. I know Brazilian hospitals don't take good care of babies—there's nobody to hold them. It is like he is already my child (*tearful*) and here he is in Brazil. I am frantic.

My visa is supposed to come from New Orleans and hasn't arrived. I call there and ask if I can come to the Consulate, pick up my visa and passport, and fly right out of New Orleans on Tuesday.

"Well, we close at 3 o'clock."

"Would someone be willing to come to the airport with my visa and passport?"

"I'm sorry," she says, "we can't do that."

I remember something my therapist had said: "Sometimes it's useful to burst into tears." So I cry.

She says, "Let me see what I can do." It seems the head of the Consulate agrees. I can come to her place and pick up the documents. Tuesday, I'm on the 1:30 plane to New Orleans, get a taxi to take me to her house, then back to the airport, and fly out of Miami that night.

In Rio, I was met at the airport by a Brazilian family who facilitates adoptions. They drove me to their house where there were seven babies. Two mothers were there—one had adopted two children, not related. Another mother was in the hospital with her sick child. A man was standing with another family and his baby girl. Nobody smiled. Nobody said, "Welcome. Are you excited about your baby?" I heard something about having trouble getting passports for the babies but it didn't register. It didn't dawn on me that anything was going on.

Pretty soon here comes Sally, a very animated American woman. She was excited about taking me to see my baby. She drove me to a small private hospital. I walked into the maternity section to find my son in an incubator, an IV in his head, and his arms held down by bandages so he wouldn't pull out the IV. Two-thirds of him was mouth, and it was wide open, screaming.

I wondered what would happen when I held my baby for the first time. I didn't know whether the stars would shine and the band would play. They put him in my arms and he immediately stopped crying. All I could think of was, "You are so ugly (*laughs*), but we're going to make it." I stayed with him all day.

Sally invited me to her house for dinner. Her husband worked for an American company in Brazil. They lived in this gorgeous penthouse on Copacabana Beach and we had a lovely meal. But all I could think of was, "I want to get back to my baby." And finally, I got back to the hospital.

Paul was crying again. I picked him up. Right away, he stopped. The doctor had come in the afternoon. I had pushed for Paul to be discharged. He had had an infection but was getting better and they had taken out the IV. The fact that I spoke Portuguese was to my advantage. The doctor let us go the next afternoon.

We went back to the Brazilian family. By adopting through this family, you have a choice of going to Brazil to get your baby or having your baby escorted to you. There were five babies waiting to be escorted to the States. Those mothers who had come for their babies and were waiting for the children's passports were expected to feed all the children during the day and take turns at night feeding them every 3 hours.

I wanted to take my child upstairs to sleep with me but that wasn't allowed. It would disturb the people trying to sleep. So Paul stayed on the first floor. I could recognize his cry and when I heard him I would fly downstairs.

I found out that an investigation was beginning into black market adoptions and all foreign adoptions of infants were being frozen. We were told this would be resolved within a 3-week period. Things quickly became hectic. That first week we had to go to the police station to testify that we had not paid the biological mothers and to our knowledge they had received no money for the children.

Meanwhile, my partner back in Chattanooga wanted to know when I would be home so she wouldn't have to be on call every night. Staying in a house with an emotional Brazilian host family became increasingly depressing. They were under a lot of stress and started yelling at each other. We were all exhausted.

About 2 weeks after I arrived, one of the Brazilian daughters went to the northeast part of the country where the babies came from to see if she could find out from the state police what was going on. She came back real late at night. I remember it was 11:30. Paul was asleep. The word was that no one knew when this would be resolved and we should go back to the U.S.

"You need to go home," she said.

I went and picked up my son and walked and walked with him and thought, "I can't go home. I can't leave my child." Yet there was this constant feeling of guilt: "You can't stay. You have to go back because your partner needs you there. But I can't go back. But you have to go back." It was a war inside me.

The realtor in Tennessee phoned. What did I want to do about the house I had planned to buy? Fortunately, one of the loans I applied for I couldn't get. I backed out of the purchase. That was easy to get out of and I could do it without guilt. A Catholic background gives me high stakes in the guilt field (*chuckles*). I made the decision not to leave.

Roger, the man who had adopted a little girl baby, had originally been staying with the family, too. But they didn't get along. So Sally let Roger and his baby stay with her, since his daughter's passport was expected any minute.

Roger was a mechanic and had two children and a wife in Tennessee. Mechanics don't have benefits. Their money was rapidly running out. The plan was for him to go back to Chattanooga and Sally would take care of Cindy, his baby. Then when I could leave with Paul, I would bring Cindy home since I lived in Tennessee.

After 3 weeks, I was in a severe depression, fatigued, getting up at night to feed the babies, and not wanting anybody else to feed my baby.

Sally and I had become friends. She said, "Roger is leaving. Come spend the weekend with us." I arrived at her house on a Friday afternoon and she said, "Here is a room for you. What would you like to do?"

"I want to sleep."

"Stay here as long as you need to." She closed the door to my room. I curled up in a fetal position with my baby next to me. I slept and I slept and I slept. I was physically and emotionally exhausted.

Just before I was to leave, thinking, "How can I go back to that house?" Sally came to me and said, "We can't let you go back. Stay with us." I stayed for 2 months, and the only thing I had to pay for was Paul's formula. I ate with them every night—these lovely meals. I didn't have to do anything in the house at all. The maid did our wash—mine and Paul's. I became very good friends with the maid.

During the day, I would go for walks. I had no idea what would happen.

One night I got a phone call from my best friend in high school. We had been very close and after college lost contact. Ann had called my mother who told her I was in Brazil with this terrible problem.

So Ann called. "How are you?"

And I said, crying, "Fine." Any time anybody called I spent 10 minutes crying on their money to Brazil.

And she said, "Do you need money?"

"No."

"Are you sure? I have lots of money."

"Can you send me $75?"

"I'll send you $400." She and a friend of hers became The Committee to Keep Vera and Paul Together.

They set aside $5,000 for me to use as I needed. Whenever I

needed money, I'd call her up. And she would call me whenever I said I needed her to call.

One night, she asked, "Well, what are you going to do?"

"I don't know. I need to go home but I can't go home."

"You must stay."

The police were threatening to take all of the babies away and put them back in orphanages 'til they got this resolved. I said to Ann, "What will I do if they take him away?"

"You will move next to the orphanage and you will go every day and take care of him."

"What if they won't let me do that?"

"You will hire someone to go and care for him for you, and you will get permission to see him at intervals." She was very clear. It was at the point where I needed somebody to tell me what to do.

It was hard calling my colleague and saying, "I'm staying here and I don't know when I'm coming home." She was furious, as well she might be. But I couldn't leave my child. Once that decision was made it was much better.

We got in touch with the American Embassy in Brasilia. Originally, the Ambassador said he couldn't help us because the children were not American citizens. That was in July when I had arrived. In September, Ronald Reagan appointed a new Ambassador. Ambassador Anthony Motley appointed this wonderful consular official to help us. Pablo was encouraging and incredibly helpful. He gave me his home number and would listen to me cry.

Finally, Pablo said, "There is nothing we can do. You need a lawyer."

Someone put us in touch with a lawyer who turned out to be mentally ill. He did terrible damage pleading our case with the federal police in Brasilia. At one point, this lawyer told us the police were coming to get the babies and we should go into hiding. Another mother and I hid in this lawyer's tiny apartment. We had to boil water and make formula and sterilize bottles for these babies and there was no place to set anything down.

We were right by the elevator. Every time the elevator opened, I thought, "It's the police coming for the children." After 48 hours, I said to myself, "I hope it's the police. I can't stand it anymore."

Once again, Sally and her husband found another place for us. A third mother joined us with two children. So here were these three depressed and desperate American women and four babies in need of care.

Something in me knew this lawyer was crazy and going about this in a way that was harmful to us. Finally, the others figured out that something was wrong. We had this horrendous meeting where we fired him. We called the Embassy again and they recommended a new lawyer who was wonderful—a Brasilian lawyer.

Meanwhile, an American woman whom I had met, Martha, invited Paul and me to come and stay in her house. I would only have to buy our food and pay the maid a little extra. I liked Martha a lot. I thought that would be wonderful.

Now Roger calls and says, "Vera, Sally's husband has been transferred and they are moving to Chile. We're counting on you to take Cindy."

I thought, "As much as I don't want to do it, if it were reversed, what a terrible thing it would be if Paul were to go to somebody else." I said, "Okay," and Cindy, Paul, and I moved to Martha's house.

I can remember just sitting there crying the whole time when Sally came to say goodbye. She left me this bag of chocolate chips because that's my very favorite thing. And the interesting thing was I never made chocolate chip cookies while I was living with Martha because I knew I would have to share them, and I thought, "I need every one of those chocolate chip cookies for myself." So I brought the chocolate chips home to Chattanooga.

I stayed at Martha's 5½ months.

Martha and her family were very nice and caring. They made it clear that the care of the babies was mine, which was fine with me. It was still incredibly difficult. Their house had

3 stories. So to go in and out I had to take two babies up two stories and down two stories. I was so exhausted I was in bed at 6 o'clock every night. Then I'd be up at 6 in the morning. It was impossible to pass the hours. I would live for the mail at 10:30 in the morning. I would live, first of all, for breakfast, and then I would live for the mail.

Did you have regrets?

Never. The idea was to live through it.

After 5½ months at Martha's, we received news that the passports would be released. At immigration, we found out that our names were in a computer and we could not leave the country.

Our names were there at the airport, too. We would not be allowed to leave if we had the babies. The head of immigration in Brasilia said he would rather the children die than leave the country. In *Newsweek* magazine, a Brazilian juvenile court judge was quoted as saying he had no proof that the children would be happy when they got to this country, and, for all he knew, the children would be used in pharmaceutical experiments or used as slaves. It didn't seem to matter that Paul's biological mother had testified to the police earlier that she had not been paid and that she was unable to care for him and didn't want him!

I never believed we would be safe until I was in Miami. It had been so awful. My fantasy was that the Brazilian military would come and make our plane turn back (*laughs*).

But we did fly out! I had the two babies—Paul and Roger's Cindy. As soon as our plane took off, Sally called Roger, who left right away from his home to drive to Chattanooga. They were there when we landed.

It was mid-December. I wanted to go back home to Seattle. So Paul and I went home for Christmas. Afterward, back in Chattanooga, my mother came and stayed a month with me. My colleague was still furious because she'd been on call ev-

ery night for all the time I was away. I found a young woman
from France to take care of Paul. She was studying English.
She was like my daughter. It was wonderful. And she loved
Paul.

I'm not sure how I decided to adopt another child. I think it
was because I was a wonderful mother. I could have been the
mother of the year. I was patient, kind, loving, gentle, sympa-
thetic. I was incredible. So I thought, "Well, I'll do this
again." But if I'm going to do it, I'm going to go live near my
family where my child will know my brother and his family
and my sister and her family and be near Grandma.

So I moved to Seattle and got a job teaching at the university. I bought a house, this house. I had started the second
adoption homestudy in Chattanooga and had it updated here.
Then started one of the most difficult periods.

I was adopting through a new group in Brazil. This woman
called and said, "Would you consider a 9-year old?"

I said, "Sure."

I left Paul in the care of my mother for a week and flew to
Brazil. I went to the orphanage and the minute I met Luke I
didn't like him. He told me I was ugly. He told me I couldn't
speak good Portuguese. He was all over the place, and I
thought, "Something is wrong."

There was another mother there adopting two children, and
these three children were absolutely uncontrollable. They
would be underneath the table in restaurants, running up and
down the aisles. There was nothing I could say to them, even
in Portuguese, that would control them. I wanted to hit Luke.

So I called the woman in charge and said, "Something's
wrong."

She said, "You need to be sure about this. Do you want to
leave him here?"

"I don't know." But then I thought, "This child has been
twice abandoned by his birth mother at critical times in his
life. What will happen to him if I leave him here?" So I took
him. It was awful. He was awful.

He wouldn't do anything I asked him to do. He was destructive. No toy was safe. He would take anything apart—clocks, locks. I'd tell him to go to his room. He wouldn't. One day, I tried to physically take him up to his room and I had him in front of me with my right arm across his chest and he was bracing his feet against the stairs—and he bit my arm! (*Laughs*)

At last I took Luke to the social worker and asked, "What is going on and how long will this last?"

He said, "It sounds to me like you have a child who is pretty independent. You thought you were going to get a child who would need a lot of loving and cuddling, stuff like that. He doesn't seem to want that."

I discovered Luke had a major hearing problem. He had three surgeries that first year. In the hospital, after surgery, he woke up at 1:00 in the morning, screaming, "Mama! Mama!" That was the first time he called me mother! Before, he would call me "auntie," the word Brazilian children use for any woman.

I knew something was wrong but I never knew what. He was in special schools and was always a problem in school. His behavior kept being awful. This is when I questioned, "What did I do to myself? What have I done . . . and all these years to come?" It had never occurred to me not to go through with the adoption.

At one point I said to myself, "You've got to send him back." And then I thought, "No, there's hope because he's nice to Paul." He was wonderful to 2-year old Paul. Still, I never wanted to touch Luke, and I was glad he didn't want to touch me or want to be cuddled. I didn't want to be with him. It was an absolutely awful time, particularly after I had thought of myself as such a wonderful mother.

After about a year and a half—I have no idea why—I decided to adopt again. No idea!

I can remember going to New Mexico to meet Gabriel. All the way there I kept thinking, "Don't do this. You are crazy." When I got to Albuquerque where a good friend lives, I told her how scared I was and she made an appointment with her therapist that afternoon. This man was wonderful. He helped me separate the stuff from Luke.

I went to the airport, petrified. The woman who was the head of the agency was there. She was up close to the window, looking out. The plane from Rio had just arrived. I was as far back in the waiting room as I could get.

She called to me, "Come on, come on!"

I went up to her and said, "I am petrified."

She said, "This is a child who is so different you can't believe it."

He was from the same orphanage as Luke but this was a year and a half later. The minute Gabriel got off the plane he called me mother. Every 30 minutes I got a hug. He has been an incredible child. Luke continues to be a problem. And life goes on.

Two years later I formed a support group for single adoptive moms and a resource group for single moms who want to adopt. And soon I started getting "that adoption feeling" again.

I got to know the names of all the kids who were pictured in the agency's adoption magazine. I saw a picture of a black child with the most incredible smile and an incredible name: Sugar Ray Lewis.

Soon after that, Jill, from the agency, calls. "Vera, we have a child who needs a home. If he's not adopted immediately he will be sent to an orphanage. He's in our transition house right now."

"Who is it?

"Sugar Ray Lewis."

"I'll take him."

"I understand you don't have any money."

"Jill, I have no money at all."

And she said, "We'll help you." So she started the Bring Sugar Ray Lewis Home Campaign by asking people who had adopted through her group for donations to pay for his airfare and expenses so I would only have to pay for mine. I went to Brazil with one of my friends and brought Sugar Ray Lewis home.

At this point, Ray and Gabriel are both 11, Luke is 9, and Paul is 2.

Ray is one of the world's most incredible children. He's also given me all kinds of problems but they're different from Luke's. Ray has stolen. He has been incredibly disrespectful to teachers. He would have temper tantrums, threaten to kill himself. But always I knew it would be okay.

The first time he was angry with me was when I made him wash the windows. He had agreed to wash them as a way to make some money. I had given him the money ahead of time and he hadn't washed the windows.

Three days later I said, "You must wash the windows now." He got to washing them but he was furious.

He looked at me and said, "You're not my mother. You're not even black." I tried not to laugh; but I did.

One night, he was terrible. I was trying to get Paul and a friend to sleep. Ray was angry with me. He was being loud and kicking things. I told him to go to sleep downstairs on the couch. He finally went and it was quiet. I went to bed and pretty soon I heard Ray stomp upstairs. He grabbed his covers off his bed, went down to the landing of the stairs, and curled up with his blankets over him.

I went down. "Go sit on the couch," I told him. "I'll be right there." I checked on the little children upstairs and then came back and sat next to him. He wouldn't let me touch him. He was facing away from me and I put my hand on his back. He pulled away. I said, "I'm going to leave my hand here."

Paul, now awake, came and hollered over the stairs, "Are you okay down there?"

I looked up at him and said, "Are you afraid I'm going to spank Ray?"

"Yes." So Paul came downstairs and nuzzled up on one side of me. Ray eventually relaxed and I was just real quiet.

I said, "Sometimes it's hard to be adopted."

He didn't say anything for a few minutes. Then, "I wasn't mad at you. I was mad at my other mother."

"If your other mother were here, what would you say to her?"

"I wouldn't talk to her at all."

"Oh, you have to talk with her."

"I wouldn't talk with her if the judge had a gun at my head." This mother, when Ray was 7 years old, had taken him to the judge without telling him ahead of time and said, "I can't take care of him."

And I said to Ray, "The judge has a gun at your head; what will you say to your mother?"

And he spat out, "I hate you. You were mean to me." So it's that with Ray. I know he'll be okay. Although I hate it when the school calls and tells me he's called a teacher a "fuckin' asshole" again. I hate it.

He's how old now?

Fifteen. He's bright. He's the social person in the class. The clown.

Where is Luke?

Luke is 16 and is in a home for emotionally disturbed boys. His behavior got worse after Ray arrived. I called CSD (Child Services Division of the State Health Department) because they have an emergency program where they will come to your home and do therapy. After about three sessions with all of us here and Luke disrupting every minute of it, we realized something had to be done.

They were able to place him in a group home for 2 months for further evaluation. The recommendation of the group home was that he be placed in a residential facility. I couldn't face giving him up. I wasn't ready for that. But then the children said, "Mom, we can't do this. You have got to do some-

thing about Luke." And I finally was able to realize that that
had to happen.

Vera, you have a family now. Are you going to do this again?

If I had the money, I would do it one more time. They are
wonderful. Because the more I've done this, the more I realized what an incredible leap we ask these children to take.
You grow up in an orphanage for 11 years, have never been to
school, have never had to behave politely or with manners,
and all of a sudden there are all these restrictions on what
you're allowed to do. Plus it's in a different language. It's
quite incredible.

I wonder what would have happened if I had left Luke in
Brazil. There's part of me that says I should have for his sake
as well as for mine. And there's part of me that says he's doing well where he is right now. This child has a chance for a
life that may have been ended by now in Brazil. He could have
easily been into robbing and he might be dead.

What is the most important piece of this whole thing for you?

Knowing how important I am to the children. We have frequent conversations about what if I die, what will happen to
them? I worry about dying and another loss for them. So it's
being wanted and needed and loved.

It's being challenged in ways I have never been challenged
before. What do you do when the supermarket calls you and
tells you your child has shoplifted and he's sitting in the office in handcuffs waiting for you? How do you handle that?
What do I say when Ray steals for the twentieth time to help
him realize he can learn not to do that? He just hasn't learned
it yet. And how to come up with appropriate consequences?
It's especially difficult with these children because I struggle

with how to discipline them in ways that won't hurt their self-esteem which is so low to begin with.

Seattle is a mixed ethnic community. Has that been helpful in terms of the fact that you adopted foreign children?

Probably. For three of the children, anyway. For Sugar Ray Lewis, I don't know. He is black but he's not Black-American. He's Black-Brazilian, which is a completely—he's more Hispanic than he is black. And how that will be for him in his future, I don't know. We don't have black friends, but he has black friends at school.

What has been the perception of the world around you—your personal and your work community—about you, as a single mother adopting children from another culture?

They think I'm crazy.

I feel they don't know what they're missing. I think they are influenced by having seen Luke and his behavior. So they see him before they see the others.

What about your original family?

My mother coped well until I decided to adopt a black child. Interesting to me is that when I was going to adopt my second child, I told the agency I did not want a child with black features. And look what I was ready to do a few years later!

My brother called me and said I needed to reconsider what I was doing 'cause of Mother. I went over to Mother's house.

She said, "I don't think I can accept a black child. I don't think I can love a black child. I know it's not Christian." This is a woman who says the rosary every day. And for a while we weren't welcome in her house. She was afraid of what the neighbors would say. And now, he spends the night at her house.

My sister and I rarely see each other anymore as a result of Luke. His behavior was so awful. I didn't realize what was happening for my sister and her husband. She has two children—one that I helped deliver. I would invite her children to come over to spend the night. She would never allow them to come.

I finally said, "We need to have a meeting. What's going on?"

She said, "I won't let them come because I'm afraid I'll have to invite your children over to my house. And we can't have Luke."

I tried to say that there could be something between the two of us without the families but it really never worked. So we are cordial to each other.

My brother is willing to accept whatever I want to do. Although I would like my children to be more involved with him on this little farm that he has, he never invites them up. But that was also a result of Luke. He and his wife kept Luke and Gabriel one weekend and it was just terrible—the way Luke insulted his wife and stuff.

So that legacy is with us. . . .

Have you ever thought of marriage?

Yes. I was dating someone 2 years ago and decided that's what I wanted to do. And the children loved him dearly, too. But he decided that that commitment was not something he could make.

I would love it for my children. They really need and want a father. And there are people who would say I shouldn't have adopted because they don't have that male influence. That doesn't bother me either because they are children who wouldn't have had a whole lot of anything otherwise. I think a little bit is better than nothing.

4

Sally and Roberta

Sally is perky and pretty. She is 35 years old, has short, blonde hair, bright blue eyes, and a daughter, Kimberly, aged 6. They live in a luxury townhouse in Tucson, Arizona, which they share with Roberta and Roberta's 3-year-old daughter, Alexis.

The front of their split-level residence is completely closed to the outside world except for the front door. Once inside, a wall of windows gives on to a panoramic view of the desert and distant surrounding mountains. The contemporary furnishings and decorative color accents reiterate the desert earth tones and mountain blues, the fiery orange-reds and deep purples that typify the landscape and sunscapes of the American Southwest.

Sally offered us a quick tour of the house. The living room is a few steps down and the bedrooms a few steps up. The daughters share a bedroom filled with children's toys and games, stuffed animals, and assorted dolls. We returned to the middle level and sat around a breakfast room table surrounded by four comfortable beige chairs. Neither Roberta nor the children were present when the interview with Sally began.

Throughout my life, I would have this series of dreams where I had a baby. The dreams were tactile. It had been an idea germinating for some years. I had my feet on the ground about having a child, and was impatient with waiting for the right time. In fact, I was in a fine relationship when I was 27 and I almost had a baby.

When I became pregnant, he announced, "I guess I'm more

traditional than I thought." He didn't want me going to Mexico where I had a grant to do research on the Center for Intercultural Documentation, an institute set up in Cuernavaca by Ivan Ilyitch. Anyway, it ended in a miscarriage.

About a year later, the opportunity to have a baby presented itself. My two sisters were also having babies, and I knew the family's reaction would be more positive because of the coincidence of the three sisters all having babies at once. I thought that might soften the blow of my decision to have a baby on my own—and it did. There was shock at first, but the family as a whole—mother, father, sisters—have been very supportive. I camouflaged it initially by saying I intended to get married, which put off their questions for many months.

Although this was a serious relationship, we had difficulties. He became very possessive and wanted me not to finish my two masters degrees, but to adapt to a very reclusive life in northern Arizona near a huge Navajo reservation. I would not be allowed to go hardly anywhere without his permission. We argued a lot—had disagreements about religion. If all those difficulties could be worked out, fine, we could stay together. I was sure it wasn't going to work. Whether we got married would have been another issue for me.

He has a lot of fine qualities and, as far as Kimberly is concerned, she has a great father. He is a musician and one of those very able people, very talented, could fix anything, which I found fascinating. But he's explosive. Kimberly has seen him when he gets upset, starts yelling. It was good for her to see that side as well. I worry that maybe I build him up to be this perfect person for her sake.

We've made the effort to involve him with Kimberly but his focus once again becomes me and our relationship. That creates a lot of tension, which is one of the reasons I left. I don't want to raise my daughter with that sort of tension. But I'm toying with the idea of initiating visits again.

We have no formal legal agreement. He pays no child support. He had been married before, and had a child he was very close to, but he lost total contact with this child. I think a lot of his not seeing Kimberly is based on the fear of becoming emotionally attached to her. I'm often criticized for not forcing him to provide child support, but I feel I understand where he's coming from. Still, there is the responsibility side and he could be doing more for her. Finances have always been a problem.

Is being a parent what you expected?

No! No! It's an adventure, and my life has always been an adventure. This one changed everything. I had never had any interest in having dressers and beds, couches, and dishes. I had nothing. Now I am very materialistic. Even the business of eating regularly. But most of all, it is engrossing. Nothing had ever captured my attention so totally.

I remember the midwives trying to trick me into ways of diverting my attention like, "Why don't you read a book?"

And I said, "I don't want to read 'cause I might fall asleep."

I remember having her—at home—and not sleeping for days. I didn't want to lose the whole experience of the birth. Here was this little creature and she was real.

I love being around children. They do not stress me out. I can have five of them in the car at once and it's great. Some of my pat sayings are like: "My daughter is my double martini; my daughter is my Porsche." I work in a very stressful business. To get in that car in the evening and go to this other level of conversation and perception—the way she sees the world— is just a very rich experience.

For me, relating to my daughter, the aspects of understanding how she relates to the world, sharing with her what life is, what spirit is—it took all of my learning, all the years of academic thinking, and all the years of studying in spiritual areas, and brought me to watching an incredible process. At first, this little being and I, we just looked at each other because we couldn't talk, right? And gradually, while watching each other, communicating began to happen.

For the first few years I was so focused on her that I really did not have a social life. Being a single parent is very isolating. You're always picking up the child, taking him someplace, doing something connected with maintaining that child. An adult, if they don't want to eat they don't eat . . . they don't want to sleep, they don't sleep. That's not the case with a child. So it's a constant watchfulness.

When did you go back to work and what arrangements did you make then for Kimberly's care?

I finished my master's degree and started to work when Kimberly was about 2. I put her in an in-home care with four other children. At that time I was living with my father and commuting to Tucson. My brothers and I were all trying to force my father into retirement from the family business which he refused to do. It was an auto body repair shop. But he had the flexibility of taking Kimberly to the daycare keeper in the mornings by way of the coffee shop where they had pancakes or waffles. That was a great experience for her.

My parents have been divorced for 17, 18 years. I was raised in a family with absolutely no religion. My mother was a high school dropout and turned her back on religion, and my father had no formal education. My mother was 14 when they got married. There was no heavy cultural environment growing up in Arizona.

As I look back, I'm very grateful for what I just described. I have not been encumbered by religious structures and values that I might have had to work out. I gobbled up any metaphysical books and philosophy for a number of years on my own. All of this came from an inner desire. Of course, early seventies literature wasn't hot like it is right now. It was a very different type of literature.

Okay. So I had a BA in Philosophy and then got a Master's in Public Administration. From there I went directly to work for the Secretary of Finance and Administration in state government. I did management analysis and legislative bill analysis for the Governor's staff. I was then offered a job in a very large company which does political polling, public opinion, and market research. I designed questionaires and analyzed and interpreted the results, putting them into a report that's easy to digest.

The job was also very flexible. My employer has a daughter 3 years older than my daughter. We actually have in our research focus group an adjacent room for viewing. In there we put a television, a VCR, videos like "Cinderella," "Casper the Ghost," art supplies, a cot, some blankets. So it is not unusual for one or more children to be in there. These are very nice corporate offices.

There is an interesting thing about this. I think the perception is that it is the employer who is not open to that kind of a facility. But younger women have commented that the older women don't want this in the workplace. It could be that the older ones didn't have these opportunities and they may resent it. It might be that they've raised their children and don't want children around now. So it's not always the employer.

One day my daughter commented, "Mom, you only take me to the office when I'm not feeling well." I started taking her to work when she was feeling well, and she quit getting sick.

Now she goes to school full time—kindergarten, at Montessorri. I take her in the morning anywhere from 8 to 9 o'clock and pick her up at 5. I find, though, that 8 hours is a bit tough, because she's in a school that is very stimulating and she stays busy all day going from one project to another. The morning is taken up with math, reading, that sort of activity, depending on the level. They have multi-level stages in her class, and they have something they call theater workshop with play-acting lots of parts. Also, she's become very familiar with animals. The school has been wonderful about bringing in live animals, tarantulas, snakes, ducks. When they got too big, someone had to volunteer to take them home. Guess who! It's a wonderful experience. It's an expensive school but. . . .

Is the father involved now?

No. It's been a year and a half since Kimberly and her father have spoken. He came down for a dance recital. We had been up to where he lives a few weeks before. She would go through this period of tension and bedwetting in anticipation of seeing him. I decided we should probably either do something regular so she becomes comfortable with it, or cut it off altogether. That might not have been a good decision on my part. Now that she's 6 I feel that she could probably handle the "sporadicness" of it and would be more relaxed.

What do you consider the good aspects of raising a child alone and what is not good?

Let's start with the good. There's just the delight, the pleasure, that's just immeasurable. So many women say to me, "Oh, aren't you lucky. You only have to raise one child." Now I have not been married, so I've never had to take care of a husband. I'm also not taking care of another adult which so many marriages do come to. This is an interesting thing and I have observed during these 6 years that it is true. So I suppose that that is one advantage. My energy goes to Kimberly and myself. I like the flexibility of being able to pick Kimberly up and just go off wherever we want and not check in with anyone. It's also the learning, the pure pleasure of it, the understanding of life—that is, human development, relationships, having this experience of being a mother.

On the down side, it holds you back in various ways, from the very mundane, like jumping in the car and running to the Circle K, or making a decision to move to Washington for a job where you wouldn't have the support system. So, it's on the entire spectrum of actions.

The thing of being held back and being restricted, there was something else I was thinking of. There are advantages to waiting. I was almost 30 when I had her. A friend would say, "We're going skiing—but no children!" "We're going to do this—but no children!" And when you're 30 and you've had 10, 15 years of being independent, you say, "Great! I'm staying home with my kid. Have a good time." And you feel that way. I've really loved the excuse of saying, "I've got to go home."

And yet, part of what precipitated my wanting a roommate was the realization that I needed to branch out somewhat from my daughter. We were so much a twosome that other than my professional life I didn't have a social life. The combination of being a workaholic and being with my daughter left no time for anything else—no going out, no movies, no lectures, no other adults. As Kimberly became more independent and able to draw away from me, and as I realized I was very attached to her, I knew I needed to create a separate life for me.

I reached a point where I said, "Aha! I need to get back out in the world again." I really had secluded myself. I was ready for a change and definitely thought that having some adult company at home would be good. Also, Roberta and I were spending a lot of time on the phone. She was going through a divorce.

It took a lot more time for us to adjust to one another and get comfortable than we ever imagined. But the children had a great time. It was interesting that the things each of us does or doesn't do balance out. On a superficial level there are things Roberta enjoys doing that I don't, like shopping. Some of those things just magically cancel themselves out. I'm more of a thorough cleaner type. I'll get lost in scrubbing something for two hours while my mind is wandering. Roberta's more the type that tidies up the kitchen and gets the dishes into the dishwasher.

Do you all eat together?

It happens on its own. That was something my family never did when I was growing up. Roberta's family did. I come from a very low socio-economic. . . . No structure.

In this setting, does the absence of a male matter?

Only from things I see outside. For instance, my daughter reacting to another father, or my daughter reacting to Alexis's visits with her father.

I dated one person off and on so he's been a constant. It would be nice to have someone around when the doorknob breaks, or something like that. I think I'm vacillating. Three years ago I swore to observe marriages for a year. The next year I vowed to consider it. I really vacillate on this issue.

(Roberta arrives. Though she is in her mid-forties, she looks considerably younger. She is a tall and graceful woman with light brown hair and light brown eyes. She wears no makeup, but her tanned face has a healthy glow. She smiles readily and is at ease, assured, and sits down to join us around the table.)

Sally: Both of us questioned whether or not we could have relationships, live-in relationships, with people of the opposite sex. We decided that we couldn't, that we were really independent souls and needed to be by ourselves. Recently, we've reached a nice balance. There's respect for each other and each other's children. And the children have reached this balance, too. We function now very much like a family.

Roberta and I joke about whether, if this were a lesbian relationship, people would be able to figure it out, as to which was the man and which was the woman. I'm the one who is never two feet from her lipstick, but I'm the one who goes out and shovels dirt. I bring home my two newspapers tucked under my arm each day. And Roberta sure isn't waiting with my slippers or a pipe.

Roberta: We change roles. It has really created a bond.

Sally: She's mellowed out and I try to be more assertive. One of my attractions to Roberta was her up-frontness. I was very evasive and I was very nice. And then, of course,

I would reach a point where it would just blow. We were still trying to adapt our ways. Roberta has pointed out to me that you can waste a lot of time in your life not being direct . . .

Roberta: . . . and be misinterpreted! But then there are also ways Sally has helped me to distance myself from the issue, to give it some time, to see it from another perspective. In the beginning, if I thought Sally was upset with me, I would follow her around the house asking her what was wrong. She would not be able to articulate it yet 'cause she wouldn't quite know what it was. So this would just add to her frustration over the whole thing.

In terms of our relationship and how it affects the kids, I think we're showing them two things: one is that a family can consist of different kinds of people. It doesn't have to be a mother and a father. We are indeed a family. We function as a family. Secondly, this is a temporary arrangement. At some point, we both want to live separately. But we will always have this experience that will always keep us close. The children will always have this relationship.

Sally: My daughter doesn't hesitate to refer to Alexis as her sister.

(Sally excuses herself and disappears to another part of the house. The interview continues with Roberta.)

My father died when I was 28. My mother remarried. Then she died when I was 35. My grandparents were also gone. There's just my brother and me. I had never really thought about having children. I think I felt like a child myself. I was busy exploring life and I didn't really have time for that kind of responsibility. But when I realized that I really had no family, with the exeption of my brother, I started thinking about it. Also, I was getting older.

I came to Tucson from New York City to do research for my dissertation and found something I didn't have in New York—a kind of spiritual quality. In New York, I think I was eaten up by the day to day activities of racing around in taxis and making money and being an overachiever at Columbia University. Out here, there's—it's like a period in a sentence and there's silence and there's space. There was a dialogue inside me that I hadn't been able to hear before because of all the distractions of the city. I also decided that what I wanted was the opportunity to make films and to have a child. And these I said consciously.

I've been here for 6 years. I made films and I had a child. I wasn't quite sure what kind of arrangement I wanted to have for this child. But on a subconscious level there was this need for family. I had had two major relationships out here with men. After 6 weeks of knowing the second one, I became pregnant. I was 40 years old and decided I would just go with it. We got married. The marriage didn't work out.

I had just turned 41 2 days before Alexis was born. I had had amniocentesis and felt relieved with that, too. If I had been under 35, I probably would have wanted it anyway. I was going to an accupuncturist as well as a traditional OB/GYN. I felt I was real healthy. I guess my only concern about having a child at this age, without having any other family with the exception of a brother, is the fact that both my parents died in their early fifties. My father had emphysema and my mother had cancer, but I've lived my life very differently from the way they did. I have come to feel that disease is related to imbalances in one's spirit, that their fate won't necessarily be mine.

I had no knowledge of infants. My daughter was born 6 weeks premature. She was in intensive care for 2 weeks because she developed apnea, which is a condition where they stop breathing. Back home, she was hooked up to a monitor for 6 months. I was very anxious because of the medical problems and also because of never having been around children. I had read so much about SIDS (Sudden Infant Death Syndrome). Had the monitor not been attached to her, I think I would have been in her room every 5 minutes. At least this way I knew. The whole introduction to parenthood was terrifying.

I had a nurse for Alexis for the first 2 weeks that she was home. I found it very uncomfortable not knowing what needed to be done. I felt more comfortable by the time she left.

I had one other friend who had a child—most of my friends are childless or they have older children—and I would call her up. Her son was a year older than Alexis. I would say, "When Brian was 6 months old, did he do x, y, and z?"

And she would say, "You know, Roberta, I really can't remember."

And I would think, "How strange that she can't remember all of this."

In a birthing class, I had met a nurse who was having a child and we became friendly. She lived around the corner. So, at 2 in the morning, I would call her to find out what to do 'cause I didn't have a mother to call. Now I provide those services for women who are having children. It's a network we have.

A friend will call in the middle of the night and say, "Timmy's been up all this while, coughing and running a fever. Do you think I should call the doctor or should I put a vaporizer in his room?" Most of the people I've become friendly with, except for Sally, are transplants. So nobody really has immediate family out here. We've all kind of hooked into each other and have created a large extended family.

There is a concern on my part that Alexis will not have a good guardian should I die. Because of the relationship with her father and our differences it concerns me. But then I feel I'm giving her a foundation right now that would allow her to assert her needs and that she would feel. . . . What I'm trying to create for her is an environment that's nurturing, that reinforces the fact that she's free, and that no matter what goes on around her, no matter what is crumbling and falling apart, it has nothing really to do with her, and that people love her for herself. I want to give her a sense of self-esteem and self-confidence so that should I not be here she could fend for herself.

Alexis's father, Arthur, and I had never gotten along. As soon as we got married there were problems. We went to four family therapists. All of them said we should not be together. We had different styles. One of them did some testing and found that Arthur had a personality disorder which was treatable but with professional help.

At the time Arthur and I were getting divorced, there was one particular judge we happened to be assigned to. She doesn't believe in sole custody. I went along with the joint custody which the judge had determined because I do believe Alexis should have access to both of us. However, other people we know, such as the day-care provider, witnessed Arthur's bizarre behavior with Alexis and how he was dealing with me. He would follow me around all summer; he would stand outside of men's houses whom I had seen the night before and scream at them. He was very much out of control.

Alexis wanted to go to school with Kimberly at this Montessorri program. Actually, the school's headmistress had wanted Alexis to come because she thought it would be good for Kimberly and Alexis to be at the same school. She had met Alexis on several occasions and felt that the program would be appropriate for her. I had spoken with Alexis's father and he had agreed to it. So I put her name on the list and her number came up.

When I got the call that there was a space for Alexis, I called Arthur who said that he had decided that he didn't want her to go there. With joint custody, I couldn't do anything about it. Her life then remains status quo. With sole custody, I could have said, "Well, we discussed this and I made the decision to send her there." Without it, I don't have that right. It's more than moving out of the state. It's day to day. He would make agreements with me and then back down, and it would be directed not at Alexis but at me.

So I decided to go for sole custody. In order to get sole custody you need a psychological evaluation which costs thousands of dollars. I paid to have one and the evaluator determined that I should have sole custody. But when I spoke to a lawyer about an appeal, I discovered that that costs a great deal more money which I don't have.

We've had occasion to deal with all of this in the present. What I suggest to Alexis is to say to her father that she loves him and that she loves me, to say that she dosn't really want to hear a lot of the bad things which she translates in her 3-year-old way. I think she's been able to handle it.

On occasion, when things have really intensified, she's had tantrums. I have difficulty seeing whether or not they're developmental or if they're situational. But we've been able to work through them. When we did a custody evaluation, the psychologist found that Alexis was very well grounded, meaning that she wasn't being disturbed emotionally and that there is a workable reality about all of this.

PART II

Adolescent Mothers

The vast numbers of unwanted pregnancies among the young for the most part evidence a troubling pattern passed along from one generation to the next, usually for social and economic reasons. There are no effective remedies as yet for this extremely serious problem for both the individual and society.

A disturbing increase in adolescent pregnancies continues. In 1991, 10% of teens between the ages of 15 and 19 became pregnant; four out of five of these girls were unmarried (U.S. Bureau of the Census, 1993; Women's Action Coalition, 1993). In 1992, the number of pregnant teenagers rose to 13% (Guttmacher Institution, personal communication, December 1994; National Center for Health Statistics, 1994). The total number of teen births for 15- to 19-year-olds in 1992 was 505,415, and of these 70% were unmarried (Child Trends, personal communication, January 1994).

In instances of accidental pregnancy, when the decision is made not to abort, it is not necessarily for ethical or religious reasons and the pregnancy is not necessarily "an accident." Loneliness and the lack of a nurturing family can subconsciously motivate a girl to have a child on her own to ensure that there will be someone for her to love and someone to love her.

The two adolescents, Nola and Manachan, have been included to represent this category for two reasons. First and foremost, to call attention to what must clearly be recognized as an aberration in the evolution of the family; and secondly, as a practical matter, to indicate the importance of reckoning with cultural and educational differences and the need for constructive intervention of social programs that will work to break the cycle of children having children.

One concept, foster care, is not without problems, but the data regarding the numbers are significant. In 1986, 280,000 children were placed in foster homes, and by 1993 this figure rose to 460,000 (National Foster Parents Association, personal communication, November 1994). Thoughtful programs designed to help adolescent mothers cope, such as Teen Insight, Teen Fathers Program, Parent Teen Program, and Young Parent Program exist in various locations around the country. For the year 1993–1994, there were almost 63,000 persons between the ages of 16 and 18 who were enrolled in the Job Corps Training Program (Department of Labor, Office of Job Corps, personal communication, January 1995).

For those young mothers who succeed as a result of these programs, their experiences are encouraging. It is the adolescent mother's enlightenment in this new circumstance that is depicted here and not an evaluation of the child's benefits, or lack thereof.

Nola and Jackie

5

Does the Eagle know what is in the pit?
Or wilt thou go ask the Mole?
Can wisdom be put in a silver rod?
Or Love in a golden bowl?
                              —William Blake

Buried among commercial properties, alongside a major road, is a small, weather-beaten, gray house. The paint is peeling. The yard is cluttered and weedy. Inside, the rooms are small and the furnishings are mostly old and threadbare, but the atmosphere is cozy. The air smells of stale cigarettes. Present are three women and a baby, Isolda, who, after being introduced, is carried off for a nap without protest.

The house belongs to Jackie, a solidly built woman who looks worn out. She wears a white shirt and dungarees. Her thin hair is in a pony tail. In a Barca-lounger near the front door sits Jackie's mother, heavy-set and flaccid. She and Jackie remain quiet and protective throughout the interview with Nola, the adolescent mother of Isolda.

Nola's large brown eyes have deep shadows underneath and the couch she sits on as the interview begins engulfs her fragile frame.

I'm 17 and I've always lived in Seattle. My mom went crazy doing drugs. She had to go to the hospital—three times. Last time was about a year ago. My dad, I don't really speak to him. Once in a while we talk. He's in a biker gang.

One of my sisters—I've got four sisters—two of them I don't know. One, she works at Safeway. She's a straight A student. She graduated from high school. The other one has a 3-year-old and she don't do nothing. (*Laughs*)

Did she have a child as you did, meaning not being married and not in a long-term relationship?

Yeah.

Was this your first pregnancy?

Yes. I was going to get an abortion. I didn't think I'd be able to take care of her. I was really bad into drugs. I didn't think I'd be able to make a good life for her, the baby. I didn't want it to grow up living the life I lived. I grew up in a terrible life—a drug world—where I didn't have any opinion of myself or anyone else.

I knew I wouldn't want to give the baby up when it was born. I wouldn't have been able to. At the same time, I just couldn't go and do it—get an abortion. I canceled three appointments 'cause I just couldn't do it. But I was going to try to act in the best interest for the baby.

How did you feel when you made the decision not to get an abortion?

I was happy. It made me feel good.

Were you taking drugs when you got pregnant and throughout the pregnancy?

Yeah. Mainly pot. Once in a while I did a little speed. I didn't do drugs when I was having my contractions. Going into labor I wasn't on any drugs. But I did some like a couple days before. But the baby didn't come out deformed or anything. She was 6 weeks premature. But my sister's daughter was exactly 6 weeks premature too, and she don't do drugs whatsoever. Both my sisters don't do drugs.

At first I was worried about my daughter's health but she's fine. I'm in a treatment right now—the first time. I started January of '91. I already had the baby.

What about the father?

Well, I was with this guy for a long time and we don't get along. I'm seeing another guy now—Marty. I've been going with Marty since I was 2 months pregnant. He's helped me. He's supported me. He tried to keep me off drugs—except for pot. Pot doesn't hurt the baby. I'm still with him to this day.

Where did you go after you had the baby?

I was staying where me and Marty was hanging out for a while, up the street. The baby was in the hospital for 2 weeks. She was premature. They weren't going to give her to me 'cause she was premature.

Marty and me—we were fighting a lot because I didn't know what I was going to do. I was going to go live with my sister and her boyfriend but her boyfriend is a real jerk. She wanted me to live with them. He didn't. So she got really mad at him. About 2 months later they split up.

So I didn't have nowhere to live. My other sister, her landlord is like really strict and I couldn't live there.

If it wasn't for Marty and his mom, I probably would have lost my baby. Social Services got into it. Marty asked his mom to help me. And she did.

That's his mom (*Nola gestures toward Jackie*).

Jackie's been helping me get my life together. Yeah, Children's Services Division (CSD) was going to take Issy away from me, but I went to Jackie, and she said she'd take me and the baby in. She went to court with me. Then we went and picked Issy up and we've lived here ever since. I'm staying off drugs. I'm watching my baby grow up.

How do you feel about that?

I love it. I was going to give her up and I didn't; and now I'm watching her grow and she'll be part of me for the rest of my life. I really like it. Yeah! But I got lots of help. I got Jackie and I got her daughter—and Marty, once in a great while. Jackie watches Issy when I have to go to my appointments or school and stuff like that. Jackie will take care of her for me; and so it makes it a lot easier on me.

Why would Jackie do this for you?

Because she loves us. I don't know. You might want to ask her that. I don't know. She loves us, I guess—felt sorry for us, or something.

How much schooling have you had?

I quit school in seventh grade. I was going to a program here to get my GED (Graduate Equivalency Degree) and then I quit that 'cause I didn't like it. So now I'm starting Job Corps. It's an outpatient-inpatient program for job training and GED. They help you train for a job. I've been there and I like it. I start tomorrow.

They get you a GED. They give you 6 months to a year training. I'm going to take computer training. After that, after 6 months to a year, or however long they think you need to be in there, they give you 2-week job training. And after that, if you didn't get the job, they help you find a job, and they give you money for a month. They help you with things you need, like clothes and stuff like that.

There's a Teenage Insight Program. Did you get involved in that?

Yeah. Through CSD. They said I had to go to the infant and toddler thing, classes they have. You spend a half-hour with your daughter and the rest of the time you go in another room and someone else watches your child. They talk about everything to you and your child. I don't like that, so I don't go. I speak to Dan quite a bit. He's a counselor.

Did he make arrangements for the job training?

No. Jackie did. She went to Life Skills class, and I was going to a Life Skills class—a different one. The one she was going to told me about Job Corps. So I went to Life Skills for 2 weeks and now I'm starting Job Corps.

What does Life Skills teach you?

(*Nola turns to Jackie.*) Jackie, I think you can explain it better than me.

No, I want you to explain it, please.

Well, they teach you about—about how to cope with your problems. Like when you get angry at somebody, how to cope with it. If someone is rude to you, how to say something back, but not get into a fist fight or something like that. They teach you how to cope with life better—to understand.

Do you feel you benefitted from that?

Yeah. Then comes job training.

Have you ever had a job?

Dairy Queen—for a couple of weeks. That's the only job I've ever had.

How did you get your drugs?

I knew lots of friends. I got them free. All of my friends— they always had them.

Has that changed at all?

I don't hardly see anybody I used to know.

What's not so great about having a child?

Well, I don't get to do what I want. Well, I do; but I don't get as much freedom as I used to have that I like. That kind of makes me mad sometimes, but I deal with it. I don't get to sleep in. Jackie takes care of Issy at nightime but in the mornings she wakes up early and I like to sleep late. I can't sleep late. I got to make sure she gets to her doctors. I got a big responsibility that I never used to have. That's the negatives. I'm all hooked up with CSD and all these other programs that I really wish I wasn't hooked up with.

I never had a responsibility like this. I just can't get up and leave. No way. Well, I can, but I wouldn't do that.

Why wouldn't you?

Because I love her too much. I mean she's my life. She's the only thing I really got of my family. The only thing that's really mine, I guess.

Had you protected yourself against getting pregnant?

No. I was with this guy for over a year, and I didn't think I'd get pregnant. I never thought about it, I guess. Well, I probably knew I would sooner or later but I never really thought about it at all.

Maybe you wanted to have a child?

Maybe I did. I don't know. I didn't speak my mind. He's a real jerk. Now he's going out with my best friend, and *she's* pregnant with his kid now. He doesn't give me child support or anything. He won't give me nothing. He wants to see her once in a while, but we always argue and fight 'cause of it. Once in a while I get nice and let him see her. I'll let him take her for the day—when I want some peace and quiet for my own. But that's about it. His mom sees Issy whenever she wants.

Has your family seen her at all?

Mmmhmmmm. They love her. Well, my mom, she's mentally ill. My dad, he sees Issy. He spends time with her. My sisters would see Issy every day if I would bring her over. Well, except for my little sister. She's always working and never has time for that.

How do you support yourself?

Jackie supports me. She gets money from the government—$1,000 a month for me to be here. They give it to her, not to me, 'cause she's my foster mother.

What do you think a pregnant 17-year-old woman ought to know?

Being pregnant is terrible. It hurts. It's a miserable pain that you go through. But if you want it and take the responsibility of it, I guess the only thing I could say about being pregnant and having a kid is that being pregnant's the worst part of it.

It depends on what time of the year you're pregnant, too. The summer's the worst. But I wouldn't really know 'cause I wasn't pregnant in the summer. You're always grouchy when you're pregnant. Well, I was. Always grouchy—really moody. Anything would make me mad.

Actually, after I had her, I have been pretty moody. I used to never get mad over nothing, about anything. But after I had her, I'm still moody. People say something to me wrong and I get really mad.

Are you angry a lot of the time?

Just when someone makes me angry.

How does someone make you angry?

Well, a lot of things, I guess. I don't know about that one.

What are your goals for yourself now?

My goals? I'm doing my drug program. I'm going to stay clean. I'm going to go to school. I'm going to make something out of my life, and I'm going to make sure my daughter has a good life for herself when she's older, and make sure that she goes to school and stays in school. Those are just about all my goals.

(The interview shifts to Jackie.)

I've known Nola since she was 12—through my son. He was a friend of hers. They've always liked each other. Marty went to Idaho to live with his father for a few years and Nola was off doing her thing. When Marty came back, he and Nola got together again. She was pregnant and then went into labor.

When she had Isolda, the hospital got CSD involved because the baby was premature and she still had the drugs in her system. They figured since she was only 16 she needed something. She had no supervision in her life, no place to live other than with friends.

So Marty called me. He was real upset, 'cause they didn't want to give up the baby. Nola was crying. I went over and talked to them and told them I would do it—you know, that I would go to court and try.

What made you decide to do that?

I don't know. She was upset, and she was young, and she deserved a chance with her baby. I just couldn't see someone just coming along and taking the baby. You have no chance with your child.

I was a young mother myself. I was married though. My husband sort of worked, off and on. I didn't know what it was like for someone who's a drug addict because I wasn't a drug addict. But when I got divorced I was all by myself. It was hard. I decided she needed someone to give her a chance.

When we went to court, they gave me custody of Isolda when she was 2 weeks old. The agreement was that Nola could live with me. Nola was supposed to do certain teen programs. She went, but they weren't the programs for her. She just didn't like them.

They were going to certify me as a foster parent and it took them like 6 months to do it. It was a really slow process. Finally, they started giving me money to take care of them. Actually, it's a really good program. They give you $1,000 a month. They pay me $400 a month to take care of them, and then $600 is for maintaining whatever they need. Like $225 is for rent, so much for utilities and food, and they only give you like $35 for recreation, which isn't very much, but she literally doesn't do much anymore either.

It's called a mutual foster home—the mother and child can live together with a foster parent. See, normally they would take the child away from the mother and they would live separately until the mother gets her life together. Well, this is a new program. The parent can live with the child.

How long will they continue to live with you?

Well, what happened was that the last time we went to court, Nola was really upset. She has been staying with her drug program and staying clean. So Nola was hoping she would get custody of Isolda. But it didn't work out because she didn't go through her schooling.

The judge asked her, "What are you going to do?" And Nola didn't have an answer. She didn't know because she had no schooling or training of any kind. So the judge just said "No." Nola was really upset. She was crying and she was sad.

I told the judge I knew of this program that Nola might be able to get into and stick with it 'cause it's a really good program called Life Skills. The judge agreed to another 120 days of keeping Isolda in my custody still—and Nola could live with us. Nola has to go through Life Skills and stay with the drug program. Those are the only two things she has to do now.

We went directly to this friend of mine that runs the Life Skills program. Actually, I was in the program myself a couple years ago. A lot of women that were there were either drug addicts or alcoholics or abused women. And I wasn't any of them, so I thought that some of the program was monotonous 'cause I had to sit through these drug programs and drunk classes. But I learned a lot. Some things that people go through is really sad.

Anyway, I took Nola up there to talk to Rosemary and Rosemary told us about some other programs. That's where it started and now Nola's in Job Corps. Tomorrow is her first day, and, hopefully, July 18th she'll get custody of Isolda. She'll be out on her own then. They'll help her get a place.

Your role as the custodial parent and the foster parent will end?

Right. It will end living with me but Nola and Isolda will be part of my life. You know, it's like she's got herself a second mother and she's not going to lose it.

What in your own life brought you to this place where you could do this?

I don't know. That's kind of strange-feeling. That's a hard question to answer. It's just that somebody needs help and nobody else would do it.

I've seen a lot of bad things. I've had a lot of bad things happen in my life but not as bad as Nola. You know, her family—not that I'm putting her family down—but a biker for a father and a mother gone crazy 'cause of drugs. And nobody would help her. Nobody. I mean she was really upset when she came to me. And somebody needed to help her. That's all I can think of. I mean it was just somebody came to me for help and that's what I usually do when people ask me for help.

How old are you?

Thirty-three.

Did somebody reach out and help you?

Sort of. I divorced my husband. About 6 years later—I had just got my GED—his mother called me up and she paid for my way to go to L.A. She supported me for almost 2 years, while I went to college and she supplied everything—food, clothing.

That's the only thing I can think of. Other than that, nobody's really helped. Well, my parents helped me. My father passed away. Now I'm taking care of my mother. So my mother-in-law's pretty much the only person that's ever really helped me. My father always gave me a place to live when I needed one, but money-wise they could never help me.

Do you work?

Not right now. I just graduated college. It's been exactly a year now, I think.

What's your field?

Accounting. I'm not working right now because I'm taking care of Issy while Nola does everything. I *was* working and I didn't like my boss, so I just quit. It's hard to work with somebody that's always on your back, constantly giving you a hard time. So I just didn't go back one day. Which probably wasn't the right way to do it, but. . . . As soon as Nola gets custody of Isolda I plan to go back.

Do you think you'd ever do it again?

Possibly. It would depend on the situation, I guess. If it was another situation like Nola, yeah, I would. I don't think anybody deserves to have a baby taken away and not have a chance to be with her and see what it's like.

It's been kind of rough at times—when Nola gets in her moods. I've had to pretty much put her in place. Well, I'm not the unmoodiest person either. I can be a real bitch at times, you know, but I'm not used to a teenager just telling me flat no. And she's done it a few times. She's gone and told me she'd be back in an hour and didn't show up till 8 hours later. That kind of made me mad. I'd tell her exactly how I feel about it. I'm pretty straightforward with her. If she makes me mad, if she does something wrong, I let her know.

I have a 17-year-old daughter and she's in school. She lives here. Actually, compared to my son, she's a perfect angel. It's not good to compare your children. Candy has her problems too. She's always had a lot of attention. Now there's a baby here that needs attention more. Nola needs the attention because Nola's had more problems and Candy has never had any problems other than "what-to-wear-today" type problems.

So it's been hard at times, but we're managing. Yeah! We do okay. We get in arguments. Candy and Nola have had a few arguments. Nola and I have had quite a few arguments, but we all get along pretty good. Everybody gets mad at Grandma because Grandma gets her way all the time. But that's just the way it is. If you want to live in my house you have to live with my rules. They don't always get obeyed but we try. I pretty much take care of Isolda at night. She kept me up all night last night. I woke up just before you got here. But we all do okay.

(*After Jackie's interview, Nola becomes less shy, more open. A friend had come in during the interview with Jackie. Nola whispers to her, "I'm going to be in a book." Nola and Jackie now answer a few more questions.*)

(To Nola): *Jackie wasn't involved with drugs. She had to get her GED. She went through the Life Skills and Job Training programs and graduated from college. Do you see any of that for yourself?*
Yeah.

(To Jackie): *Do you?*
I do. I see it for her.

(To Nola): Have people been disapproving because you had a baby and were not married?

No. If I get custody of Isolda, Rosemary said she's going to help me get a place. She'll probably put me on section eights where it will only be like $50 or $40—depends on how much your rent is. You only have to pay like a quarter of it, or just a little bit of it a month. I'll be on Welfare for a little while until I finish my job training and get a job.

If I stay in school and finish my drug program by July 18th, well, I've only finished my drug program. But if I sustain my drug program and go back to school, they'll give *me* custody of Issy this time.

(A few months after these interviews a note came from Jackie: "... Thought you would like to know Nola and Issy moved out of my home on 7/1/91. Nola's in the Job Corps now and doing very well. ...")

Manichan 6

The interview is held in a Home Economics room at the high school Manichan attends in San Francisco. She is of slight build, wide-eyed and dark-haired, a Laotian girl who applies cosmetics noticeably, creating rather a doll-like face. She wears a print dress, high heels and, at first, holds her purse in her lap as if ready to leave at any moment.

Soon, however, she settles down. Though her grammar is faulty, she expresses herself freely in English. She is bright and animated and gestures frequently with her hands.

I t was just the beginning of school—just a month—everybody was started at school. I go to the teen health clinic where they did that process for me. I learned I was 3 months pregnant, not knowing who the father of the child was. It was just one of those things where I went out and I got drunk, and I had intercourse with somebody that I did not even know. Someone that was maybe an acquaintance. I got drunk and did not know I was pregnant.

I was a senior at the time. I was 18 years old. It was so sudden I didn't know what I was going to do, what my decision was going to be. I had no plans. It was scary.

Then, I'm seeing all these young kids—and they're young!—having the good life as a senior and here I am being tired, being lazy, because I was pregnant. I dropped out of school. For almost a year I did not do anything. Through all that time I was home day after day, doing nothing. I took care of my nephews and my niece. I was depressed.

To be honest with you, I never liked birth control pill. I never liked using condoms. One of the things that I've learned now is that the most important thing for someone who is going to be in intercourse, is to use those things. During that time I was a kid, very rebellious. I was having fun. I didn't even think being pregnant could happen all of a sudden. I thought, "Just a one-time? It could never happen!" That was a mistake. I should have been aware, and I was not.

I'm thinking, "What am I going to do? I'm 18 years old. I don't have a high school education. I don't have a diploma. I'm not in school. I'm a bum." That's what I thought. My mother and father took it very hard, and they took it hard on me. They think I was terrible and horrible just because I came home pregnant. It was hard to believe they were ready to just not have me, not want me in the family anymore—just disowned, period. They told me to get an abortion.

I was frightened. I am carrying this child inside of me and my parents want me to get an abortion. At the same time, if I have the child, my mother wants me to give it up for adoption.

I wouldn't do it. I believe abortion is a sinful thing. It's not just destroying your child but it's destroying you at the same time. Maybe I should have got an abortion but somehow I thought this child should live.

This child had to be part of my life. Yes. And then after making the decision I cried, of course. I cried because I was 18 years old. I wasn't ready. But anyways, I kept my daughter.

Do you have sisters and brothers?

I have six sisters and one brother. I have three that's younger and four that's older because it's an every-year thing.

From my sisters I did not get much support. My sisters didn't care what happened to me. They thought I was a terrible girl who does not know what responsibility is, who does not know what education is. The whole view of my family was that I didn't belong in the family.

What counts in my family is education, respect, knowing your responsibilities. They thought having a child was the stupidest thing because I was not financially ready and I didn't have education. They thought I would be in a slum, especially not having the father of my daughter involved. To them, school was everything, and going shopping, and things like that. Out of eight in the family, I was the one out of the circle. That's how I felt when I was pregnant.

I didn't have much support. My parents didn't want to accept me and I didn't—it's so hard to say—I didn't get the support from them. I felt lonely and empty because I did not listen to them.

I tried talking to my sisters. They wouldn't listen to me. And then again, I was afraid to talk to my parents. They're not as Americanized as we are. We grew up here and they're more into the old culture—the culture from Laos. They don't realize we grew up here and what we learned and how we adapted to the new culture of America.

It was so hard for me to talk to anybody. But somehow I managed. I was by myself and here's my child. I felt abandoned by everybody. I didn't have contact of friends. I didn't have contact of teen-parenting program to help me. I mean, it was nobody. I went through this thing all by myself. And that's what the hardest thing is.

Finally, I talked to my parents and I told them, "You know, I am your daughter, for goodness sake. I'm going to have this child. I need love and I need support and I need understanding." And I says, "I don't think it's a mistake to have this child. I choose to have her and I know what's coming. I know what kind of responsibility I'm going to face everyday. But it was an accident. I did not mean anything." I told them that.

My parents told me I should be on Welfare. I should get my own assistance. They told me I could live at home and would have to pay half the bills after I had her.

When I was 4 or 5 months pregnant, I went to Welfare. So I was put on medical assistance and on food stamps and all that good stuff to help me get started. I went to San Francisco State University Health Science for my pre-natal care. I was kind of frightened at the same time, and I didn't go through all those classes that I was supposed to. I delivered her up there.

When I was about 8 months, my parents accepted the fact that I'm going to have a child. And they learned to accept the fact that I'm not going to give this child up for adoption because I've been carrying my child for almost 9 months. And so after I had her, they learned to be supportive. They learned to accept that this is going to be their grandchild.

I went through a lot of tears from just having her.

When I first saw my baby I was shocked. I didn't want to hold her. I didn't want her near me. I just pushed her away. I was not happy when I had her. I was not happy when I was lying in the hospital for 2 days and 2 nights. They asked me if I wanted my daughter and I said, "No. Just leave her where she is." It's just the saddest thing a mother can feel about a child.

I felt a lot of hate towards myself, a lot of hate towards those who didn't give me support. I did not know what I was going to do next. Here I am with a live child, a mother who does not want this child yet does not want to give it for adoption. I want myself to give the love that my daughter needs, not anyone else. I want her to know who her real mother is.

Back home, every day, every night, I was in my daughter's room—a room where my mother would always have me be. She would turn the heat on. She would help me take hot baths, hot tea, and things like that so that my body can heal a lot faster; and my daughter was there next to me, and I look in her eyes and tears are coming down my face and I hope to myself, "I hope I will bring this child up in a good world, not a bad world."

And from then on my mother was helping me take care of her, and the only time I would hold her was when she needed her milk and when she needed her diapers changed. I fed her by bottle, and I would only change her diapers or hold her when she would cry, and sometimes I wouldn't even hold her then.

Slowly my feelings changed. I learned and grew with her. I've learned to love her, and I've learned to understand her, and I'm trying to get myself together, you know, "Hey, you are a mother now. You can't abandon your child like this." Somehow I learned to be strong.

What is your daughter's name?

Her name is Mala. She's 17 months. And we live in my parents' home.

When Mala was about 4 or 5 months, I went looking for a job. I went out everywhere—jobs at the bank, jobs at the office, places that I liked to work, places that I liked to be. They turned me down; everybody turned me down because I did not graduate from high school.

I did not have the education I needed. And from looking at Mala and from going out to get a job and they turned me down, I says, "I need to go back to school. This is not working out for me. What is going on? What am I thinking? I'm 18 years old and I'm having this child and I'm not even ready. I don't have a job and I'm on Welfare. I don't need to put my child through this."

And so after this year of 1990, I decided to come back to school and this is where everything began: the Teen Insight Program, how to take care of your child, how to go back to school, how to get a high school diploma. And Terry, from the college, would come to teach us job-training, job-placement, how to be financially independent. We learned about medical care and day care for your baby—whatever you need to take care of yourself and your child and whatever you're ready for. And this is where I knew exactly what a teen-parent mom is.

What is a teen-parent mom?

To me, being a single teen-parenting mother and especially at such a young age, I think it's work—24 hours of responsibility, a lot of stress, emotions. Just learning how to strive, learning that I'm not only responsible for myself, but I have a child. I have a daughter who is part of me now, part of my life, who is going to be part of my responsibility for 18 years. That's what teen-parenting mom is to me.

I've learned a lot. I've learned to deal with a lot of criticisms from other people—from other kids at the school—that says, "Oh, it's stupid to be a young mom. What are you going to do with your life? Why do you even want to have a child?" It's hard. I don't know how to explain it.

It's like I'm a baby and I'm having a baby at the same time. I don't see my daughter as a mistake or regret her. I love her dearly. Without her and not having the choice to keep her, I would not have learned anything. I don't think I would have grew up. But then again, I believe I grew up a lot faster than I should have.

She has made a whole new outlook of my life. She has put so much strength to me. I look at my daughter and I think of a lot of things I do—and that I want to do for her and for myself.

Who takes care of your baby now?

Daycare does. I got it through AFS, Adult Family Services. I did not have the financial system to be paying for my daughter's daycare. Adult Family pays for it. That's Welfare.

I take Mala there at 8:15 in the morning and pick her up at 3:15, after school. And if it wasn't for the teen-parenting, I would not have been able to be in school today. I want to be able to go out in the world and graduate and have that diploma. I say to myself, "Okay, Mom and Dad, this child has made me grow up. I realize what the terrible things are that I did. But I'm making it in the world. I'm going to have a career after I graduate."

What are you going to do?

I'm going to be a bank teller.

So it is very nice. I never thought I'd make it this far. When I was pregnant, my parents, my sisters, they always put me down. They said, "You're never going to finish high school. You're going to be as dumb as ever. You're going to be a bum." And all of this terrible things.

And now, I'm looking at myself. I graduate in 1990. So what, maybe I'm a year behind. But I'm going to have a good career and my daughter is healthy. And to me that's a progress. I've been in such a slump for over a year and now I'm lifting my feet up and doing so well. I feel strong and I feel very happy when I talk about it.

I see other 15-year-olds coming to school pregnant. Like at the teen parenting program we have now. We have freshmans who just had a baby and freshmans who are coming in and they deliver. Honestly, I truly think it's terrible for a 15-year-old to become pregnant.

And these kids, they say to their self they're ready to have a child. They don't have a mind of an adult. Maybe they will be delivering during the middle of school, the semester. Say I'm 8 months pregnant and school's not out yet and there's 2 more months of school left. I'm going to deliver. That's 2 months of school and they're going to have to start the whole year over again.

I'm an 18-year old who dropped out of school with nowhere to go. I was not ever ready for this child. And I didn't have an abortion and I didn't give it up for adoption. And I'm 18.

It was very hard for me to come back to school and do well. I was put in so much pressure because of my daughter. I was striving so hard to get good grades and to make it out of high school and to get into the real world. And I'm growing up but then again I'm still young. Do you know what I mean?

The teen-parenting program and Insight, and Terry who helps with life skills, and child care skills, and all of that—it's all there for the 15-year-old, right? But the 15-year-old isn't old enough to take it in.

What would you say to the people responsible for the education of young women and young men to help them understand that becoming pregnant is something that ought not happen?

That's a hard question. We can't really prevent it because I think America has given each individual so much freedom. The schools offer classes on health. The teen health clinic has put out so many ads, you know, "Don't get pregnant!" "Be careful when you go out on a date." Things like that. I don't think the school can prevent this. Each individual of the female side can prevent from being pregnant and having a child.

My Mom and Dad has never sat down with us and taught us about the birds and the bees and what it was like to have a child. So I learned these things in school. Then again, I did not listen and I was not careful. That was my problem.

If your mother and father had been able to give you the necessary information and you could always go to them and talk, would it have made a difference? Would you have listened?

Yes, I probably would have listened. It was like we see each other every day, you know, Mommy and Daddy, but we really never had the eye contact. For me, I was embarrassed to talk about sex. I was embarrassed to talk about condoms, you know, what it was like. And to them it was embarrassing. It works both ways.

I think it has to start with the mother and father. If they are more involved, emotionally, and if they communicate with their children, I think there would be less of pregnancy. Everybody needs that communication between mother and daughter.

And if there wasn't so much anger! For example, my mother was very, very angry that I was pregnant. She screamed at me. If she gave me that little support, you know, the love that I needed through my pregnancy, I wouldn't be as bitter as I am now. I feel bitter, really bitter. They never really sat down with me. They never gave me the support I needed, that love.

I would have not known where to go, what to do, if I didn't come back to school. The school was for teen-parent moms who want to go back to school. They would keep her attendance records. If we were missing classes, we would have to have excuses because they don't think we should take advantage of it.

And it's expensive these days. It's awfully expensive to have a child.

If, somehow, I can get my words out to these young kids today, "Condoms and birth control pill—use them! It is so important. And if you're going to bring a child into the world, for heaven's sake, be prepared—emotionally, physically, financially, be prepared."

Everybody in this world's going to have sex. I mean, today, in this society as I have seen, they're starting out from seventh and eighth grade. I don't think anybody can prevent these young kids from having sex. I don't think anybody can prevent these young kids from having a baby because it's their choice. And if they decide to have it, it's a need, it's a want and desire that a human being has. Why didn't I say no? It was hard. I don't know why I didn't say no.

You said that the night you became pregnant you had been drinking.

Yes. Drinking. Oh my goodness! That was a problem because you just don't know what can happen. I was so drunk that if somebody did something to me I would not have known what was going on. And then after waking up and being sober and later realizing that I'm missing my period, my menstrual period, I knew I was pregnant. I think saying no to sex would be the hardest thing to say, especially young teens today.

What do you see for yourself, say, 10 years from today?

I see myself being successful in the career, banking career, that I am in. I don't want to go to college. I think college is scary. But I can probably see myself going to school that deals with the banking system to move myself higher up to become a loan officer 10 years from now.

And I see myself raising this child so where we can have the mother and daughter relationship. And where we can be happy. I want my daughter to have all the things that a daughter would want in a mother. I want to raise this child up so that she can learn what her mother has went through. I want to teach my child to grow up to be smart and to learn the right things and the wrong things. And especially, I don't want her to be a young teen-parent like I was.

How will you prevent that?

Giving her a lot of love and talking to her. Say no when you have to.

When I go pick her up at daycare I feel—I look forward to it every day because it's like picking up my, you know, picking up my life. She knows every time at 3:15 that Mommy is going to be there and she's ready for me. So I feel really happy and I look forward to it.

When my daughter was very young, I felt bad putting her at daycare. I felt like I didn't give her enough time to be with me. But it had to happen because I needed the education. It's such a dramatic change in my life. My daughter has helped me to learn a lot of things that I did not know. I mean, from just the beginning of me not wanting her, and now she's like the love of my life, and it's really great.

And if I decide to have another one, I don't want it to be the same way. I want to be able to love my child the very first day she's born. This creature has brought me so much . . . don't know what to say . . . so much happiness.

Do you see yourself married?

That's hard to say. I can see myself married, yes. And I can see myself being ready this time with a good relationship—with families and things like that. I probably see myself having two more kids.

I notice you wear a wedding band.

Oh, this? My mother got this for me. They're really traditional. Every woman has them. It's not a wedding band.

When you go out in the world do you feel that the world looks at you as a single mom and as bad?

That's a good question because when I see other single moms and I see them not well-dressed and their kids are crying, in stores, I judge that mom as a bad mom. Sometimes I keep my appearance so well that people don't even think I'm a single mom if I'm not with Mala. In public, I like to be careful. I like to show my daughter the love that each single mom would show. And I never think that anybody would judge me bad as a single parent.

My parents have come to love Mala. They've come to spoil her. So they learned. My sisters are very impatient with my daughter. And sometimes it makes me sad because it is important to be patient and they just don't know what it's like to be a single parent.

The hardest part about having a child at such a young age is the fact that she's always going to want and always going to need the attention that my daughter draws from me. She's bugging me. She just wants me to hold her. I guess it's time. I never have time for myself. It's time and patience.

I need my social life and I need to be around people and sometimes I drop Mala off at my aunt's so I can have that time.

This is the hardest age—when they're almost reaching 2 years old. They want everything and I yell and I scream. But then again, I have to realize that this is a baby you're talking to, not an adult. Yelling at her and taking things out on her, not taking that time, is no good. I feel bad after that. I feel really, really bad. But I'm learning to cope. I'm learning to be a mom who is going to know almost everything there is to know about a child.

PART III

Fathers as Caretakers

More and more fathers, whether married, divorced, or single, are involving themselves in the care of their children from birth on, a far cry from the traditional detachment that was the accepted norm until about three decades ago. The feminist movement which gradually changed the role of women in the home led inexorably to a modification of the role of the man with regard to fatherhood. Many support groups for fathers are available today. Men see themselves more and more as competent nurturers, deriving great pleasure from a close relationship with their offspring.

In addition, the demands of the two-income family often necessitate the father's involvement in the rearing of their children. In 1990, it was reported that there are 2.2% of married fathers with children under 18 who are the primary caretakers while their wives are in the labor force (U.S. Bureau of the Census, 1993). In fact, 58% of mothers with young children worked outside the home in 1990 (Bartholet, 1990).

Fathers who are divorced or separated and who wish to remain involved in raising their children now head 14% of single-parent households, up from 10% in 1980 (Johnson, 1993).

Unmarried fathers living with children more than doubled from 1980 to 1992 (Johnson, 1993).

Many fathers have gained increased understanding about what it means to parent, anticipating and responding to the

needs of their growing children. Recognizing this development, custody cases are awarded to the father if it appears to
the judge he can offer the better environment for the child, an
outcome previously unheard of except where the mother is
proven to be adulterous. For the past 20 years, American fathers who fought for custody increasingly won up to 70% of
the time (Chesler, 1994).

Some fathers are determined to give their children a different experience—a more tender, less competitive relationship—from the one they knew growing up. Not surprisingly,
more men seem to appreciate what women have been doing in
the home and for the family for ages. There can be no doubt
that a child who receives the benefits of an involved and caring father is more likely to become an involved and caring
adult—an important benefit to society.

Chet

7

Chet is 26 years old, white, married, and the father of two preschoolers. He is of medium height, slender and sturdy with straight brown hair that falls around his serious, pleasant face. He is the primary caretaker of the two children of his marriage. This interview took place in our office, and this gentle-mannered young man began matter-of-factly.

My situation is unlike much of the people we know. Those few men who do stay home, usually can't stand it anymore and they go back to work. Right now, on my refrigerator, I have the names of three fathers who stay home but I haven't contacted any of them. I have the desire to reach out to talk to other people but (*laughs*) I don't have the time. It's really frustrating.

My wife's in school. She's gone all day most of the week. Sometimes she has a half-day, but a lot of those days she'll spend in the library. She leaves in the morning and gets home anywhere from mid- to late afternoon. So I'm home with my 4-year-old and my 2-year-old. All day. When she's on vacation, suddenly I have a lot of time, but when she's back in school and returns home, then I go to work—5 days a week. I go in at 6 and work anywhere from 10 to 2 A.M.

Last week I was there until 5 in the morning. It plays havoc with my sleep but over the last year I've gotten used to it by taking catnaps. If I don't get enough sleep, I let my kids watch

Sesame Street and sit next to them on the couch and sleep. I have a guilt battle with that 'cause I don't like using TV as a babysitter. I feel strongly about that. You know, there's a choice. Either I can get no sleep and yell at them a lot and be an ass for the rest of the day, or I can try to get a little sleep and probably be much better.

I work at a natural food store. My title is Senior Grocery Staff which means, basically, I do everything. Myself and another woman, we work at night and spend most of our time cleaning and stocking and getting the store ready for the next day. The managers all leave around 5 or 6 P.M. We're essentially the night managers. We're responsible for locking up, taking the deposit, and handling any sort of question that comes up during the night. Things like that.

Mostly, it's the people I like. I work with different good people. It's also the kind of work I've always liked to do. I've never liked working in a situation where I have a boss. In this case, my boss leaves when I come so I see him for maybe 10 minutes a day when he mentions things that need doing.

Until I found the natural food store, we really did not know any people who were in our situation or were much like us. But at the store there are people, not necessarily with children, but people with the same kind of outlook about life, so that was a breath of fresh air.

I was born in Birmingham. My parents moved here to Nashville when I was a couple of years old to get away from all that violence. I grew up in Nashville, graduated from high school, and was determined to get as far away from here as I could. So though I grew up about two blocks from a university campus, I went to Grinnell College in Iowa. A wonderful school. That's where I met Sandra. She's my wife. I went there 2 years and transferred to Tennessee State for a lot of reasons.

Grinnell is a place to cultivate personal growth, and we were basically very much a couple. More, we were planning a life together. That was not possible there. We wanted a place of our own. That would mean living off campus and commuting, and people were not willing to accept you as a couple.

You were supposed to be independent, individual, and all this stuff. So, in a sense, we were paying $10,000 a year to commute to campus and take classes. Hell, we could do that at TSU and have our own life and pay half as much. That's what we did. In a lot of ways we regretted transferring and in a lot of ways we didn't. Grinnell was a much better school.

Sandra and I have been married 5½ years. We met when I was 18. We knew after about a year or so we'd end up being married and I guess we were engaged for a year. We got married and took a year off. We knew we would have children soon and thought, ideally, it would be after we graduated. We weren't being very careful. When we did get pregnant—it was more or less an accident—we were really happy about it. It wasn't a bad situation.

I didn't know the specifics of what it would be like, but it wasn't a particular adjustment we had to make. We knew we would be giving all our time and energy—would be giving our lives to our children.

After Sandra had the baby, she started going to school half-time and I was going full-time. We were undergraduates. We'd be on campus, and she would hand off the baby and go to her classes. In the middle of winter, when Loren was less than a year, I would just wrap him up in my coat so he wouldn't get cold and we'd walk downtown or I would switch him off with Sandra, and she'd go back home. It was difficult, but it worked out well. We arranged our classes and things so that we used a minimum of babysitters. Those times that we really couldn't work it out and switch off we used my parents. They live here in town. I'm sure there were other couples like us in town. We just never saw them.

It's sort of complicated. When I was a senior she was still a junior. She continued part-time and eventually finished her undergraduate degree in biology. Meanwhile, I got a scholarship to graduate school. I got my masters and a teaching certificate and went looking for teaching jobs. I was a physics teacher. High schools, if they have a physics teacher at all, usually there's just one and he's been there 15 years or something. I did not find a physics job.

Eventually I found a job in the middle school as an assistant math specialist. It turned out to be very unsatisfying, so I quit, but a couple months later I went back because a math teacher was pregnant and leaving. I took over her job—taught and finished out her year—and did not like it at all. I was working 12 hours a day. My kids would be asleep when I left, and they'd be asleep when I got back and I'd still have work to do at home. I finished the year and decided I didn't want to teach, at least not for a while. I was stressed out.

During the year that I was looking for a teaching job—a quote real job—I started working at the food store at night and weekends. After I found my "real job" and realized that that wasn't what I wanted to do, I went back to the store. I got switched around at the store and into the position I have now. That's where I've been for the last 2 years and I like it a lot. Working at night enables me to be home during the day.

I think I have a very strong maternal instinct. I think it's more than maternal. It's always been there. I wanted a family even when I was in high school. I wanted to settle down and get married and have kids which set me apart from my friends 'cause that's the last thing they wanted. In a lot of ways this isolated me, but I knew from the start that's what I wanted to do.

I was 21 when I got married, 22 when Loren was born, and 24 or 25 when Melinda was born. Sandra is the same age as me. She is now in her last semester of nursing school. She wants to be a midwife.

I see friends of mine that are older settling down and having kids. They've got their jobs and their social life which they don't really want to give up. They squeeze their kids in on the side. I just don't see that as working very well. Kids take too much time. I mean most of it's good time which I don't mind giving up, but you still give it up. I don't think it works to try to hold on to the freedom you had before you had kids.

Usually on weekends Sandra does the majority of the childcare; and she's got them in the evenings. She's gone a lot during the week, so she misses them, and I'm sort of sick of them by then. I let her take care of them, and she doesn't get pissed at me for not doing more, and I don't feel like she's meddling. I sort of stand back. It works out pretty well. If both of us are home and Melinda is the slightest bit cranky or tired, she clearly prefers Sandra to me.

Sandra says when she gets out of school she wants to be home more with the kids during the day and I've thought, "Now wait a minute, I want to be home." Is this traditional, non-traditional, transitional, or what?

Do you and Sandra have time to be together?

No, no we don't. During the worst of it, when I was working at night and she had a lab at night, I think we had one meal a week together and maybe one weekend day. I mean we don't see each other much at all now. We're growing apart not seeing each other. Right now our marriage is kind of unsteady.

Actually, this weekend Sandra and I went away. We're trying. We're seeing a marriage counselor whom we've seen before. We both like her and we're both hopeful.

My parents will help with the children. They'll babysit unless they have somewhere they have to be. They're very supportive. Sandra's parents live in Virginia and we see them fairly often.

It is so pleasant being with my kids—just more quantity time. You see enough to know their highs and their lows, and you see them grow up, and it's wonderful. That's the best! I also like having them in the day.

I still have to take the kids with me where I go and worry about their going to the bathroom and cleaning up the mess, but I can arrange it how I want. And I still get a lot of work done during the day which is good. I like to be doing things— paper work, paying bills, household stuff. We live out in the country in an old house, and we're putting a bathroom on. I don't get much work done on that during the day. But I did put brakes on our car the other day.

The aspects that are not so pleasant are the isolation and not having time to myself. Up until recently it's not bothered me but I think over the long run not having any time to myself has made me very restless. Really, I have not had any time for myself for 2 years now.

I believe there are other young men out there like me doing the same thing, but I haven't actually personally met any full-time male parent. One of the women I work with at night is at home with her kids during the day while her husband works. We both joke about how it is a vacation to come to work. All we have to do is worry about ourselves and our job, and we don't have to worry about two kids running around. It is nice to be able to talk about it and be mutually supportive.

Do the problems outweigh the pleasures?

If I had the opportunity to do it over again, I'd do it.

I generally prefer the company of women over men anyway. They seem to accept me more readily. It's usually women I run into because I'm doing errands—a woman bank teller, women receptionists, cashiers, checkout clerks. Most remarks I get are innocent. I'll be at the bank and somebody will say, "Oh you're babysitting today." I never say anything. I just nod or smile.

What gets me upset—it's usually the women who do this—like last week I was at an insurance office. My two kids were with me, which is the way it is every day. I know their limits of behavior and when to say no and how to—I mean, I'm their parent. I know how to do it. I'll be somewhere talking to a woman and I'll tell one of my children to stop doing something and the woman will say, "Oh, it's okay. They'll be fine." Like she knows—because she's a woman, and I'm the father! Because they're female they think they know more about kids and that I don't quite know what I'm doing, so they have the right to advise me.

The men I run into are generally repairmen. They usually say something like, "I've got two kids at home and I miss them a lot" or "I did that for a few years." Or the men will come to the house and see my two kids and say, "Oh, it's your day with the kids." But it's usually women who are more likely to assume I'm just doing this for the day or I'm doing this but not out of choice.

Several times Sandra's father has thanked me for letting Sandra go to school. I always say, "I'm not *letting* her do anything. She's going to school on her own." And he'll say, "You're right, you're right." He doesn't say it as if he means it. I think both her parents believe we would be happier in careers. They have a problem accepting that staying home with kids can be satisfying—satisfying enough for someone to be happy doing it. They think it's what you do until you get old enough to get out and finally "do something." To me, it's not at all a sacrifice. It's something I want to do.

Is it all for the kids and seeing them grow up or do you want to avoid going to an office at 9 o'clock for the rest of the day?

I've thought about that a lot. I don't like 9-to-5. I never have. I much prefer to do what I do even though my night job is hectic. I've always been happier doing lots of little things or doing something unusual. I can stay home with my kids. I don't have to think about making a whole lot of money and supporting a family. That's not my job.

But on the flip side, if I realized it was just an excuse and I either forced myself to or wanted to go out and get a 9-to-5 job, we'd have to hire somebody to raise our kids and that's pointless. Why pay somebody to do something I can do better? I would get a lot more out of being home with my kids than somebody else would. It would be a lot cheaper for me to do it and the kids would be better off.

A lot of our friends' kids are in daycare. One of our very close friends did daycare for a while. She would go to people's houses during the day and watch the kids for them. She is one of the best parents I have ever seen. If I had to drop my kids off somewhere or had somebody come to our house, she would be the one. This woman is very patient. She takes the time. Her children will come up and if they interrupt her she'll say, "You're interrupting me." But if they are respectful and polite, she will squat down and look in their faces and explain and talk to them. I respect her a lot.

And still, even her—you just don't treat other kids the same way you treat your own. You don't have the same drive.

Loren goes to preschool twice a week, so he has contact with other kids. He's learning all about ninja turtles and superheroes and all those things he's been isolated from. He absolutely loves to watch TV. We don't let him watch cartoons. Loren will watch the Financial News Report or something like that. All day he's, "Can I watch TV? Can I watch TV?" and it drives me up the wall. He likes Sesame Street and Reading Rainbow. Sesame Street I think is a good show. I like watching it, too, with him.

Generally, there's so much violence on TV, and Loren is just sitting there, staring at it. His mind sits down. You can see it happen. His eyes glaze over. He stops thinking. If he's been watching too much TV, he'll get up from it and he'll walk around the house. It's like his creativity checked out. He hasn't had to use it. It takes him a long time to get it back.

If he's not obsessed by the TV, he'll be in here with Melinda, drawing. I tend to ignore them, sort of go about my business of washing the dishes, cleaning up, and letting them fend for themselves. It'll be wonderful when Loren is in school full time. Wonderful, because I so rarely get to be home alone with Melinda. She acts very differently without her older brother around. It will be easier.

It's isolated living out in the country. At the same time there's plenty to do. I do lunch and breakfast. Sandra does dinner. And that's changed too, because I would make them a nice lunch and set it down and they wouldn't eat it and then 40 minutes later, "I'm hungry." It became too frustrating. I'd get too angry about spending all this time making lunch and them not eating it.

I felt I had to change my strategy and be mature enough to know what battles to develop and which to have the patience to keep quiet about. So about a week ago I just said, "Screw this. When lunch time comes along I'll make them a sandwich and just sit down."

I grew up in—I guess you could call it a non-traditional family myself. My father went to work and my mother went back to school. We drove around in a Volkswagen bus and she's marched and all that. They started their own school 'cause they didn't like public school. So for a while I was in a private, very small, very liberal, very alternative school. That lasted for a couple of years. One year I was at home with a tutor. Eventually I ended up in public school. I had an adjustment problem for about a year.

My father was 17 when they got married, so he had been pretty much living at home. My mother had moved out of her home the year before they got married. They were not at all hippie-dippie. My father had a full-time job and a house and a mortgage and kids and all that, and they had values. They had a family and considered themselves responsible.

My father retired in his late forties. He was into computers. He's never been to college, but he was an assistant professor at a university and did a lot of consulting. My mother was trained in public health and worked at the hospital as an expert in child sexual abuse. She did that for 9 or 10 years and then she burned out. She is now starting to get back into research in the same field. She wanted less hands-on.

What does being a good parent mean?

Endless patience, but at the same time drawing the line when it needs to be drawn. Kids need a lot of patience but they also need discipline. At some point you have to say, "No! You've got to stop." They need to be taught manners and respect and all that sort of thing, but they also have to be loved. Just being able to do that all day is. . . .

I try really hard. I don't know how successful I am, especially when I don't get enough sleep. Maybe I yell too much. I ask my kids, "Am I a good father?" and Melinda says, "Sometimes." I think it's a pretty good response. Nobody's a good parent all the time. I think I'm a good parent most of the time.

Aaron

8

The interview with Aaron was conducted in the library of the small New Hampshire law firm in which he is a partner. He is 45 years old, a trim man of medium height with sandy-colored hair and an open, direct countenance. His rolled-up shirt sleeves and knotted tie seemed appropriate dress given the demeanor of the earnest and dignified person who began to speak.

I am married. It's the second marriage for me, and we have one child who is 5½ years old. I have no children by my first marriage. Both my wife and I felt it would be a natural thing for us to do, to have a child. I'm not sure the basic assumptions were questioned. The idea of raising a child was appealing. I think we had an intuitive sense of it being an enjoyable thing. We knew it would be a lot of work but felt like it would make us feel more complete somehow.

Did it make you more complete?

Oh yes. I would say I'm significantly involved. A little background might be helpful here because I'm not sure it would have been significant but for some accidents of history.

Ann had been accepted to med school about 3 weeks before we met. I was 36. She was 33. That was in '83. We were married a year later, during her first year of medical school. She had been a physician's assistant for about 5 years and had done 2 years of training for that. So she had been leaning in that direction. I was very busy at that time in many respects, practicing law and doing a lot of community work.

Caleb was born just 10 days prior to Ann's graduation from medical school. She stayed at home from then until she began her internship 9 months later. That was actually a longer time she had with him than a lot of her friends had with their children, and then, of course, we just made this incredibly dramatic change where she had almost no time with him.

For 3 months we had somebody living in and he was cared for at home, but it didn't work out very well for us. In the beginning of her internship, I was getting Caleb up and taking care of his needs in the morning—washing, dressing, breakfast, whatever. Caleb started at daycare placement when he was a little past one. I would get him there sometime between 9 and 9:30, and I would pick him up at 5; and that was a real hard thing for Ann and me. Neither one of us really felt that that was right, but there wasn't a whole lot of choice.

So I was thrust into a primary caretaking role. I have continued that role pretty much. At first, it was because of her schedule, and now I wouldn't have it any other way. I guess it has to do with what a child can give you, and it has a lot to do with spontaneity and kind of a refreshing openness to the world. I feel like I adopt that posture when I'm with him. Of course, I don't do it every time. I like the total silliness—the nonsensical things you do and say when you're a child. I tend to do them also. It pulls that back out of me. It's great fun— that unabashed joy he has of discovering something or telling me about somthing. It's infectious.

Could you describe how your wife's internship affected the family?

No, it's indescribable. The hospital gives most of the direct patient care to the interns, so she was on duty all night every third night, and she was technically off the next day. What that meant was that she had no new patient write-ups that day to do, but she was often at the hospital after an all-night tour of duty or episode 'til about 6 or 7 o'clock the next night. So the second night, when she was technically not on, she was still doing write-ups and would often be there 'til about 11 or 12 o'clock. It was hard on everybody.

I have to add another dimension in this. The additional thing in our life has been Ann's suffering from a rather severe case of PMS. She has significant personality alterations, mood swings from severe irritability at certain times during the month to severe depression. And when you add to that no sleep it was almost unbearable. That was another piece of it that complicated our lives.

She actually did her third year at medical school studying that whole question. She has a vested interest. It was not a mere academic exercise. PMS takes such different forms in different people and even different in the same person, sometimes from year to year and even month to month. For Ann, somtimes it was aches and pains but mostly it was moods. It's really a strange and varying malady.

Have you been able to overcome this real obstacle?

Oh, I don't know. We worry a lot about it and have no idea whether we've really taken care of it or not. I have consciously tried to change my practice to make it less demanding. So we try to make adjustments here and there. I mean it's worked in the sense that I think I've been able to make more time for Caleb.

The caretaking responsibilities are beginning to shift back more. It's about fifty-fifty now. Ann gets Caleb to the preschool sometime between 8:30 and 9:00, and I pick him up somewhere between 4:00 and 5:30, and that varies a lot. One day a week it flips; Ann picks him up and I take him. For the next 8 months, at least, we'll work it that way. I try to organize my time so that I get up early to come to the office and work when people aren't here. I'm more efficient doing it that way. Then I can get out of here at 4 P.M.

Ann is just finishing up her residency this July. My hunch is that it will be easier. I think it's very hard for her to be in a kind of student role at age 42.

Who fixes dinner, who markets, things like that?

I do most of the grocery shopping, and we often, Caleb and I, do that together. Typically, we do it after church on Sunday. For a while we had a day during the week when I would pick him up and we'd go grocery shopping. I try to turn it into as much of a fun thing as you can. We'd read and look at numbers and stuff like that as we shopped.

Most of the time I fix Caleb's meals. I will cook for Caleb and me and, not knowing when Ann's coming home, will not cook for her. Either she'll fix her own or we'll do it together when she gets home. I fix Caleb's lunch. I do his supper and she is mostly responsible for breakfasts since she takes him.

Did having a child turn out to be different from what you had in mind?

I would say I had not really planned on its having the impact that it did. The one place where it's caused me the most problems is in my community activities, which have always been such an important thing for me. I get a lot from those activities, and I've had to really restrict those more than ordinarily.

I was really heavily involved in politics for a while. I've been on the board of this, that, and the other—volunteer agencies, nonprofit organizations, and in a couple of cases helped start certain social service groups.

One group that's kind of floundering right now has to do with volunteer foster care. I picked up on a model I found in

Massachusetts, where community people would assist the governmental agencies responsible for placing children. There was the tendency of agencies to let kids drift without making plans for their permanency. So this whole notion of permanency planning in public agencies came into being. Short term foster care families would be recruited primarily out of churches and service-oriented groups. The community people would assist them in training and keeping availability calendars, stuff like that. So it was a way to assist the agency in doing the things they didn't do very well.

The system is changing. It not only encourages but mandates plans for the child's permanent placement. That means a place where the child will probably be for the remainder of his or her minority which is to age 18. My translation of what that means is to pay attention to the kid and make the plans you need to make to get him to a place where he can feel like it's really home.

It's not so much an emergency anymore. One of the things that they've started doing is using families to serve as respite families for kids that may be in long-term foster care. When their foster families need to take off a weekend the kids need a resource which is where the respite families come in. That's becoming a typical way of using the families. So I helped put that together—kind of got it going in the first place.

When Caleb was about 2, we started getting more involved in the church and then I got heavily involved in Adult Education courses. We belong to a Presbyterian congregation. My church roots go back a long, long way and so it is partly something familiar and homey. Ann is from a Catholic background and has not joined the church. I'm now on the governing board of the church and I'm also teaching a class on Sunday mornings. It's kind of a new way of doing Bible studies. It's a more meditative, reflective way rather than discussion and debate about the meaning of passages.

See, I'm seminary trained, and I really enjoy biblical studies, but I've kind of gotten away from it because it all seemed so intellectual. It's the most exciting thing I've ever done in terms of relating to the Bible.

You seem to have a deep concern for children and their care. Where did that come from?

I'm not sure. I'm not sure, quite frankly, if it is related to the process of building something as much as it is the subject matter which in this case is placing children. They kind of go hand in hand. I like the challenge and the satisfaction of bringing something into being. I'm not the force that sustains it. I'm not as good at keeping it going once I've started it.

I must admit that I think the need to take care of Caleb has helped me realize that doing some of these things wasn't so good for me on a personal level. I think I've gotten to a point in my life where I don't need to be doing that anymore. I need to be paying attention to other things—personal, spiritual development, quiet time.

It's kind of interesting how it happened. I think my taking care of him gave me the opportunity to disengage from some things and pay attention to the good coming out of that.

Beginning with this past summer, Ann had started reengaging more. That's been really great. As I said, it's fifty-fifty now. She'll be finishing a psychiatric residency. A piece of her would like to go on and do a child fellowship. I think she's found great successes and joys in working with children which was really unexpected for her.

I think what she does will present dilemmas for as long as we have kids. I must say the same is true for me. We're professional folks. Both of us get a little fire in our bellies about whatever it is we're doing and have a tendency to get overcommitted. So there's this constant warfare going on within ourselves and sometimes between each other about who should be taking what. I think whatever she does, she will want to do it to such an extent that there will be some conflicts with her parental role. But that's true for me, too.

I think it's a struggle for Ann and me to find time, you know, to take time for ourselves. There's actually a piece of me—it may be stronger in me than it is in her—that wants us to do everything together as a family; and there's a piece of me that knows, first, that we need to get away, and desires to get away, on our own together. And that's just hard to do.

Ann's parents are in Canada and mine are in Massachusetts. They used to live here in Hanover, but they've been gone for 4 years. I mean it's not a weekend . . .

One of the sacrifices we've made because of our personalities and the demands on our time plus other things we're dealing with in our relationship, is the real loss of a social life with other adults. We talked about that recently and about needing to rekindle friendships. We find we have to be fairly rigid about our time. So Friday night is usually the night we target to do something like that. But I must admit, I find it real hard to leave Caleb at home. It just doesn't seem right somehow.

I guess the hardest part for me in dealing with him is what he's going through right now. He's got a real temper, and he's got ways of dealing with his frustration where he instantly blasts. It drives me crazy. I can't stand it. I am really struggling to figure out how to deal with that. So it's not all roses, obviously. But the whole experience, I mean even being involved with him on the darker side of things, is a—"treat" is not the word—it's real important for me.

Do you want to have more children?

We're in conflict about that. I think both of us want to have other children but I don't see how we can manage it. I, in particular, have been the one putting the brakes on it. I sometimes feel like we really don't give as much quality time to Caleb as I would like. I don't see how we could do it with two.

I'll strip it down to it's barest form. I think it will produce more demands, and I think I'll be the one that will feel the pressure the most to pick that up. I've been basically making the judgment. I don't think I can handle more and still do what I'd like to do.

I'd like to be a good parent to Caleb, and I've got these other things that I want to do as well. But that's really complicated. That doesn't have as much to do with the structure of things, that is, two professionals, one of whom has had a particularly demanding 5 years. It's what our interaction, Ann's and mine, has been partly as a consequence of that. We just have a lot of difficulty with each other. What I resent is when I have done extra stuff and hear that I'm not supporting her enough. I think it's as much a function of her personality and our relationship as it is the demands of a two-professional household. And it's kind of hard to keep all that assigned responsibility to the different components. But that's how I see it.

In handling custody cases, I see a lot of the kinds of pressures I was just describing, the pressure of two careers—you don't even have to call one or more of them a career, just call them jobs, just a 9-to-5, 5 days a week, two people doing that. That puts a lot of pressure on a family; and the pressure to keep up financially is tremendous. Plus, I think the pressures to spend more money, and to be content with that, and to find joy and satisfaction just in family life is more difficult now than ever before. Financial difficulties don't get any better when families split up, they get worse.

For about 15 years I handled divorce and custody cases as well as child neglect cases for the Department of Social Services. A few years ago I made a transition and handed that work over to an associate we had hired in our firm because those cases are labor intensive. And I, partly for financial reasons and partly for satisfaction reasons, began divesting myself of that work.

I keep only one such case at a time in my caseload and they're usually cases involving property distribution and not child custody. But at the time I was involved in it, I saw an increasing interest on the part of men to have more involvement in the lives of their children after the divorce; certainly more now than when I first started practicing. That has some real positive aspects. It also has created more problems.

It used to be Mom would get custody and Pop would get visitation rights every other weekend. Now the structuring of the time with children and parents has become much more complicated. It may be that in two-career families men have more of a taste of parenthood or involvement with their children than they used to, and therefore know more about the loss they'll suffer if they don't maintain contact. I also think there's sometimes more of a show on the part of the fathers that doesn't always pan out. The reasons for it I think I'd be hard pressed to know. Sometimes you get results which you really don't think are in the children's best interest.

Have you found any explicit or implied criticism or judgment about your role among your peers?

Well, what was negative was real subtle. It came in unusual ways. I must say, first, that this law firm has a lot of children in it. In fact, our Christmas party is for the kids. So people here not only understand the needs of family, the process of involvement with their family is very much a part of them. I'm not the only one in this firm that has a greater role with his children. In fact, I would say that probably there are men here that have greater weekend involvement than I do. I have had to cut down during the week, but then have to work on Saturdays a good bit to make up. So let's not put the halo on myself.

I'm really trying to change that, so I can have more time so we could go away for a weekend more often, that kind of thing. But here's where it creates a rub. When Ann first went back to school for her internship and I started taking both ends of the day caring for Caleb, that brought me into conflict in a very practical way with some things that were happening in the firm. We were having a partners meeting one day a week at 8:30 or 9:00 in the morning. There were times when I just didn't make it, and everybody would say that's okay. But you're out of the league. That's irritating. There's an inevitable conflict between your kid's world and your world.

Quite frankly, you can say our approach—it feels more like survival than approach—is that you kind of do what needs to be done and that's the way it feels. I've adopted—and I think Ann's adopted—the approach that we'd like to have as much time, good quality time, with Caleb as possible. A small example of that is when I got a call at the beginning of this school year from a father of a child in Caleb's class. He said "I'd like to work out some carpooling for school and daycare."

And I said, "You know, I'd be happy to pick up your child, but I don't get enough time with my child as it is. I don't consider it a chore; I consider it part of my life with him and I don't really want to swap off." I guess that's an example of approach. I guess anybody that deals with custody cases and reads any of the literature is confronted repetitively with the phrase "best interest of the child," and it begins to sink into your psyche after a while. Just having that focus, I think, has helped influence my thinking about where my priorities are going to be.

Geoffrey

9

The interview took place in Geoffrey's office at the City Planning Department. At 27 Geoffrey is an attractive African-American—well-built, personable, easy with himself and easy to talk with. On his desk was a color photograph of his 5½-year-old daughter dressed in a dancing costume. "If you had come to interview me yesterday, you would have met her," he said. "There was an electrical blackout in the city and I had to leave the office to fetch Katrin because all the schools closed. She spent the rest of the day here with me."

I guess the best place to start is how I became a father. When I was a senior in college at Ohio State, I was popular on campus. I had a lot of affairs with women. One young lady became pregnant. I didn't know about it 'cause I'd stopped seeing her. She came knocking on my door 4½ months later to tell me, "I'm pregnant."

You know, I'm like, "Well, gee, that's too bad."

She said, "Yeah, but you're the father." I knew her well, but she wasn't like my—like my special—so that made it quite difficult. We went through all these tests and examinations and questionings with doctors. They pinpointed the exact day and there was no question that I was the person. I talked to some of her close friends. They assured me she was telling the truth.

In the state of Ohio, abortions are legal up to the 20th or 22nd week, so legally that still could have been an option. Because she was that far along she didn't feel that was something she wanted to do, and I wasn't going to ask her to at that late date—4½ months, which is about 20 weeks.

So I told her if she wanted to keep her child she should. I had no problems with that and I would make sure the child would be well taken care of financially. I wasn't going to bankroll her, but I was certainly going to pay enough child support voluntarily to make sure the child would have the things she needed. So we agreed to that. I said, "Call me in 5 months, or whatever." and we went on our merry way.

I wasn't into spending a lot of time with this. Quite frankly, I wasn't really all that concerned. I felt like that was just something that happened, and I was going to do the right thing in terms of financial support. I know a lot of women who take care of their own children under worse circumstances. I figured this was the best I could do. I said, "You take care of your child."

Late down on the wire, I mean, the 7th or 8th month, I received a letter from an attorney asking me to sign a release so the child could be put up for adoption. That was no option. The choices were either, "You take the child or I'll take the child." So I called this attorney and told him under no circumstances was I going to sign adoption papers. If the woman didn't want to take the child, I would take her. So we were back to the original agreement. But then, at the last minute, she called my family and told my mother she couldn't take the child and I would have to take her.

Katrin was born on June 9th. On June 12th, graduation day, my father drove up from New York. We met at the hospital, picked up the child, and the three of us drove back home to Syracuse. All the way I kept thinking, "Here I am, 21 years old—actually I was 22—an athlete, graduating from college with full scholarships to graduate school with a lot of things going—a trip planned to Europe and some other places, and all that has to be set aside because now I have the responsibility of taking care of a child."

At the hospital, the mother said she felt she was doing the right thing. I told her she could visit the child. There would be no problems whatever. But I made one major mistake. Even though I was advised by some legal people to have the necessary papers with me at the hospital and have them signed before I left, I didn't do that. I felt that would be kind of insensitive to the woman who I thought would be going through a lot. I didn't want to have her sitting up there at this time signing everything in triplicate. I figured after a few weeks I could send the papers to her and she'd send them back and it would be no problem.

It didn't turn out that way. After a few months she began to have anxieties about giving up her child. Earlier she had given certain definite reasons that would interfere with her raising the child on her own: her career, personal finances, and just her personal well-being. She felt she couldn't do it.

I told her, "You know, you said you couldn't do it. Nothing has changed about that. I think you may be feeling some anxiety or something personally. But in terms of who brings up the child, how do I know within the next 2 weeks, if I do give the child back to you, that you won't say, 'Oh, I can't do it. Oh, I was right.'?"

I said, "We made an agreement. We had made a decision that we felt in the best interest of the child. I think we should stick to it." So, subsequently, there was an 18-month court battle about this.

The legal battle was here in Syracuse, since this was the child's established residence. It cost me a great deal of money, time, energy, dealing with the legal system, especially being a male. You know, the judges, the whole court system, is biased against males in these kinds of situations. Being an African-American and the woman being European-American also complicated matters.

So it was an interracial . . .

Well, yeah. If that's what you want to call it. I mean, I don't look at things that way, you know. Children are children. But certainly that was the case within the whole legal system.

It turned out that the reason she couldn't take the child was that her parents were adamant about it. My family had asked them to take the child home for a few days while they came up for my graduation. Then we—my family and me—we were all going to go over to pick the child up at their place in Akron and then drive back to Syracuse. But they wouldn't even take the child home from the hospital. That's why my Dad drove up to meet me there. We had to drop the child off here in Syracuse and then I raced back to Ohio in my car to go to my graduation and then returned immediately to Syracuse. As a result, my parents missed the ceremony. They had to stay home and watch the child. It kind of ruined my college graduation.

You said judges and the courts don't look favorably upon the male.

Yes, here in New York State . . . as a matter of fact, I had one legal action thrown out. I had to take it to the State Supreme Court 'cause it was a biased decision.

What happened was that when we first went in, the judge ruled that, yeah, we were going to have a custody hearing. This was about 6 or 7 months after my daughter had been living in our home. The mother had made no arrangements for the child. She talked about going to Social Services. She did not know what was going on and had shown no indication of having any kind of support system to help her. The judge ruled that, in the interim, before the hearing, the child should go back to the mother. It was based on nothing, really. I mean, he gave no decision.

So in the 2-week period before that transfer was to take place, I hired another attorney, a more specialized, more high-powered attorney, took him to State Supreme Court, filed all these papers against the ruling within that 2-week time period, all of which, believe me, cost plenty of money. And then, when we got it to the State Supreme Court, they threw out the lower court's decision—right out, 6–0. It was an erroneous decision. They just threw it out, dismissed her lawyer, and reassigned another.

Sitting in the bullpen there, waiting to go to trial and going to these hearings, I found a lot of men there in the family court system, and 95% of them are trying to get out of something—to get out of child support or get out of custody. Many of the men were probably from lower educational and economic backgrounds, and a large percentage were African-American. So here I come into court, upper middle class, from a professional family, well-educated with a pretty high-powered attorney, and in a legal battle with this European-American woman who is kind of, you know, working class from Ohio with nobody helping her—you know, this whole thing.

I felt again like this judge looked us over and thought, "Who do these people think they are, doing this?" And it wasn't a case of my doing anything. I was just looking out for the best interest of our family. So I think that explains how come he also allowed so much erroneous testimony and disallowed other things during the course of the questioning afterwards.

Luckily, a new judge was assigned, and, as it turned out, right before we go to trial the mother and her attorney conceded they didn't have much of a case.

The court case brought up very negative feelings that I have for another individual, being the child's mother. I'm not comfortable with having such feelings but they're there. Even though things turned out for me, I just have no confidence in the legal system. A lot of how things turned out for me had to do with the fact that I had a great attorney. But the great attorney cost great money and if I wasn't in that kind of a situation where I could afford that and if things had turned out differently, as I firmly believe they would have, Katrin's life would have been much, much more difficult and certainly I don't think it would have been as good. It probably would have been a life filled with Social Services and . . . just not the things that . . . it just would not have been as good a life. It's scary to see how much power is in these systems that are run by men, a lot of not very honorable men, a lot of men that don't really give a crap. They don't care. That's very, very disheartening. Also, seeing how many people in this society are in similar situations! You know, really it's scary. It made me to some extent bitter and cynical about the system.

You spend a couple days in family court and listen to other peoples' stories and you're like, "Jeez, what is this society coming to?" Family courts are packed. It took me months just to get on the docket 'cause there are so many domestic problems in this society.

In terms of getting through this experience, my spiritual relationship with what I call God, which could easily be hallow or anything that's higher or better than you—that's how I look at God—something that's above me and man—my faith in that has helped. I mean, it certainly has helped a lot. It's helped me answer those questions that I really can't answer or nobody else can really answer 'cause there's a lot of fear when you're going through the situation that I went through.

One thing my mother always taught me is that God will never put anything more on you than you can handle. So it may seem like this is a big . . . but if you believe that God's a loving God, He, or She, or whatever, wouldn't put you . . . would not put you in that kind of a situation where it would just destroy you. So you really have to dig down deeper and find some resolve that you may not necessarily . . . I certainly did not know that I had. I always thought I was a tough person, but I had no idea that I was this tough. It took a great deal of toughness to get through 18 months of this court stuff, and to change your lifestyle, and to change some of your plans, and to have the kind of patience that it takes to raise a small child. There's times when you really need some help, and because of circumstance there's no one there, and you just have to get through that time. I never knew I had that in me. I reached out.

The most influential thing in my life has always been my family. Even though I believe in God, God is supposed to be the highest thing—my family is the highest thing I will have to deal with on Judgment Day. I can make a strong case for that.

My family has been so supportive of me. They have taught me and brought me up in a way in which there are no gender rules. In growing up, I never experienced "the mommy does this, the daddy does that, because mommy's a woman and daddy's a man."

My parents are both professionals, both pioneers in their fields. My mother was the first black principal in upstate New York at a very young age. My father's tops in his field, and they're both very busy with civic activities in the community. As a result, we all had to share in making the house run effectively.

That did not mean that Mom came in every night to cook and clean and that Dad—what does a dad do?—dads sit around and drink beer. That didn't happen. I mean we all did what we had to do. Certain things my mother usually did, like the laundry. She did it 'cause that's what she does, not because she's the woman. She does it because that's . . . I do it! It's no big thing. We all pitch in to keep the house clean and the yard nice. We just kind of live our lives.

In terms of aspiring to goals, my sister and my brother and I were never treated differently, never once told, "You can't do this because you're a man" or, "You can't do this because you're a woman." We were brought up to believe that there was really no such hierarchy. It sounds corny and some people don't believe it but that's just the way it is, and it's not because my dad is a great feminist or anything. He's just such a good guy. He respects my mother for herself and for her skills—who she is as a person—and he sees that she has so much to offer the rest of the world that she should not be so

tied up with taking care of the family that she can't share all
she has professionally with society. It means we all have to
share in dealing with different things within the household.

My sister, the oldest of the three of us, has played a special
role in my father's life. My father was not able to go to the
medical school of his choosing. He grew up in the South. After he fought in the war against oppression and all that other
stuff and came home here, he wasn't able to go to the specific
medical school in the South because they didn't allow Afri-
can-Americans. So, being discouraged about that, he chose
another career path which turned out good. But he really
wanted to be a doctor. So when my sister graduated from
medical school that was a great day for him—and one of the
best days in my life because I never, to this day, have seen him
more happy and proud of anything than when his daughter
lived out the dream that he really wanted.

My sister didn't become a doctor because my dad wanted to
become a doctor and couldn't do it. She wanted to be a doctor
because that's what she wanted to do; and she was encouraged to do that.

My brother's an artist so he does his thing. And there's
never been a time in my life where I've felt that I cannot do
certain things within the family unit 'cause I'm a man—that
there are things that are strictly what a woman does and by
doing such you make yourself less of a man. So it was easy. It
was natural for me to assume the role of a parent. We really
didn't have a mother and a father; we had two parents in the
household.

Certain things I shared with my father because that's just
the relationship two men—you know, a man and a boy—will
have. It doesn't make it any better or worse than the relationship you have with your mother. It's just certain things, like
when you're going through puberty or when you're experi-
menting with sex and stuff, you're just not going to have those
conversations with your mother. You could. I felt like I could
if I wanted to, but it was my choice to have those conversations with my father.

Anything that I am that is good is because of this. I mean they've been so supportive. Even now, I came back with a baby and. . . . It's tough because, you know, they're a little older. But that's okay. They feel like this is the hand that's been dealt us. There's no reason in the world that we should make the child suffer because of my indiscretion. It's our blood, and hopefully my child will grow up to have those same kinds of values that I was brought up with, and it will make her a better person. It will make her have the kind of commitment to your children that you need to have.

I've seen my family, my mother and my father both, live their lives for their kids. I've seen the things that they've had to give up for their kids. We talk about some of their contemporaries, some of their peers, who are in the same kind of economic bracket, and how some of them have a little bit more stuff than we have. The main reason is—and they don't say this to these people—is because my parents spent so much money and stuff on their kids. They did. I mean, they spent a lot of dough on us. They didn't begrudge it.

My career has got off to a slow start. I'm not as far along as I thought I would be. There are a lot of things I would like to do full-time which I have to do part-time, like graduate school. Even though we live in my parents' home, I have full responsibility for Katrin. They are rarely home, so I usually do the cooking for both of us, take her shopping, pick her up at school, take her to ballet classes, and when she's sick—to the doctor—and if she has to stay home, I must arrange for her care.

In terms of vacations and a lot of other little stuff, I really can't do—well I can do if I want to but, see, I don't feel comfortable right now. If I'm going to spend a lot of money to go somewhere or to do something, it has to be something that my child can be included in. Right now I can't afford to do that. For my daughter and I to do it and do it like I want to I just have to sort of . . . so we'll wait.

I miss traveling down to New York City. I did that a lot, just kind of go and spend a weekend with friends and do stuff down there and kind of act silly. But those are things I don't feel I should do right now. Basically, the real down side has been the changes that have happened in my career.

Establishing relationships with other women is not an easy matter. I don't need anybody to help me raise my child, yet a lot of women kind of come at me with that. In order for a woman to get close to me, she's going to have to have a good relationship with my child.

My mother and father have been married for over 30 years and they're like kids. If my dad has to go travel for something, he'll call three and four times. It's so funny that after all these years they are still so close. They get along so well, and they really, really are in love, so that has given me and my sister high expectations. As a consequence, she's had a couple of marriages that didn't work out. At least I didn't go that far, but it's very difficult for each of us to have the right relationships with people.

The biggest problem I have is that I really want a woman who will push herself and see how well she can do with her own life. I don't want a woman to live her life for me. I don't want her to say, "Well, whatever makes you happy makes me happy." I don't want her to shape or mold a career around my goals. To me that shows a weakness or something. I think people should try to find out what they can do in life, how good they are.

A lot of people say that I want somebody like my mother, which is natural. I think a lot of people do. I would like to have a woman who is really confident and has a career, too, and feels good about herself and wants to do the best she can with her own life—not necessarily do great things—but, I mean, if she's able to do great things, she should reach for those great things. I think the problem a lot of people make is that they never find out who they are, so they can't do what they can do. And from my point of view, if a woman doesn't know who she is then I don't know who I'm loving yet. And as I find out, it may not be what I wanted.

It's the same thing that happened to my sister. She has such high expectations, and she has certain standards about what she's not going to do. It's not in her upbringing to play the subservient, submissive, subordinate role that a lot of men want, and they can't deal with her strength.

My mother is probably the strongest and toughest person I've ever met in my life, and my sister is probably the second. It's their own kind of toughness. They're not bitchy or anything like that. They're just great people. If they were men they would be called assertive, "go-getters," the kind of guy, person, that's going to go somewhere in life, and that threatens a lot of guys.

And on my side, I think I scare some women because sometimes I say, "You know I have more confidence in you than you have in yourself. You could do so much. You're as educated as I am. I mean you've got the same degrees, or you could get them, or you could do what you want. Don't limit yourself."

My daughter is so protective of me. She's funny. If we're out somewhere and run into somebody I know, Katrin kind of, you know, gives her the once over. With the friends that I do have, once Katrin gets to know them she warms up to them and really enjoys spending time with them, but first we have to go through that little trial period.

People always tell me, "Jeez, you know, I'd hate to be a teenager trying to date your daughter."

PART IV

Homosexual Parents

Homosexuals make up an increasingly visible segment of the American population. When one considers how much else there is about human beings besides their sexuality, it is not surprising that much of what gays and lesbians long for to enrich their lives is very like that which heterosexuals desire. For the homosexual community, parenthood presents numerous obstacles. So far, only a few local governing bodies in this country assign legal status to the union of same sex partners—and that only relates to property deeds—even when the relationship has lasted for years and indicates continued commitment.

Domestic partners (DPs) who are gay and decide to have a family may connect with lesbians also interested in family and thereby establish a dual household for the offspring who have the benefit or confusion of two mothers, two fathers, with one of each sex being the biological parent.

Adoption is another route for gays and lesbians who wish to have children. Here, the problems they face are that DPs cannot adopt as a couple, so only one partner can be the legal adoptive parent; few agencies will decide in their favor because of their sexual orientation; and those agencies that do usually offer choices of children nobody wants. As with heterosexuals, importing adoptees from other countries has been an answer for some homosexuals.

Lesbians have other options beside adoption such as a sperm bank, or a sperm donor who may be a willing male friend, or, preferably for some, a gay man. The knowledge that the father is not a nameless, featureless gamete may be of importance to a child, and is of concern to many a prospective mother choosing artificial insemination, whether lesbian or straight.

Prejudices abound. For example, ordinarily simple arrangements for daycare of the children of homosexuals are subject to unsubstantiated accusations of abuse of one kind or another. It is difficult not to be impressed by the pain this must engender in the parents who wish to do their best for their children. With that in mind, gay and lesbian parents often seek out or develop extended families which include both homo-and heterosexual friends and parents, to ensure an accepting, empathic community for their children and themselves.

Statistical data are incomplete. They suggest the following: 10% of the male population is gay; about 6–7% of females are lesbian; 20% of the gay male population has been married once; 20–50% of this group has had children; and between 1.5 and 3.3 million of the lesbian population are mothers. The number of children from both homosexual groups is estimated to be between 6 and 14 million (Gonsiorek & Weinrich, 1991).

Franklin

10

Franklin is 42 years old and lives in Charlotte, North Carolina in an established neighborhood. Baby carriages, tricycles, swings and sand boxes are scattered around the grounds of a three-story modern apartment house. Franklin is finishing his dinner, explaining he was unexpectedly detained, and offers to share his food. Camellias float in a glass bowl on the dining table. Before the interview begins, he shows a photograph of Laurie, his 4-year-old daughter.

When I was a kid, I had a lot of friends my own age, but I really enjoyed hanging out with the younger kids in the neighborhood. I was the only boy who babysat, and was one of two or three eighth graders who worked in kindergarten.

When I got to college, I did not know what I wanted to do. There were the usual routes—law school or business school—but nothing really grabbed me. One summer I worked at Head Start. I decided, after that, I'd like to try elementary school teaching when I finished my degree at Princeton.

I moved to Boston but didn't pursue the teaching right away. I had spent a lot of years, primarily in college, with this strong sense that I was a homosexual and very upset about that and wanting to change it; but by the time I graduated I was keenly aware that sexual identity is an integral part of one's personality and not something that can be excised like some tumor. So that year in Boston was spent figuring out who I was and getting into some therapy to help me come to grips with it.

This was 1971. There wasn't a hell of a lot of support at that time for people making that decision. When I talk about a decision, there was no choice in terms of my sexual orientation. There was a choice in terms of "Do I want to live a life that affirms that I'm gay, or do I want to try and hide it?"

I decided I wasn't going to hide it. However, a recurring theme for me in therapy was the sadness I felt about the improbability of my ever having a family.

I picked up my intention to teach elementary school, did a Masters at Tufts, and landed a job in a large suburb of Boston. The environment was more than I could handle—the worst of public school teaching in a lot of ways. I wasn't becoming the kind of teacher I wanted to be, so I moved to an alternative school in downtown Boston and taught there for 4 years. In this wonderful little school, I could work with people I really respected who helped me to become a good teacher, I think. I loved that work, and I loved those kids.

Nevertheless, I really did not want to be an elementary school teacher for the rest of my life.

I left teaching for a career in Public Health just about the time I turned 30. Leaving teaching meant leaving kids. That was a sadness for me. I resolved that I would figure out a way to "people" the next generation of my life. I wasn't quite sure how that was going to pan out. The most likely scenario was becoming good friends with a single mother who wanted her child to have some sort of male person in his or her life.

I befriended a single woman in the School of Public Health and hung out with her son some. I could have been more involved in their lives, but I was extraordinarily busy with school and began thinking this might never work. I started exploring some options—talking to people about adoption.

I attended the National Gay and Lesbian Health Conference in New York City back in 1984 or '85. There was a workshop on gay and lesbian parenting that was exciting—just to hear the stories of other people. It was also discouraging because I found out how hard it was for a gay or lesbian to adopt a child.

One woman, from New York City, successfully adopted a child with Down's Syndrome. They couldn't find anybody else to take this handicapped child. She took him in as a foster parent. He was there that day—an infant. He seemed like a delightful little kid. She loved him and she adopted him. That was her story.

Then there were two men out in Arizona who adopted a little girl. They had done it all under the table and 2 years later were still living with the risk of having their child yanked from them at any moment.

I went right from there to friends in Boston to find out about becoming a foster parent. Then a critical thing happened. A woman I knew—lesbian—came to me. She and her lover wanted to conceive a child. They had had artificial insemination. She was pregnant and looking for someone to be a significant person in her child's life. I was intrigued and flattered, but I didn't know this woman well and, though I liked her, there wasn't a real good connection. Besides, the timing was all wrong—I was in the middle of my doctoral studies. I said, "No."

Not long after that, a friend of a friend, also lesbian, came to see me because she knew I worked at a health project concerned with AIDS. Pat and her lover were also planning on conceiving a child. They had an anonymous sperm donor—someone gay. She wanted to know what questions to ask this guy about his health in order to protect herself and the baby. I told her what I knew.

Before she left, I said to her, "You know, I've always loved children and always wanted to be involved with them. If you decide that you would like someone to be more than a sperm donor, and this doesn't pan out with this guy, give me a call because I would be interested in talking to you."

Within 2 weeks she called. She and Meg had thought about it, and decided it would be better to have a man involved in raising the child. I was nearing the completion of my doctor-

ate. Ahead of me was the dissertation. We began getting together on a regular basis to get to know one another, which
was in August of '85. We had dinner together once a week for
about 4 months—the three of us.

I was in a relationship with a guy named Jordan, who was
not excited about all this, but he also knew how important it
was to me. Finally, he said, "Well, if this is what you really
want, go ahead." He was not interested in being a co-parent,
but he wasn't going to stand in my way.

By the end of October, Meg, Pat, and I had gotten to know
one another well. Basically we saw eye-to-eye on parenting issues. We had similar philosophies of child-rearing and felt
real compatible with some common interests. So it was big
decision time. Do we go ahead with this or not?

That was a soul-searching time for me. All of my self-
doubts came to the fore. Would I be a good parent? Did I deserve this? I had chosen to live my life as a gay man. Being a
parent isn't part of that package. What right do I have—do
any of us have—to bring a child into this world in a family
that's not going to be traditional? I mean, is this kid going to
grow up to hate us for doing this to him or her?

And my feeling was, "Don't do it. It's not right."

I went back to my therapist and worked on it. I came to the
conclusion that those negative feelings were mainly internal-
ized homophobia. If I really wanted to be a parent, I deserved
to give it a shot.

But there were fears. God, what if I'm HIV infected? Of
course, we wouldn't move forward with any of this without
my being tested. But how accurate is the test? After counseling about it for a long time, my feeling was that there is no
guarantee, but if it's what I wanted I should do it. Do it as responsibly, as thoughtfully, as carefully as I could. But do it!
That was the decision on my part. Pat and Meg felt the same.

That was November. We began all the medical stuff. I went
for tests—was tested twice for HIV. Negative both times. It
was real scary stuff. I had other kinds of routine physicals.
Pat had physicals. We decided to go ahead.

In January of '86, we started attempting conception. I was working on the proposal to my dissertation at that point and was thinking this was going to take probably 6 to 9 months to conceive (*Author's note: the baby, not the dissertation!*) I was 37. Pat was 34. I thought it would take a while. The second shot she got pregnant (*laughs*).

The logistics were ridiculous. It involved me masturbating into a little jar—this is mid-winter—at my house, wrapping it in a wool sock to keep it warm, driving across town with the goods, and ringing the doorbell. Meg would meet me at the door and I would say, "There it is," and she would say, "Thanks. See you later." It was really comical, but it worked. Before we knew it we were dealing with the fact that our plan was going to work, which was exciting and terrifying at the same time.

Pat was nothing if not methodical about all of this. She had taken her temperature every morning for a year. She was committed to doing this as carefully as possible and it paid off (*sighs*).

There was still a lot of emotional stuff going on. I had a good friend dying of AIDS in the middle of all this. I'm still fearful that those tests weren't accurate. I've been tested twice since then—even though I've only—I mean, at that point I was in essentially a monogamous relationship. But I was concerned about prior—and, you know, there has been evidence from time to time that this test might not be as accurate as it is cracked up to be. That fear has plagued me.

The bargaining I did with God, or my heart, or whatever, midway through all this was, "If I'm HIV infected, okay, I can handle it somehow. But please—please, God, do not let me infect this baby or Patricia." So, yeah, I fear for my own health. No man in his right mind wouldn't, but there was this whole other layer. It qualified my enjoyment of Pat's pregnancy. My anxiety level got so high about midway through the pregnancy that I went to get tested again even though I—I mean it was a done deed, a done deal, at that point, but I was just—I got tested a third time. It was negative.

I have been tested a fourth time in the last couple years, and it's still negative. Still, there's this recurrent nightmare that somehow all of this is going to come crashing down. You know, fears that we all carry around, totally irrational.

But, having said that, there was loads of really wonderful stuff. After Pat became pregnant, Jordan got really excited about it as well and became part of the birth team. After Laurie was born, he became involved with her care. He and I split 2 years ago. That was difficult. The hardest part was that we would not be sharing Laurie together.

I was afraid Jordan was going to drop out of the situation altogether, but that hasn't happened, and Laurie clearly loves him. She thinks of Jordan as a second father. She is comfortable with the idea that she has two moms, and she thinks she also has two dads. She sees Jordan that way, although Jordan does not. But regardless of how he defines his relationship to her, she sees him as another father.

According to our legal document, Pat, Meg, and I have equal say in all the significant decisions in Laurie's life. We have an agreement that we will do whatever we can to stay in the area until Laurie is at least in high school. Laurie's legal last name is the same as Meg's. That was a way of saying that Meg, the non-biological parent, is as important.

Pat and Meg were real adamant that we split expenses a third, a third, and a third, even though at that point, I was earning more money. They did not want to introduce an element of inequality. We have a savings fund for Laurie and what we kick into that reflects what we earn. But the day-to-day expenses, child care, and the rest, are split equally.

What about your relationship with your daughter? You saw her born?

Absolutely—was part of the birth team—was there at the birth. It's always fun to think about this. It's the best decision I've ever made, and I am very much a part-time parent. She spends Tuesday nights, Friday nights, and all day Saturday with me, and then I usually see her again during the week. If Pat and Meg need somebody to provide child care, usually, I'm the first person they'll call. My schedule's pretty busy, so I haven't done as much as I'd like.

When Laurie gets sick, as little kids do a lot, we split who takes time off from work. Right after she was born, I struck a deal with my boss. I took every Friday morning off so I could provide some child care and get to spend extra time with Laurie. I did that for the first year.

To tell you the truth, I had no experience and not much interest in babies, although, once she was born, it was fascinating. I could sit and pretty much do nothing with her for long periods of time. It keeps getting better and I enjoy her more and more because I can do more with her. She's really a neat little person. I credit Pat and Meg for most of it, since Laurie spends most of her time with them.

But the time I spend with her is precious. I don't schedule anything else. When she's here on Tuesday nights, occasionally I'll have a friend of hers over, but rarely do I schedule anything for me during that time—and the same with Friday nights and Saturdays—that's her time. So, I think that in a lot of ways I probably spend as much quality time with her as fathers who live with their kids all the time, have busy lives, and only get to spend a couple hours a week with their kids. The conception (*laughs*) and birth of this child—I don't think any child has been born with more thought and more intention than Laurie (*laughs*). We have a neat relationship.

I have other friends who are single parents. Some of them treat their child as a "best friend," and the lines get blurred. I need to be the parent here. Laurie's only 4 but, knock on wood, I seem to be somehow maneuvering around that. When she's here, it's often just the two of us and so there is that danger. But it doesn't happen. I'm perfectly comfortable saying to her, "Well, it's time to go to bed."

"No it isn't. I'm not going."

"Yes you are."

"No I'm not."

And so I give her another 5 minutes and then I say, "Well, that's it, Laurie. It's time for bed."

"I'm not going."

"Yes you are and do you know why?"

"Why?"

"'Cause I'm your father, and I'm a lot bigger than you, and that's that!"

She accepts that. It's real clear that she loves spending time with me and that I'm real important to her.

The biggest down side for me was after the split with Jordan—not having someone. It was lonely. There were so many wonderful things happening. I wanted to share that with another adult.

I was worried after Jordan and I split up. "How could I cope as a part-time single parent?" Jordan was always very good with the concrete tasks of parenthood—getting the meal together, getting Laurie changed. All of a sudden I had to do everything. I was worried that I couldn't cope, but I negotiated that just fine. What was really hard was not sharing that with another parent, yet it evolved into something very special. I think Laurie and I bonded in a new and different way as a result.

I'm seeing someone now, and he's wonderful with Laurie and really enjoys spending time with her. Bob doesn't come over often on Tuesday nights, and he doesn't come over on Saturday mornings. Friday nights the three of us do something—have dinner and play—and then he'll come over Saturday afternoons and we'll all do something.

Are you ever together as a family unit, meaning Pat and Meg and you and, perhaps, even Jordan?

Yeah, not too much anymore. On Laurie's fourth birthday, we asked her what kind of party she wanted. She said she didn't want a party, she just wanted to spend time with her family. She defined her family as Pat, Meg, me, and Jordan, and the four of us spent the good chunk of her birthday together.

Christmas was really neat. This was Pat and Meg's idea and I loved it. They came over on Christmas Eve. Laurie has a Godmother, an older woman who is in her early seventies—a dear friend of all of ours. She joined us along with another friend of mine, and we all had dinner together. Pat and Meg and Laurie spent the night here. They had lugged all their presents over, and we had a Christmas tree. So Pat and Meg and Laurie and I spent Christmas morning together. On Christmas Day we had dinner for 14—just invited a bunch of friends. It was wonderful. We did that sort of as a family.

When you take Laurie to the doctor, who is identified as her family?

Well, some of it's easy, some of it's hard. Her doctor is a lesbian, a friend of Pat and Meg's, who understood from Day One exactly what we were trying. She's also my personal physician as well as Laurie's pediatrician. Often, if I can't see her, I'll see another doctor in the same practice—family medicine. They're a fairly enlightened bunch.

Day care is a whole 'nother story. We've had some colossally negative experiences but she's now in a day care almost 2 years and loves it. They know the whole situation and they're very supportive of us. It's a stone's throw from here, and I can walk to pick up Laurie. It's just worked out beautifully. Prior to that a couple of daycare centers didn't pan out.

In one daycare situation, the woman knew that Laurie lived with her biological mother and another woman, and that she spent time with her biological father and another man. We began to feel the woman didn't like us and that it was affecting her relationship to Laurie.

So we pulled Laurie out of there and put her in this other daycare that has an excellent reputation. We were up front with the director because we didn't want a repeat.

The director said, "I appreciate your telling me about Laurie's home situation and there's no problem with it. But I suggest there's no need for you to share this with the teachers."

So we never told the teachers. Unfortunately, because they were not informed they became suspicious. They didn't trust us, and that lack of trust really affected their relationship with us in ways we didn't fully understand. It led to their reporting us to Social Services for neglect. They didn't trust us enough to share with us their observations about Laurie's physical or psychological well-being.

Laurie was just getting potty-trained and had developed a urinary tract infection. She cried whenever she peed. We took her to the doctor who put her on antibiotics to be given in the morning and at night. We shared this information with one of the teachers who failed to communicate this to the other teacher or to the director. The director, not knowing otherwise, thought we were being neglectful by not taking Laurie to the doctor. Rather than calling us to find out, she called Social Services and reported us, instigating a complete investigation.

There's another part of this that is just more horrifying, as far as I was concerned, as far as all of us were concerned. I'm not really comfortable talking about it. But it was an awful incident. The social worker who came out was very clear. She said, "I don't know the full story here but it really seems like you people are getting the shaft." So we confronted the daycare people about all this. Lack of trust in us on their part and lack of communication with one another made them come to the wrong conclusions about us. GRRRRR! I'm still furious.

We pulled her out. I had an idea and I'm proud of this. We decided that Pat, who was unhappy in her job anyway, should stay at home with Laurie. So for a year, Meg and Jordan and I paid Patricia to stay home and take care of Laurie.

Eventually, we put Laurie in another daycare center for three afternoons, so she could have some time with peers. Otherwise she was at home with Pat. It worked out beautifully. Now Pat is working part-time so she's at home with Laurie in the mornings, and Laurie goes to daycare from 12 to 6.

What about your own family?

It was an interesting evolution. They did not know of my intention to have a child. We're a small family. It's just my parents and my sister and me, and yet, it's never been easy for us to share things. It's a little better now than it used to be. They've known that I'm gay since my mid-twenties. In any event, I did want to tell them about this. I didn't talk to them about it until Pat was pregnant.

They came for a visit, and I kept postponing telling them. It was their last night here. We went out to eat. Unfortunately, my father's hard of hearing. So there I am in this noisy restaurant screaming at the top of my lungs this story of how I'm going to become a father and the more I say the quieter the restaurant becomes. Maybe it's just my imagination, but I'm assuming that more and more people are picking it up.

My mother is clueing into what is going on here. She says, "In other words, Patricia is going to have your baby."

"Right. You got it!"

She just went, "Oh, my God!"

My father goes, "What? What?"

"Dad, Pat's pregnant."

And he goes, "PREGNANT!" in this very loud voice. "How the hell did she get pregnant?"

I yelled, "Artificial insemination!"

"Why didn't you just go to bed with her?"

"Because she's lesbian and in a relationship and I'm gay and in a relationship."

He looks at me and says, "Franklin, I'm getting too old for this shit."

His major concern then was that I was going to get arrested, that this couldn't be legal, that somehow the authorities were going to find out and they were going to throw me in jail. And, in fact, he was worried.

"You know," I said, "I hope that when the baby comes, that you'll come down and visit."

"Will it be safe?" He was dead serious.

My mother was sitting there sort of rolling her eyes. I mean, she was just dumbstruck. She wanted more information. But she was a lot more open to the idea than my father.

Laurie was born on November the 11th, and they came down for Christmas that year. It was love at first sight. All of my father's misgivings evaporated. It was amazing to watch. He could not hold her enough. They're grandparents! It saddens me that they're as far away as they are and they don't see her all that much. They usually come down here in the fall and then again in the spring, and I usually make it up there sometime in the summer.

My sister is just a year younger. She's divorced and has no kids—and I think she really wanted a family. It's bizarre that her gay brother ends up with a child. But she's quite good with Laurie. On my parents 50th wedding anniversary, we all trucked off to Bermuda for a 4-day weekend—my sister, me and Laurie, and my folks. Laurie and my sister had a great time together.

I wanted to tell you my story because we've got an incredible amount of support here, wonderful friends—heterosexual and homosexual. Laurie is sort of this community kid. Everybody knows her. People tell us, "That is such a lucky kid." I mean, there are just so many people in her life that clearly love her and give her such wonderful attention. Basically, I think she is a very happy kid.

She has issues, but. . . .

(The interview with Laurie's two moms follows.)

Meg and Pat

11

We parked the car under one of the trees along a street in this residential neighborhood. The houses are of a vintage several decades old on modest pieces of land and mostly in need of repair. We walked around a plastic tricycle left on the concrete path, up the wooden steps to the porch where the varied collection of brightly colored toys were strewn.

A delicately built young woman with short, dark hair opened the screen door and invited us in. "I'm Pat," she said, smiling. Inside the house stood another young woman. Her frame and features were larger, her short blonde hair was less trim, and she didn't smile. Pat introduced her as Meg. The four of us sat down in the kitchen. Pat got us each a mug of coffee and began the double interview.]

Pat: For a long time Meg and I didn't talk to each other about having children. It was a hidden desire that we'd given up on. We were lesbians, and figured we couldn't do that. But hearing about lesbians out in California, and even single women not in relationships, having children however they could, ignited a spark of hope. It became a possibility. You have to have a dream, a vision of something that can happen so you can proceed on it. That's part of decision-making. I bet we thought about it for 3 years.

Meg: I would say 5. We've been together for 13 years. When

I hit 30 I started thinking about our having a child. We both wanted it. We had good relationships with our nieces and nephews and had been around kids a lot. I knew I would feel sad if I didn't get it. I felt it would be the main thing homophobia would have taken away from me—a sense of something being stolen from me.

In San Francisco several years ago, I remember hearing on the radio that 500 lesbians had had children that year. But here, when we started, people were thinking about it, but the technology and the family structure hadn't been figured out yet.

If there had been a way that felt clear for me to get a child . . . if we could have adopted and not have the state so implicated in it where we felt like we were in a third world country and stealing their children . . . if we could have inseminated each other, it would have been no problem. We would have had several kids by now.

Since I was older, I thought I would do it first, though I didn't have any attachment to my genes being in the world for posterity. I just wanted a child to love. But figuring out the sperm donor was the biggest part of it. As it turned out, while I wasn't so attached to the actual physical birth, it was wonderful. I'm glad I had that experience.

Are you the birth mother?

Meg: No—but just the experience. (*Lots of laughter from both.*) I was more hormonal.

Pat: The longing to parent was there, and I'm sure the way we socialize somehow plays a part in that process. Girl children grow up with the expectation of having children as part of the reflection of life. I've talked to people who've had this desire all their lives and know that they're going to have a child some day. I'm not sure that in my mind it was that deliberate.

I realized at some point Meg had given up on getting pregnant. One of us had to do it, and that was me.

Meg: We couldn't figure out about the sperm or who the father would be. We brought it up to our gay men friends, and they would freeze. I mean they wouldn't answer the phone when we called. They were alarmed. We made it clear that the method would be artificial insemination. They may have wanted to be our friends but not the fathers. We learned that. The person I negotiated with the longest was ambivalent, and Pat had some questions about him in terms of trust. I just gave up. At that point Pat picked it up.

Pat: Meg went to Nicaragua, and while she was gone I put an ad in a local paper for sperm donors.

Meg: "Long fast-swimming sperm wanted."

Pat: We knew exactly what we needed. The ad got 13 responses. To keep it anonymous, a friend screened the responses and corresponded with the people who answered. We used a health form for people to fill out, including essay questions. We asked for physical characteristics—how tall and color of hair, weight, stuff like that. Health kinds of questions, like, do you have cancer in your family? Do you have heart disease in your family? We had gotten this form from a woman in Tennessee who was a friend of mine who had had a child by artificial insemination. The information is shared, passed around. So we copied the form.

One line asked, "Would you be willing to let this child know who you are when she (sic) reaches 18?" That answer was important to us. I mean, I didn't want to have somebody say at some point, "Who's my Daddy?" and point to the sperm bank.

Our friend got all that information. Then she interviewed, actually talked to the people we'd decided would be best. No one identified themselves as gay, but we read between the lines. The man we first chose to work with was gay.

Twice I inseminated with this anonymous donor.

Meg: Actually, (*Meg turns to Pat*) you started inseminating, and then gay men friends asked us if the donor had been tested for AIDS. We said, "No." They said, "You have to stop. You cannot do this anymore."

Pat: At that point I approached Franklin. We needed information about AIDS and AIDS testing and what to do to protect ourselves and our child 'cause we were dealing with anonymous donors. I had already met with Franklin a couple of times. I liked him a lot and was really excited about the person he was. Meg was more dubious about him. She hadn't spent time with him.

Actually, Franklin lived with some other gay people in a community we used to live in. I knew of their existence. I had heard their names a lot—Franklin and Jordan—and I knew one was one, and one was the other, but I never knew which was which.

Meg: Yeah, but we also had this other piece of information about him—that he wanted to be a parent. We didn't tell him that right away. The relationship with Franklin has grown up around our mutual desire and intent to have a child. It's worked in a different way, I think, than it would have with the earlier men we had approached with their other meanings and entanglements.

The first time we all had supper together we discussed the AIDS questions, and then he very tentatively brought up that he wanted to have a child in his life, too. First he said, "If you do have this child and you need a man to have some relationship to it, I would be interested."

Pat: And then he added, "or if the sperm donor doesn't work out. . . ."

Meg: Yeah. It was kind of a proposal. I can't remember what else we talked about. We didn't really want to go into it until we had a chance to talk about it ourselves.

Pat: Another time, when he came over to have supper with us, he almost cried when he talked about how much he wanted children. A man that wants children that much! And Meg said, "Amen."

Meg: For both of us, family had been important, if conflicted. We didn't want to truncate half of it. Also, would it be better for a child to know who the father is or not? There are so many weird images of men in the culture. If you have to put one together from what you get in the culture, it would be a lot more dangerous than somebody in the flesh, someone you'd have a relationship with and had some choice over.

Franklin was somebody in the flesh who was interested in being a parent himself and willing to take an active role. That was appealing. So we began to shape an agreement—what he would want and what we would want.

I would be the nonbiological parent. Bringing a man in who would be on the birth certificate and who would have more legal claims than I would, put me in the most vulnerable position. So Pat left it up to me to decide, and I decided we should do it.

We got back with Franklin. It became more of a possibility than any of us had gotten to before. At that point we had to start working out the details.

Pat: We made out a contract—nine pages that we formulated together. We had a lawyer check it out and tell us things we needed to add. But we did it.

Meg: We worked off of other contracts. A lesbian from another state had just had a kid and gave us all her information, the legal things, different contract forms, "how to get inseminated" stuff. It became the basis for our working things out.

The main reason to go to the hospital is that they have the sperm. If they don't have the sperm, there's no reason to go there. It needs to be sanitary; it doesn't need to be clinical. Why have this whole institutional thing when it's

incredibly simple technology? It's like turkey-baster
baby. We used syringes. He puts the semen in a sterile jar
and brings it right over. You know it's coming (*sic*) and
you're ready for it. So you just put it into a syringe, in-
sert, and then lie with your hips up for 30 minutes.
There's a lot of oral history on how to do it.

Pat: There are also articles, little pamphlets—not slick
information. We're part of the lesbian network, so we
have access. There's a whole generation of lesbians who
came out in the seventies who were hitting their biological clocks about then. So places where there were heavy
concentrations of lesbians, like San Francisco, were coming up with the technology.

There was this whole population of aging lesbians who
didn't know exactly what to do or how to do it. A lot more
lesbians than heterosexual women use the technology. Intercourse would be more of an option for the single heterosexual woman. She could just go and get knocked up
if she wanted to.

Meg: We had to start figuring time lines and time ta-
bles. Franklin got tested three times for AIDS plus all
these other tests. We started talking about it in the summer and started inseminating in January. So it took
about 6 months to put it all together.

Pat: I had tracked the changes in my temperature
daily for a year. And I did a lot of spiritual work during
that time. When I used to jog, that was my time to do a
lot of internal work and spiritual work, preparing to welcome this new soul into the world.

I grew up in a real fundamentalist Baptist home, but
that's not how I experience my spirituality now. Some of
that I kept but it was prayer-like meditation. I continue it
today, probably even more so.

Meg: I remember how I alternated between excitement
and terror. Because Pat was going to be the biological
mom, she had a kind of internal focus that was different

for her than it was for me. She knew her temperature. She knew her body. She was really focusing in on it, and she got pregnant the second month. It worked.

Pat: Meg was gone, out of town, when I found out I was pregnant. I had kept close track of my monthly cycles and I was 2 days past due. So I went to the store and got one of those early pregnancy tests. I tested positive. I phoned Franklin.

He said, "It may not be."

So I went over to his house with this thing, and he said, "Well, maybe so."

And I said, "Franklin, I'm pregnant." I called Meg up. (*Pat turns to Meg*) I called you before I went over there. Meg was pretty excited.

Meg: I was ecstatic.

Pat: Well, the first 3 months I was pretty sick so I wasn't very ecstatic.

Meg: I was ecstatic for both of us.

Pat: Part of the infrastructure was that our doctor was a lesbian. I went in 6 months before, and had a check-up, and told her what I was planning to do. So when I came back 6 months later, she was real excited and said, "Well, that was quick!" And she was right there all the time.

Can you tell us about the birth?

Meg: For the first 17½ hours it was terrifying. Very hard— to watch somebody that you love and a body you know well, in labor. I think we were not prepared. We'd done all these fucking breathing classes, but I'm afraid breathing doesn't do it. Neither one of us were prepared for the intensity. It kind of snuck up on us. They had talked about packing for the hospital and taking books and games. No way. As soon as it started, it was like, games? Who has time for games?

Pat: We stayed here 'til about 4 centimeters. It reached 6 by the time we got to the hospital.

Meg: There was a point at which we both got afraid of being separated from each other. There were too many people around. I felt like we'd lost contact. That made it harder for me. To experience 2-minute intervals for that many hours was very intense. There was this elasticity to time, almost. It was scary 'cause she got stuck a couple times and we didn't know how long it was going to last.

Pat: I finally just announced, "I give up," and it was really what I needed to do—surrender to the process of childbirth. You have no control over it, and there's nothing you can do about it.

(To Meg): You were right there and watched the birth process?

Pat: She made it happen.

How did you do that?

Meg: Well, when we got to the hospital, Janet, our doctor, mercifully sent people out. They would allow only two people in the birthing room with Pat. She got stuck again at 7 centimeters. We had this plan to avoid intervention, avoid drugs and blocks, and all those kinds of things.

Janet came in after having conferred with colleagues and said, "Well, Patricia, if you feel like you need something you can either have a potossin drip or nipple stimulation."

Pat said, "I'll take the nipples."

Janet said, "You get to choose who does it." I think the nurses were very shocked when I started doing it and not Franklin. Jordan came in and out, but I was there most of the time.

We did that for about 15 minutes to get 3 more centimeters. It worked. We didn't have to use interventions.

There was about 30 minutes of intense pushing. Then,
all of a sudden, things really happened. When Laurie
started crowning, there was one point (*Meg looks at Pat*),
you just smiled. It was like you knew it was coming or
something. And when Laurie popped out, it was complete
exhilaration, going from worry and anxiety to complete,
complete joy. I heard someone say, "It's a girl!" She
weighed 7 pounds, 11 ounces. If you want a baby you take
what comes, but I had a preference for a girl.

Pat: Laurie has Meg's last name. It was an idea I pushed to
legally protect Meg's relationship to Laurie. Franklin
would have his name on the gift certificate (*everyone
laughs at the word slip of "gift" for "birth"*) and so
would I. We were concerned about something happening
to Franklin or me, or both of us. Having the same last
name is somehow a way the outside world respects of
putting two people together in a family kind of way.

Meg: It also announces to people that I wasn't to be left out—
that it wasn't to be this couple, Patricia and Franklin,
having this baby.

Has your relationship with each other changed since Laurie is here?

Pat: Yeah, in lots of ways. It propelled us both, individually,
to hope for and reach for things that we maybe had given
up on before—personal goals, aspirations. Maybe that
would have come with middle age. It's about being able
to get what you really want badly, and I think, well,
maybe you can do your whole life that way.

Meg: I expected changes to be those around responsibility
and time and having to negotiate, those kinds of things.

And they certainly are. But there's this deep level of
change for both of us triggered by the profoundness of
having a child. I don't know if it would have been the
same if it had been a boy child. On some levels it would
have. For me, it put me back in touch with this amazing
period of life that we don't remember because we haven't
developed. It's kind of lost. It's pre-history or dreamlike.
So there's this way of getting back in touch with your
dream material, to just watch this child and think, "Well,
I was like that," and then I would see things that were
about to hurt Laurie and I would have this visceral reaction to them and realize I deserved the same thing, that
same level of concern. You know, I'm going to be so protective over her! It's like learning to love yourself again
'cause you're loving somebody else.

Pat: And learning what all that involves.

Meg: It recycled fast and profoundly changed the interac-
tions. This vulnerable little thing needs so much protec-
tion and love and deserves it and maybe I do, too. It got
both of us, Pat and me, down to more basic material in
our relationship that we hadn't understood or been able
to name. It became easier.

Pat: The only real difference between us is in my being the
biological mother. I nursed Laurie. That was an experience just she and I shared.

Meg: That first year was hard for me. I felt left out. We had
a good bit of conflict over that, and it was hard for Pat.
Heterosexual friends nursed their kids for 18 months
whereas Laurie was out the door by the 6th week to
spend the night with Franklin. Once a week, every week.
Pat was having to deal with stuff around separation
while I was having to deal with stuff about exclusion.
There were fights about that. Part of it worked itself out
just listening to each other. Part of it was because there
was a period in Laurie's life when she just needed Pat a
lot more. It was hard to respect that sometimes, but it
was important. Then the time came when she opened up

and I was next in line. I also realized there were times when my being available to support them both was important.

Pat: Laurie would leave us and spend the night at Franklin's house. I would express milk. They would take care of her by themselves. I went back to work after 3 months, so I was expressing milk for her to have during the day, and also while she was gone. That was exhausting. I wasn't able to demand for myself what I needed. I felt a lot of grief about how early she stopped breastfeeding. Her life was different from other children and that was part of it.

How does it work now on a daily basis? *(Lots of laughter.)*

Meg: Fascinating and exhausting. We're on for 4 days and then we realize: "Time! We can talk to each other. We can go out to breakfast." But we're glad when we get her back.

  I think we knew all along that if we were going to do this we would need a supportive environment. There's a strong gay and lesbian community here. Also a strong progressive community, for a lot of us have heterosexual friends or families, too. We're not pariahs. Our community accepts our parenting as just another variety and has been very supportive.

Pat: That's part of what laid the groundwork for our decision that it would be okay to pursue.

Meg: We both were in jobs where we were not closeted, and Franklin wasn't either. I couldn't have had a child in a closeted job, in a closeted relationship. Too much gets passed on about fear and all that kind of thing. We knew that was important.

  We had a hard time with day care, though. I hadn't expected things to happen as fast as they did. We didn't "come out" to the day care provider. At one point she met Pat at the swings and said that because she was keeping kids in her home she needed some assurance that Laurie didn't have any communicable disease. This meant AIDS. We gave her some assurance and explanation. But Laurie wasn't happy there.

We got another day-care provider whom we liked a lot, but she quit to be a manicurist. So we put Laurie in a day-care that was supposed to be liberal, and she did fine for 6 months. But then they turned on us, accusing us twice for child abuse. The first time for sexual abuse. That was terrifying.

Pat: They were accusing Franklin. I'm an incest survivor myself, so that was like having to find a place where I could trust my intuition about Franklin. My biggest fear was that something was happening and somehow I missed it!

Meg: In a general way I had thought we'll educate people as we go along and they'll respond okay and dahdeedah. We hit this experience at day care that made us realize uhhh,uhhh, you can't just assume this. Anybody can just turn you in for child abuse anonymously, and they have to investigate.

We moved Laurie to a different day care, and that's been a difference of night and day for us and for her, too. We just have to be careful all the way along where she goes in terms of schools and give her information on it too, some tools to understand and to feel good about her family as it relates to other families.

Pat: I think Laurie knows deeply that she's wanted and loved. Sometimes she'll go through a litany of people who love her. It's this long list, and she's right in every case. These *are* people who love her.

Meg: I'm always concerned about how and when homophobia will hit her. When the stuff with the day care happened, she had been crying for 3 weeks and they didn't tell us. She knew something was going on. We didn't think it was

appropriate to explain it. We just said, "They weren't respecting us. They weren't taking very good care of you."
Also, one of the day care people said to us, "You know,
Laurie goes up to other children and asks them. 'Where
is your other mother'?" As if it was terrible!

So I explained to Laurie in terms she can understand
'cause she's always asking, "How does this get made?"
and "How does this get made?" I was hanging out with
her a good bit that week 'cause she wasn't in day-care,
and I said, "Well, Laurie, you are like every other little
boy or girl in the world. You have a mommy and a daddy
who made you, and Franklin is your daddy who made
you, and Pat is your mommy who made you; but I decided with Pat that I was going to love you. When you're
sick at night, I would get up and take care of you, and
when you're hungry I would feed you, and I work to help
pay for you, and so I get to be your mommy, too." And I
said, "Pat carried you in her body and I carried you in
my heart."

And she looked at me and she said, "And you in my
heart.' And she kind of nodded and said, "And you and
you and you."

The splitting is hard, but there are strong parts about
it. No parenting situation in this culture is ideal.

Pat: Because children aren't respected or valued much. Children need limits. I think there's a great confusion in our
society that giving in to a child's demands is valuing
them. I think we need more of respecting them as people.

Meg: Valuing women, for one thing. Valuing women's work
and having day care provided so people aren't just having
to leave their kids all over the place.

Pat: It's structured in such an isolated way.

Meg: Being born in '49 as part of the baby boom, to me
it seems like it's a baby boom phenomenon still. People
had come back from war and saw a family as this kind of
elusive security and fostered certain illusions and ideolo-

gies about the family that were not real. Now there's this whole literature about dysfunctional families from that generation.

Pat: Laurie goes through periods where she needs to be angry at one of us. We're pretty interchangeable.

Meg: I don't think she does that with Franklin.

Pat: Yeah, just within this part of her family. When she's angry at Meg, I'm her safe place and vice versa.

Meg: Then there're temperamental differences. Pat's good at physical stuff, playing rough with her and bouncing on the bed. I'm verbal and kind of imaginative. We do reading and make books together. Franklin does a whole different set of things with her. It's interesting. I don't know in the long run, like in 20 years, what she's going to be like (*lots of laughing*).

Pat: There's a way in which she has a life that's very separate. Neither one of us completely encompasses her emotionally, and I think there are dangers in that. She could fall through the cracks somewhere.

Meg: But we're not all in the same house. People who live in the same house get enmeshed, and the emotional patterns overlap in some form. Franklin's stuff is separate from ours. So Laurie negotiates back and forth. Franklin and Jordan split up at one point, and Jordan sort of dropped out of the picture. I think there's a strength in not having to be totally under one set of things. I've heard that as kids get older when they've got two households they can kind of go back and forth. They've got a refuge somewhere.

You mean analogous to a divorce situation?

Pat and Meg: Yeah!

Pat: One thing we've been aware of lately. We used to share our lives together, do things spontaneously, go to movies.

Meg: The work I was doing—political organizing, anti-Klan

organizing, traveling a lot, working long hours—I had to cut back on that. Pat asserted herself in terms of me not being absent so much. So I began to reshape how I did work. Now I want to write about what I had been doing, because I hadn't had time before. It's very hard to carve out that kind of solitude in the middle of this. I'd think, "Aha, I've got Thursday and Friday," and Laurie would get sick on Thursday.

What is the response of your original families to your family?

Pat: My mom and dad love it. They really enjoy her. It's been hard for them—something to work through. Laurie is named for my grandmother, whom I'm close to, and who was instrumental in helping things go smoothly. My grandmother loves her a lot, too.

Meg: Which took a lot on their part. I mean, this is Southern Baptist fundamentalist. The hardest thing for them was when they learned she had my last name. That was the straw that almost broke the camel's back.

Was it more difficult for them than learning you were lesbian?

Pat: I think so because they could pretty much keep that a secret. They see me as an unwed parent which is like . . . (everyone laughing). That definition doesn't have much meaning for me. I understand the values out of which they speak, of course, but that term with which I grew up has nothing to do with me.

Meg: My mother died when Laurie was 6 months old. My mother was the most supportive. She was ambivalent about it though. I found out more after she died. She'd left some notes and things. My mother always said, "Any-

one you love, I will love. . . ." The subtext was, ". . . even if
I hate her guts." She would keep up with birthdays and
holidays.

My father, on the other hand, is much more remote. My
sister has six children and my brother has two. So he has
this circle of grandchildren already. He's PawPaw. He
sends her Valentine cards and has his own strange level
of conversation and relationship with her.

I'm not really in contact with my sister or brother. So
Laurie doesn't really have a relationship with any of
them.

The first couple of years of Laurie's life I had this ro-
manticized notion of our family. We were going to be this
wonderful family, a different kind of family. We weren't
going to do any of the things that happened to us. Two
things sent me falling into reality—the stuff with daycare, and then when Franklin broke up with Jordan. It's
like he was breaking up, and I'm experiencing this
breakup and have no control over it. When Jordan took
himself out of it, I thought this man is jerking my whole
family around. The whole unit is up in the air and how
will it come down again, if it does? I was pissed.

We had to really readjust. We called a gay friend of
ours who is a counselor and also a father and set up this
session with Jordan and Franklin. He listened to everybody, and said to Jordan that if he wanted a more with-
drawn position, he just needed to be clear about it. And
he told *me* not to try to put things back together but to go
on.

So Jordan keeps up with Laurie maybe once a month.
She calls him Daddy. That was an emotional identifica-
tion she made and has nothing to do with how often they
see each other. He bonded with her in a parental way
when she was little. He is very good about details and
structures and schedule which, for an infant, provides

regularity. Of the two of them, he was her mother. He played a very important role.

I think the connection between all of this and how Laurie is doing, which I think is very well, is this was a wanted child. The amount of thought and preparation! This was no accidental fluke.

Tracy

12

Tracy's house is in a racially mixed and poor neighborhood just out-side downtown Atlanta. It is badly in need of repair both outside and in, although new unpainted windows and door jambs have been in-stalled. A few minutes late for the appointed meeting, Tracy pulls up to the curb in an old station wagon loaded with carpentry tools, a ladder, and several bags of groceries. Out she hops, an agile, stocky young woman in overalls who apologizes for being late.

We enter together and go directly to the kitchen, which is in total disorder. Tracy explains that everything under the sink had to be taken out in anticipation of a plumber's housecall. She sets the gro-ceries down on a child's highchair and shoves things aside on the kitchen table to clear a space for the tape recorder. We sit down. The outstanding feature of her otherwise plain countenance is her big blue eyes.

I turned 38 last month and grew up in Delaware, in the country. I'm the oldest of five children. I have two brothers and two younger sisters who are 25 and 27, both lesbians.

One sister and I are bisexual. My other sister has never been with a man. I was involved with a boyfriend in high school and have had some superficial sexual encounters with men since then. I tend to fall in love with women. In my last long-term relationship, I made a decision to be monogamous and haven't been with men going on 9 years now.

At first, I thought of sex in terms of bisexuality. In high

school I started having sexual dreams about my girlfriends. But I never acted on them.

I graduated from high school in 1971, when the gay movement and gay politics were just beginning to get a head of steam. People were starting to come out. I decided that when I went to college I would explore having a relationship with a woman.

I remember having a discussion about bisexuality with my father. I remember my father was a bit loaded when we had this discussion. Of course, my father—both my parents drink. He shocked me. He was much more graphic in his assessment of the situation than I was prepared to deal with. I had not ever slept with a woman or even had been physically affectionate with women up to that point. So I wasn't prepared for the idea of oral sex, which was what he talked about. All I had thought about was kissing and I was like, "What? Is that what it means to be a lesbian?"

He was an open person as far as sexuality goes whereas my mother is the opposite. Back then, he was like, "Whatever turns you on." But since I did turn out to be gay, he is the one who has had a harder time with it.

During my first year at Loyola College in Baltimore, I met a woman and sensed she had the same inclinations I did, although she resisted my overtures. We kind of danced around each other for the first semester. She had a boyfriend and claimed she wasn't interested. But on another level she was encouraging. I was in love with her. By the end of the semester, I decided I wasn't going to pursue this anymore. It was too frustrating.

Just when I gave up on it, she made the move and managed to switch roommates in the dorm so we could room together the second semester. We ended up being lovers. I was ecstatic.

She was from Atlanta. Her father was a professor at Emory. She decided not to come back to Loyola the next year. So I transferred to Emory to be with her. It was too late to start in the fall, so I entered in January and, of course, by that time we had broken up. My whole reason for coming here was gone.

In college, I had a series of affairs. None of them lasted longer than a year and a half or so. But I liked it down here. Emory was a more respected college. I graduated in '76—majored in anthropology and geology which, of course, I don't do anything with now. Now I'm a carpenter and work for a small employee-owned company.

I graduated magna cum laude. I was always an excellent student but didn't have any idea what I wanted to do when I got out. I knew I didn't want to work for the oil companies. I tried to find a job in my field with marine sources on the east coast and other places that do science, with no luck. I was tired of collecting food stamps and sitting on my butt all day. This guy I met through my roommate needed help doing roofing. I ended up getting a job as a roofer's helper 'cause I wanted to make some money.

With that experience in carpentry, I decided to move to California—just made a decision that before I have to get serious, let's just travel and enjoy life. I was really into smoking dope and having cut-off blue jeans—the whole scene. I wasn't concerned about a career.

My trip across country took 3 months. I visited a lot of different places and a lot of friends up and down the east coast, went to the Michigan Women's Music Festival—this was in 1978—and got involved with a woman at the festival who I ended up living with for the next 4 years.

Celine and I moved out to Oregon together. We settled in Portland. I thought I could find work. It was about the right size city. Large cities make me uncomfortable. I lived out there for a couple of years and weatherized homes for low-income, fixed-income people.

While I was there, I would go through periods of drinking. It would get out of hand and then I would quit. During one nondrinking phase, I started getting involved with cocaine. It was not a good time in my life. See, I've always been an educated drug user and did research about cocaine before I started doing it. It didn't become a problem until I started drinking again, and the two together were bad, very bad.

Celine and I moved back here to Georgia. I missed the east coast. I missed being close to my family. I missed my friends in Atlanta. Being away for 3 years helped me to figure out that this is where I wanted to be. Celine and I both worked for a big electrical company. We worked hard, and on our off times we did drugs and stuff.

I got laid off from that job and collected unemployment for a while. I was strung out, not happy, and not able to quit my habit either. There came a point where I wanted to stop and then realized I couldn't stop. No matter what my resolve was when I woke up in the morning, by midnight I was going to be messed up again. Unfortunately, I had unlimited access to stuff 'cause I was dealing it.

I don't think our relationship was destined for greatness anyway, but the combination of both of us being drug and alcohol abusers and kind of egging each other on—it was bad, not only for us individually, but for our relationship also. We ended up splitting. She got interested in someone else. When Celine left me I went into a funk, feeling sorry for myself and drinking a lot.

I bought this house during that period. Actually, that helped me get out of the funk. I'd been doing odd jobs for people, cleaning houses and stuff. This house needed quite a bit of work before I moved in. It gave me a focus.

When I was in my 20s, the thought of having children didn't enter my mind—partly 'cause I was a party girl, partly 'cause I was a lesbian. I was such a partier that I felt there was no way I was responsible enough to have children. Although in my definition lesbians could not have children, there were already these jokes out of California about turkey baster babies. Some pioneering couples and single mothers, too, had been having children with artificial insemination. That was just starting in California when I left the west coast in '80. I had no idea it was to become a lesbian baby boom. So having a child didn't enter my mind until I got sober. I started getting sober in 1984.

I met Lynne, who was very attracted to me. I thought she was cute and was somewhat attracted to her, too. We started seeing each other. It had been 7 months or so since I broke up with Celine and I was still drinking pretty heavily on a fairly regular basis. I wasn't doing as much cocaine. The supplies were getting kind of thin. For a while I was making a profit on it, but I was beginning to snort up all the profits.

Lynne didn't like it. I mean she liked me, she liked being with me and spending time with me. But my addiction was such that there were times when I would rather be drinking and tooting and hanging out with friends than be with her because I couldn't do any of that when I was with her. She didn't want to be around it. So the choice was, "If you're going to be with me you need to not do this stuff."

I struggled with that, especially as I got closer to her, felt more attached to her. It was Lynne who inspired me to get my shit together and shake this addiction. I don't think I would have done it for myself. I did it for her—and I did it for us. If we were going to have a chance, I needed to get sober. I knew I needed to do that anyway; I just wasn't able to act on it. I struggled. I don't think I came to terms with the fact that I was an alcoholic until that last time.

I can remember with great clarity the last time. Lynne went off for a 2-week hiking trip. I bought a 6-pack and a gram of cocaine. I was determined to have my little party with myself, so I sat down and did up most of the coke and got down to the last bottle of beer about 3 in the morning. I got really sick. That was the last time. Thank God that's behind me. Now I'm really into 12-step stuff, the ACOA (Adult Children of Alcoholics) group, and Co-Dependents Anonymous.

After I'd been sober for a couple of years, my decision to have a child led from my sobriety. I thought, "Here I am, heading into my mid-30s. I'm sober." I was still smoking pot, but compared to what I had been through and the other things I had done, I didn't think that was a big deal at that time. I feel differently now. I quit smoking pot when I got pregnant. I was clean. I even quit smoking cigarettes. I quit all the things I thought were bad for me.

Because of my drug and alcohol problems, I never gave any thought to a career. I kind of farted around, fucked around, worked here and there—never had any job that lasted more than a year and a half, kind of like my relationships.

So I started thinking, "Here you are, getting a new lease on life, getting your shit together, so what are you going to do? Do you want to go back to school, get a graduate degree? Do you want to have a career and be a professional and make lots of money? What do you want to do with the rest of your life?"

And I thought, "Nahhhh. I'm just not into it." I struggle sometimes with the career thing, and wish I made more money, but there are so many other factors involved. I really enjoy what I do. I like building; I like working with my hands; I like seeing the results of my work; I like being able to play rock music all day long. I like not having to shave my legs or my chin.

"Well, if you really don't want to do this," I thought, "if you really don't want to make a lot of money and have some hot shit career, what do you want? What are the alternatives? What's important to you?" I said to myself, "Friends. Family."

The fact was that friends and family were very important to me. That feeling of family was the one sadness I had about being a lesbian—the lack of family in terms of children.

The lesbian baby boom was in full swing. Having a baby was becoming a glimmer of an idea for me. I started making noise about wanting to have a family type scene. Lynne said, "Tracy, you've got ovaries. If you want to have a baby, you can have one." That planted a pretty serious seed.

One of my anxieties about having a kid was the revolving door of lesbian relationships. People come and go and it's like, "Well, I'm tired of this. I'm leaving now," or "She's cuter than you are," or "She's hotter than you are so I'm going to go sleep with her." It was frustrating to me how easily relationships would break up. I was feeling that marriage was another piece for me that I needed—to feel a relationship was secure and was going to last.

Lynne and I got married in April of '85. It was a ceremony of our own construction and done with friends and family in my back yard. We read vows to each other and planted a tree, and did all this nice stuff. We were feeling a lifelong commitment to each other at that point.

I was hopeful about having a stable family unit for a child. So I started thinking about a donor. It was important to me to know the father. I couldn't imagine sitting my child on my knee and saying, "Yes, your daddy was a test tube." I wanted a real person who had a real face and a name and who had a history, someone about whom I could say, "This someone helped us to have you, and this is something Mommy wanted."

All these decisions were made within the context of Lynne and I being together, made with the assumption that the child would have two parents who would both be women. It would be a stable, loving environment. I was really not interested in having a third co-parent. I felt that made things too complicated. I wasn't interested in someone being involved because it put a restriction on what I might want to do. You know, if we wanted to move somewhere or if they wanted. . . .

I mean, it's hard enough to get two parents to agree on how to parent a child, let alone three or four. It's too bulky. But I wanted someone interested, someone comfortable with being known as the father. I wasn't sure I would be able to find that.

I wanted it to be a gay man. In the event there was a court custody battle, I felt that the judge would give the child to a gay mother rather than a gay father, whereas, if it were a straight father, the judge would probably give it to the heterosexual man. That was my reasoning.

At that time, if you went to a sperm bank and told them you were a lesbian, they wouldn't give you sperm. So you had to either lie about your circumstances or figure out something else. Plus, it cost $150 a shot for what has got to be some of the most readily available substance on the planet.

I found out about Seth. Seth donated sperm to women. He was a bisexual man who had this attitude that if a woman wants to have a child she should be able to do so without going through a bureaucratic hassle, and he's more than willing to help in that project.

It turned out that Lynne met Seth in graduate school where, every Wednesday, they have "queer lunch" and get together. So she talked to him and he said he was interested. We started meeting. We had him over to dinner a few times.

I agreed that he was great and had the characteristics I was looking for—preferably a small man, and smart, and someone who had coloring similar to mine. He fit all my requirements. The only thing he didn't have was bright blue eyes—one of my better features and something I like a lot. I mean, if you've got this genetic control, why not go for it? Seth had hazel eyes, which sometimes look grey and sometimes dark blue. I thought, "This is close enough." Besides, there was the off chance that he has a recessive gene, and maybe she'll come out blue-eyed anyway. But she has exactly his eye color which—they are gorgeous. I'm very pleased with how it all worked out.

Seth had a bunch of information he had been accumulating over the years. He had contracts regarding the other inseminations he had done—specifics about what his role would be, what his financial or lack of financial responsibility would be, and the mother's wish to be full custodian of the child. It was all written down, not in legalese as a lawyer would do, but showing intent.

There's no financial responsibility on his part. He would not be part of the team who decides what happens to her. There would be no father named on the birth certificate for that very reason. I would be the sole legal guardian and financial supporter of my child.

We decided on a verbal agreement which was basically, "I won't sue you for child support if you won't sue me for custody." I decided to do it that way because if we were to bring each other to court, we would have the document of intent, and I had a witness in Lynne. Lynne witnessed us do this verbal agreement and witnessed our handshake. I felt that was as legally binding as any piece of paper we could come up with.

Second reason, Seth had two other kids who were now 4 or 5 years old. He hadn't made any moves to take either child or to be any more a part of either child's life than he and the mother agreed to, to start with. He has adjusted emotionally, physically, and in every way to this whole concept. It would have made a difference if it had been a man who had never been a donor. You can't predict how people are going to feel about those things.

I had been keeping my basal temperature for months, so I had a pretty good idea what my cycle was doing. I was ovulating anywhere from day 16 to day 22. We set up a series of days for Seth to come over. We knew that sperm is viable for three days. So we set up our first day on the earliest day that I ovulated, the 16th day, and then we set up every other day or every third day as dates for him to come over.

Lynne and I planned to use a small plunger type syringe with, of course, no needle on it—one that held about, I don't know how many CC's, what you give a baby liquid medicine with. We did our first insemination—our only insemination—on October 5th, 1988.

We invited Seth for dinner. It was nice. We had a little fertility ritual. Lynne had made up an altar with shells and stones and little symbolic things. Some were long and skinny and others were round, little seeds and stuff. Each of us put on one little earring that Lynne had bought since we all have pierced ears. We burned sage and sat holding hands, talking about our hopes for the baby and what we were afraid of for the baby, and kind of welcoming the baby into our lives. Seth's a botany major and Lynne was getting a degree in horticulture. I'm into rocks. We're all into nature so we each took turns saying what we wished for the baby. We were wishing that the baby would appreciate nature and growing things. I don't remember all the details now. It's been 3 years.

We had fears, too. I know that one of them was just the normal parent fears about whether your baby will be healthy, whether your baby will be happy, and whether your baby will have a normal mental capacity—afraid of things in the world that can happen to the child. But then there was also the fears about us being gay, and fears that having gay parents would be a terrible burden on the child, something that would cause the child pain.

After the ceremony, we put on some Celtic harp music and sent Seth into the front room with a brown jar. Light is not supposed to be good for the sperm. He did his business and handed the jar to Lynne.

I went in the bedroom and got myself ready. Lynne took the sperm from the jar and put it in the plunger. We asked Seth if he wanted to hang around with us afterward, but he had to leave. We said, "Bye, thanks," and he took off. Then Lynne inseminated me. She put the sperm inside me and we made love. I fell asleep. I had elevated my rear end to help things move in the right direction, and I didn't get out of bed until the next morning.

Next morning, I took my temperature and it had shot up. I had ovulated, because your temperature shoots up the day after. It went up very high, higher than usual, and stayed up. I didn't test positive for about 3½ weeks. But I think I knew the morning after.

How did you feel when you knew you were pregnant?

I was ecstatic, elated. I had had some pre-conception anxiety. I was 89.98% sure I wanted to be a mother. But there was this 10% uncertainty. I would ask myself, "Am I doing the right thing? Is this really what I want to do? This is really going to change my life a whole lot. Is this crazy? Is it going to be okay?"

I had a wonderful pregnancy—just the slightest amount of morning sickness for the first 2 months. I was very healthy and very happy, of course, until Lynne told me she was leaving me. That happened 6 weeks before delivery. It's funny. Seth was scared when Lynne and I broke up. He got freaked out thinking he was going to have more responsibility. I said to him, "Seth, I'm not going to change it now. Yes, the circumstance is completely beyond my imagination, but I can't change what I expect or want from you because this has happened to me. I will deal with it." It was a very difficult time. But the moment I saw Cathleen, the moment they brought her to me, all uncertainty was gone. She is just so wonderful. The moment I laid eyes on her it was like this immediate bonding thing. I thought she was the most beautiful baby in the world. Usually, newborns are ugly, but I thought she was totally gorgeous. I look at pictures of her now and go, "Tracy, you had rose-tinted glasses on."

I haven't had a moment of doubt. There's been times when it's been a little hard but since the first moment I saw her I never doubted that I loved being a mother and this is exactly what I wanted to do. I'm totally blown away by it.

Part of my wanting the experience of being a mother had to do with wanting a child, wanting to watch the child grow up, teaching it things, just loving it, and having the sense of family. I was dumbstruck when Lynne told me she was leaving. Here I am, out to here, looking like a watermelon, planning to take a year off to be with my child, and here's my partner, here's this woman who encouraged me to have this child, who made a commitment to raise this child with me, who made a commitment to me in her marriage vows, and she's telling me that she doesn't think that she wants to live with me anymore.

I'm not sure I'll ever understand exactly what happened, although I think my being pregnant had a lot to do with it. It's not in my value system to do the kind of thing that Lynne did to me. I wouldn't have considered making a commitment with someone and having a child with someone and then just walking out. Although, she still wanted to parent. She still wanted to have a relationship with the child. She still wanted to be financially responsible. I just couldn't handle that. She was talking about coming over and spending 3 or 4 nights a week with me. Meanwhile, she was screwing a new lover. I was just like, "Forget it. I can't deal with this."

Neither one of us had considered that this might happen one day. Neither one of us had bothered to sit down and talk about what we would do if we ever broke up. It hadn't entered our minds.

Being the biological mother and having absolutely no legal obligation whatsoever to Lynne, I didn't want to have anything to do with her, and I didn't want her to have anything to do with my child either. If she had left after the child was born, say 6 months or a year later, if she had established a relationship with the child and the child with her, I could never have cut that off. I think it would be wrong. But she left before I even gave birth. So I felt like, "Fuck you. Forget it. It doesn't work that way."

Who went through the birth process with you?

We kind of expanded the birth team. I ended up having a C-section after being in labor for over 24 hours. So a lot of people took turns being with me. The nurses thought we were wonderful. They were like, "You've got a real support system helping you breathe, getting ice for you, helping you do this and that, and we're free to do our work." They were quite impressed. That all went well.

Lynne offered to move back in and stay with me for a couple of weeks after Cathleen was born. I just felt like, "What else am I going to do? I need this." There were very strained relations between us. Part of me believed that once the baby came she would change her mind. I was bitterly disillusioned once I realized she was determined to go through with her plan. So after the 2 weeks, I asked her to go. I visited my family a lot that fall. I didn't have a lot of close friends. All my emotional stuff was tied up with Lynne.

I had told my co-workers I wanted to take a year off after the baby was born. I had worked up to 7 months and saved $6,000. I had some other money that I had inherited from my grandmother in stocks and bonds. So I had $10,000 that I could live off of. I was hoping that with Lynne's faculty income I wouldn't have to burn up all that money. Of course, it didn't do me much good. But I was determined to take a year off, dammit, even if it was going to be hard. I figured I would only be doing this once, although I've had second thoughts about that. I wanted to experience seeing my child grow that first year. I felt it was important for the child, too—to be there for her.

My company was fine with that. That's another wonderful thing about being a carpenter. If you need to take a year off, okay, go ahead. It's not like you're on some career ladder that you slide down. You'll still know how to do what you do. And I continued to go to meetings and be involved in the business aspect of things.

What was your parents' reaction to your having a baby?

Right around Thanksgiving I wrote a letter explaining to them that I was pregnant, how I got pregnant, my reasons for doing it, and then some explanation about how I felt this was going to be. I wrote them that I knew it was going to create some difficulties for the child, having gay parents, but that the most important thing for a child is to be loved, and I felt that would very much be the case with this child.

For 10 days I didn't hear from them. I started getting anxious. So I called my sister, "Did Mom get that letter?", and she was like, "Yeah, they got it."

"Well, what do you think?"

And she said, "Well, they're pretty blown away, but Mom's working on it. She's probably going to call you in a day or two."

My mother called me a few days later. Her first comment was that she had had to think about it for a while, but she felt she had her head on straight now and could talk to me about it. Obviously, it had upset her to start with. It was totally out of left field as far as they were concerned. My mother said she could understand, being a mother herself, just being able to relate to the maternal urges. So she was supportive during my pregnancy.

I'm still not sure what my father thought because no one would tell me. My mother said, "Well, he feels that if he doesn't have anything nice to say that he shouldn't say anything at all."

At one point I said, "Dad, I'm not worried. As soon as you lay eyes on this little person, you're not going to be able to resist." And the moment he laid eyes on her he just lost it. He said, "Oh, she's so pretty." I knew that he may not like what I had done, but I knew he couldn't hold it against the child.

They've been incredibly supportive. They offered to help me out financially when it became clear that Lynne was leaving. My mother brought it up, "If you want to get Lynne out of the picture completely, we're willing to help you out." I thought it made sense to have a clean break with Lynne.

It was the first time in my adult life that I had really asked them for anything. I didn't even ask for it. They offered. So I said, "Well, if the offer still stands, I think I'd like to do that." That was the point at which I told Lynne that maybe sometime in the future we could be friends again, and she could be involved in some way with Cathleen. However, she was not to consider herself a parent in any way. And that has been wonderful for me.

My brothers are so different. One is very stodgy and conservative, very macho. He accepts me and loves me, but I can tell it's difficult for him to swallow.

My other brother is married to a woman, and the two of them, they have a lot of gay friends. They're very liberal politically. They're Yuppies and into the cool scene of D.C. He and Janie are the Godparents. They came to the wedding and to the baptism.

Then there's Seth, Cathleen's father. I feel like I have this connection with Seth's donees. In a sense, we're related, or we're in-laws, or something. Cathleen met Eric, her half-brother, at a music festival. His mother had told him, "You have half-sisters and someday maybe you will be able to have a special relationship with them, the same way I have with my brother." Cathleen, of course, had no idea what was going on. They just got along, played together, and he was squeezing her and hugging her and kissing her, and she was eating it up. It was really wonderful. We hope to keep in contact with each other 'cause Eric and his mother live in Macon.

I expected that my freedom would be curtailed. I expected I was going to have to time my life around the baby, and I was ready for all those things. I have to be honest and say that I can't separate this question from Lynne because what I did not expect was to be a single mother. That has been probably the hardest thing I have had to deal with.

I didn't expect to have to have childcare. I can't get up and take a walk around the block without having childcare. If I'm fed up to here, I can't just say, "Hey, I'm going to take a walk. I'll be right back. Just watch the kid for a few minutes."

I can't breathe, eat, shit, take a shower. If I take a shower, I bring her into the bathroom with me. If I try to eat—when she was younger it wasn't a problem—but now I can't eat a meal without her bugging me, wanting a bite. Most of the time that's okay with me and I don't mind giving her little pieces of things off my plate. But sometimes it bugs me. Sometimes I would like someone there to say, "Okay sweetheart, let's go into the other room and play while Mama gets to do something for herself." Time to yourself has become a precious commodity to me. Also, I started back to work when Cathleen was a year old.

It's very difficult to always be the one that is totally responsible. Lately I've been trying to get people willing to do overnights with her once a week 'cause I have a new girlfriend now. It's real nice to get a break like that. And I've started running again.

I'm fascinated by this little person who is just growing and changing so fast. She just brings me joy, just pure, pure joy. I nursed her. I enjoyed nursing her and holding her close. It was 15 months when she weaned herself. I miss that, but that was a good experience for me.

Part of it, I'm sure, is how relaxed you are and how you treat your child. But part of it has to be the child's personality. She has been so easy. I feel so blessed. She's this little social child.

It taxes your ability and your resources, but there's part of me that would love to have another child. Then there's part of me that says, "Tracy, you're nuts." So we'll see what happens.

You said you went back to your religion. The Catholic Church is not very supportive of the gay and lesbian movement.

That's true. Although it has changed some since I was younger. I came back to the Catholic Church because it's my roots. It is what I grew up with. It is my culture. It is my history. I'm Irish in background. I went off on Eastern religions and Zen Buddhism, and I've taken elements from that and incorporated it into my concept of my own higher power. I feel I came full circle back to what was familiar.

I went to Mass for the first time in years. A friend of mine was in the choir. It's a mostly black congregation. They sang gospel, which I never had been exposed to as a child. I loved it; and the people were wonderful, so I kept going. I found an incredible sense of fellowship there and a sense of tradition. I'm in the choir now. For me, that music part is very important in experiencing and expressing my spirituality.

I treat the Catholic Church like I do ACOA, that is, I take what I like and leave the rest. One thing that is of concern to me is their stand on homosexuality. It is bullshit because God made me, too.

I'm concerned for my child, and I'm not sure how I'm going to deal with that. I had her baptized, but I don't want her growing up in a faith that tells her that her mother is a sinner.

You know, in "Harold and Maude," one of my favorite movies, Ruth Gordon says you've got to reach out and grab life and give it all you can. That's what I wanted to do, and I'm going for it.

Have you remained close to your own family?

Yes—well, bless their hearts, I have two alcoholic parents. Both my mother and father had alcoholic fathers. We have a long history of alcoholism in our family. I'm sure this is part of what all my problems were about. I've been to therapy going on 2 years. There are some things about the way I was raised that weren't the most nurturing environment in the world and I'm hoping I can do better.

There's a lot of sadness for me about the fact that they still drink. I've watched them be miserable for years, and I know it's because of their drinking. Still, I feel close to them and see them fairly often; and I am very close to my brothers and sisters.

I've gone home more since Cathleen was born than I have in years. We go up a couple times a year to visit. I went fairly often to see my grandmother, particularly in the later years of her life. I realized she wasn't going to be around much longer. I was very close to her, my mother's mother. She passed away 3 years ago.

Mary, my father's mother, died in '84. It took me by surprise. I started going back to church again after Mary died. That's been helpful for me with my sobriety, you know, getting reconnected with the Catholic Church. I didn't realize until later, when I started going to 12-step meetings, what the church thing was all about. But it was a reconnection for me with familiar rituals from my childhood and also an outlet for my spirituality, the feeling of fellowship that you don't get when you try to do something on your own.

Between '84 and '87 I made a conscious effort to get up to see my maternal grandmother a lot more often than I had. You see, I used to stay with grandmother, not with my parents, when I went up there. I would go to see them and get together with them, but I rarely stayed with them.

When Mary died, it made me very sad, made me very upset. I wished I had spent more time with her. Being a mother was a connection for me into the cycle of life and death and birth. It was a fulfillment.

Also, part of being a woman is this cycle that you have—the privilege as a woman to experience giving birth to a child. It's such a miracle. It makes my life so much richer. It is unique. I don't care that 5 billion other women have done this. This is like amazing! Every time it happens it's just amazing to me how this fully formed human being can come out of you from a pinpoint of a cell. It's one of the reasons I believe in God.

Ben

13

It is dark, raining, and cold. In a rented car, we sit and relish our take-out won-ton soup. We had scheduled a few appointments in the neighboring boroughs of New York City and are too early for this double interview. After finishing what is to be the evening's dinner, we mount the stoop of a greystone on a quiet, old street and ring the doorbell.

Sean, a thin, dark-haired young man, opens the door holding a little girl in his arms. She is about 3 years old and lively. Sean greets us warmly and suggests we first interview the man he lives with. "I have to give Alicia a bath and cornbraid her hair, which takes about an hour," he explains, leading us into the small front living room. The furniture is for the most part utilitarian and large relative to the small rooms.

Sean introduces us to Ben, who is husky, rather muscular, a man of about 40 with thinning brown hair. His manner is businesslike, just short of brusque, as he gestures to us to sit in a couple of chairs opposite the couch he settles into comfortably.

I 'm a 44-year-old white Jewish male, gay. I was born outside of New York. I have a 3-year-old child, a daughter named Alicia.

Sean and I have been together almost 9 years. About 5 years ago he said he wanted a child. I was extremely opposed to it. We went back and forth for a long time and realized it was not an issue you could talk about. It wasn't like I wanted Chinese food and he wanted Italian food so we could have Chinese one night and Italian the next. You either had a child or you

165

didn't. To him, being a big brother or something like that just wasn't enough. He wanted to be a full-time, permanent parent.

I have an 11-year-old nephew. I have no special relationship with him. I'm not close to my sister either. She's 3 years older than I am, and we never got along well growing up. I never had any cousins my own age. They were all 10 or 15 years younger. So I guess I was never exposed much to children and never really liked children and had no desire to have children, especially as a gay man, as a totally openly gay male. I had no desire to be a freak and go through life as a freak. What gay man has a child? I mean most gay people don't have children and most people with children are not gay, so you're a freak in both worlds.

I was very comfortable with my life. Sean and I used to go out 4 or 5 nights a week. We used to travel a lot, go out to movies, go out to dinner with friends. We'd go away for weekends. I mean we had what I felt was a wonderful life, and I had no desire whatsoever to change it.

I went along with Sean's wish. It was a combination of fear and love. The fear of being alone, especially in the age of AIDS, knowing it's more difficult as you get older, difficult to meet another lover. I was 34 then. And I really love Sean. We've always loved each other. So it's a combination of two factors. We probably should have sought counseling earlier, but we didn't. We went into adopting a child knowing that the odds were probably fifty-fifty we could adopt.

Was there an option to adopt a white child?

Not an able child. Sean works with retarded people and so he would not have wanted to have one at home, and I definitely would not have wanted a retarded child. Neither one of us would have taken a mentally handicapped child. I would have taken a physically handicapped child. I'm not sure about blind or deaf, but certainly missing an arm or leg. I don't think there were any available. Originally, there was this book

of adoptable children that we looked through. Sean applied
for several and the agencies all said there were families for
each of them when clearly there were none available. Obviously, it was homophobia. Why else would the agencies not
release any of these children to Sean?

I think on some level I never believed he would get a child. I
thought this was more like playing, and I would just go along
with it. When it became a reality . . . Again, we definitely
should have gone into counseling earlier. Everything should
have been more clear-cut than it was. "You want the child?
Fine! It's your responsibility." It's different if both people in
the couple want a child. You share the responsibilities.

Alicia was born in the hospital. She was born with syphil-
lis. Her mother basically abandoned her in the hospital. We
were called on a Friday to see if we wanted this 5-week-old
girl. We said, "Yes."

We went through a very difficult period. Sean and I came
very close to breaking up a few times. We started counseling 6
months ago. That's helped a lot. The woman we see is gay and
a parent herself. She had children when she was married, and
then divorced her husband. Sean thought it was important to
have a therapist who was gay. I didn't.

Sean and I went to this therapist without any agenda. We
just knew things were not working out. In a nutshell, Sean resented that I didn't do more for Alicia, and I resented doing as
much as I did. I mean, I never got up in the night. I would
change diapers, but I would never get up in the night. When
I'm awake, I'll change a diaper, but other things grew out of
that, such as, I didn't feel I was getting enough companion-
ship from Sean. I should say that in talking to our straight
friends who have kids—we're pretty open about our lives—
virtually all of them said, "Yeah, every straight couple goes
through that." So that was nice to hear—kind of validated my
feelings.

We've reached a pretty good compromise. Basically, for me,
I try not to do things with Alicia that I can't stand, like playing a stupid board game or ring-around-the-rosie, whereas she

and I do all the supermarket shopping. I've always loved shopping in the supermarket. I love the idea that I can go to the store and buy anything I want, and my mother can't tell me I can't. I can buy twelve boxes of Ring-Dings. If I have the money, I can do it. So Alicia and I enjoy supermarket shopping together, and sometimes we run errands on Saturday. A few times we've gone out for a pizza. Those are things I enjoy doing. But when she's with me she often asks about Sean. I can't imagine she ever asks about me.

We're very much like the 1950s television family, except that we both work. When we come home, because I run my own business, I often have work to do at home at night, or I read. I do my thing, and he's "with the children." Alicia is Sean's responsibility. Alicia is Sean's child.

If she's sick, it's his responsibility to stay home from work. If he has to reschedule, tough. I will do what I can, if I can; but the responsibility is his. We both agree that I probably do 30% of the work with Alicia, which is more than I would have suspected. Usually, one night a week or so, I go out with friends, to the movies or the theater or something. And on weekends, clearly, I have more freedom. I love to play tennis, so Saturdays and Sundays, in the mornings, I go and play tennis, and Sean takes care of Alicia.

I have no legal claim at all. We have known that it's something we should do, but we don't have wills, and we definitely need to have something in writing. If something were to happen to Sean, Alicia would come to me. Sean's family would never have an issue about it, so I don't think that would ever be a problem. But if Sean died I would kill him. I would have to take Alicia. We have another very good friend and I would probably ask her, and I think she would take Alicia.

I make quite a bit more money than Sean does. We have separate accounts. I pay all the bills and he gives me a certain amount of money every month—maybe, 35 to 40% of the bills. He sends Alicia to school. So we probably do things evenly. I think we've both worked hard to manage this.

Sean comes from a family that never had a babysitter. He

thinks having a babysitter is kind of odd. Sean and I have a babysitter one night a week. We have a standing date on Tuesday nights and go out to dinner by ourselves. Usually, one time on the weekend we have a sitter as well. I would say no other gay couple has a sitter that often.

Most of the other gay parents that we know feel guilty about what they've done to their children, feel guilty about having children in such a strange family setting. They feel like, since they work, they shouldn't go out at night. They should be devoted to their children. They feel like they need to be superparents—like having a sitter and going out is being selfish. They look at us like we're straight people having babysitters.

There's a gay parents group which we're involved with— much less now than we used to be. As I told Sean, I don't really like small talk. At this point in my life, going to cocktail parties bores me, but if I go to a cocktail party and we talk about the theater or movies, I can deal with that. The idea of sitting around at a cocktail party with a lot of people and talking about child care arrangements and diapers does not interest me in the slightest. I refuse to go.

We met two other gay couples through the gay parents group and we're very good friends. We see them a lot, but we rarely go to any of the organized activities where there are 50 to 100 people. Sean occasionally goes without me.

When Sean and I were first together, we did a lot together. He learned to play tennis. He's certainly not the ideal tennis partner, but he enjoyed it. He always liked hiking, so we used to do a lot of hiking. We travelled, went to movies, went to the theater and out to dinner—things the average New York City gay man does.

I guess the main thing that came out of our group therapy, and this is 100% true for me and Sean, is the statement, "You marry your opposite, and spend a lot of time trying to turn him into your twin, and in times of stress you resent your partner being different from you."

The thing I admire in Sean is his social conviction. I mean, I was a child of the '50s, but I outgrew it. Sean's a social worker, does good deeds. He's a wonderful, loving, caring, giving person. I resented that. And I think the thing Sean admires about me is that I'm very energetic, some people think hyper, but an outgoing, "doing" type of person. And he resents it, like, "Why do you have to do this? Don't you just want to stay home and watch the baby sleep?" So I think the differences are what I think we each admire in the other and resent.

Sean comes from a family where no one has any hobbies or interests whatsoever. They just sit around and talk about the children. Sean wasn't encouraged to have hobbies or interests. When I first met him he didn't really have any. Sean was brought up to think that the normal way of life was you grew up, you got married, and had children, and that was it.

What is your family's reaction to your life choices?

My immediate family consists of my father and my sister. My mother passed away 5 years ago. I daresay that if my mother weren't dead, this would have killed her. My mother was a very traditional woman, very proper and prim. I always described my mother as being a Jewish WASP. Everything had to be just perfect, and looks were more important than reality. I can't imagine she could have coped with this.

My father is not a baby person at all. Babies don't interest him. He cares enough about appearances so that he wouldn't feel totally relaxed and comfortable with the three of us in public. That would not thrill him.

Growing up, my father was certainly there. He was like a little league coach and he did stuff like that. But I grew up in a family where basically we ate dinner together, and you talked about current things like how we did in school, and then each person went to their own room and closed the door. I mean literally.

In the last 6 months my father and I have established a better relationship than we've ever had. We've always gotten along but we've never been close. I've worked hard to make it better. For Alicia's birthday or for Christmas he'll say, "Here's $25. Go buy Alicia a present." When I see him it's usually by myself or we'll find a babysitter, and Sean and I will go with him. He would not feel relaxed hanging around with Alicia.

A few months ago, I confronted him on the homosexual issue. "I accept it, but I can't approve of it," he said, and then he called a couple of nights ago and said, "I'm working on approving. I'm getting there, but I'm not there yet." He's talking to his girlfriend and other people, and he's really working on it. I thought that was pretty good. So he's okay with Sean. He cares about him. He sent Sean a birthday card. My father's not an easy person—not a hang-around-and-shoot-the-bull kind of person. He's formal, uptight.

My sister—I'll tell you a story about my sister. My sister is a sad person. She has no friends. She's divorced and leads a depressed and lonely life. When we first got Alicia, my sister came to visit. Not only did she not want my nephew to see Alicia, she did not want her even mentioned. A few months later she and my nephew came and Alicia was there and my nephew saw her. We said, "This is Sean's foster child," and my nephew didn't give a shit—like any normal 8-year-old kid. He's able to cope with having a black cousin!

One day we all went out to dinner—my sister and her son, my father, me, Sean, and Alicia. We went to a Chinese restaurant in this wealthy, exclusively white, predominantly Jewish suburban community—the next town over from where my father lives. My nephew is eating with chopsticks and doing pretty well. So, as we were leaving, I asked the waitress to give him some chopsticks. She gave him six sets which, to my nephew, was like getting a million dollars. As we all walked out of the restaurant, my nephew says, "Did you notice how everyone was staring at us 'cause I had all those chopsticks?"

Now my sister is fine with Alicia. She's involved in Alicia's life. She's a thousand miles away, but she comes to see Alicia. She does the right things.

One of the things I'm dealing with in my therapy right now is the difficulty I have and the resentment I have in giving to

Alicia. My parents were not very giving people. I always knew, growing up, how much they paid for all my education, but I also knew what I was entitled to, that part of my birthright is room and board and books and occasional theater tickets and all the education I wanted. But I was not entitled to go out to dinner more than once a month. It was very clear to me never to ask for something, never to ask my parents to buy me something. I always knew from day one, you didn't ask. My mother would never buy extra treats. My parents would never buy anything that was frivolous. I've come to realize I never had a childhood. I was like a mini-adult.

One of the challenges of having Alicia is giving these things to her. Just buying her toys. It's not a natural thing for me. I work at it. It's more natural for Sean.

I think I've always been a giving person with friends. I've always given. Not just financially. I've been a volunteer with AIDS organizations for years. I think it's very different giving now because it's like giving to a bottomless pit. I mean Alicia's not going to buy me a birthday present. You've just got to give and give, and that's a very different type of giving, and sometimes I resent it—a lot of times I resent it. It's not just the money. It's like, "Alicia, I want to read the paper. I do not want to watch Sesame Street." Time is more precious to me than money. Like if I win the lottery, I have no interest in a big car or clothes. The thing I would love is not to have to work so I could have all day to read books, to go out to have three-hour lunches with friends, to go to the movies. Giving to Alicia is more difficult because it's giving my time.

Do you think about Alicia's future as a young woman?

All the time. I'm concerned. Actually, when we walk down the street, I don't happen to give a shit about the people looking at us. I don't even notice. Sean is more aware of it than I am. But when she's 13 years old, I just can't imagine she's going to be thrilled about having two gay white fathers—that she's not going to feel angry, sad, hurt, depressed—that she's not going to have a very hard time. And I wonder, when she's a grownup, how she's going to feel. Is she going to say, "If you really loved me, why didn't you find a poor but loving black family and pay them money to raise me?" And I don't know how I'd answer that.

What can you say? I would agree that if we truly loved her, what Sean would have done would have been to find a poor but loving black family and given them "x" number of dollars a month, anonymously.

When I see kids on the subway or on the street or in terrible situations, I do think, "That might be Alicia," and I feel . . . I feel . . . I feel when people say, "God, you're so lucky to be doing such a wonderful thing," that doesn't really mean anything. I don't really get much out of it. There was not a void in my life that needed to be filled.

Does religion or spirituality play any role in your lives?

I'm a born-again atheist. You're born, you die, and that's it. I'm very ethnically Jewish, not religious Jewish. Sean is somewhat spiritual.

Sean is Irish?

You got it.

I have feelings for Alicia—I mean I definitely love her. I often don't like her, often don't like having her around. I don't feel she's added to my life. Being with her is definitely work. When I stay home with her, when she's sick or whatever, I don't get much accomplished.

I'm hoping one day I'll understand why anyone wants to have a child.

Sean

14

At the conclusion of Ben's interview, Sean and Alicia join us in the living room where, near the window, is a small trampoline. Alicia jumps on it to bounce up and down, looking around at all of us for signs of admiration, which she gets. After a few minutes, Sean leaves her with Ben and leads us down to the ground level where we sit down at the table in the front room, which is the kitchen.

I've been in this relationship with Ben for 9 years. I was married at one point and am in contact with my ex-wife, who has two children. I've remained connected to a lot of the various people I've known throughout my life.

Alicia is my first child. We adopted through foster care, which began when she was 6 weeks old. Just before her second birthday the adoption was final—January 26th, 1990. We had a big bash! Alicia is 3 now.

I grew up with little kids around all the time. I'm the oldest of five children, and took care of my brothers and sisters; and I've got quite a few cousins. It seemed to me being a parent was going to be a part of my life.

When I was younger, feeling I was gay, knowing I was gay, was something I didn't cope with well. I couldn't acknowledge it. I remember as a young adolescent, having dreams, waking up and thinking, "Oh no, I'm not—only one of ten—I can't be the one of ten!" I didn't want to be.

I grew up in a Catholic home. My family was blue-collar Irish. I went to Catholic school through to high school. To me, being gay was being a queer. It was horrible. I tried to push it aside—so much so that I resisted any type of sexual contact. I was always everybody's best friend. I was the guy all girls could talk to, but there was never a connection other than, "Oh, Sean, you're such a great guy to talk to." I'm sure I set it up that way.

From the time I was 13 or 14, I wanted to move out from my parents' home. All of us lived in a very small house. It would be like having a bed in this room. That was my room until I was 18. I wanted my own space. I don't know how much has to do with knowing I was gay and different from the rest of my family. I've always had an independent streak.

In my junior year at the State college, I moved out, got a studio apartment, and worked two jobs part-time along with going to school and student teaching. I was very busy and very motivated to maintain my independence, but I still hadn't been involved sexually with anybody. I mean I'd gone out with girls and done some heavy petting, but never intercourse or any type of oral sex.

When I was, I guess, 21, I met this guy who was gay. I was a counselor working with disabled children. He was another counselor. Basically, he picked me up and I had sex with him. I was freaked out by it. It was coming face to face with, "Oh, God, I had sex with a man!" Until that point I could think, "Well, maybe you're bisexual. . . ." That made me more comfortable. My relationship with this guy was fleeting. I think it was only two or three times. I was petrified.

At work, I met a woman. We really became best friends and then, one night, I was staying over there and "Boom!" we had sex and I thought, "Oh, I can do this."

It was my first time with a woman, and it was pleasant in certain ways. I was just very relieved. Almost instantaneously we started living together. A year and a half later we married. We were married for about a year and a half before I left.

For about 2 of those 3 years I coasted, feeling everything is okay, I don't have to worry now, but gradually I became aware that I really was gay, that the feeling for men was surfacing. And on some level I was tormented, conflicted, certainly in terms of the life I was living versus the life I felt I should be living.

My wife kept saying, "I want to have a child." My answer was, "The world isn't a good enough place. I don't know if I want to have children." It was my defense. I didn't want to make the situation more complicated than it already was.

I told her about the one experience I had prior to our getting together. I said it was a phase, curiosity. She's pretty sophisticated, worldly, much more worldly than I was. I guess she wanted to believe it also, so she bought it—and I bought it for a while, too. But then she gave me a deadline about having a child with her.

I was working as a counselor on a travel program for learning disabled. A trip to Spain came up at this time. They needed one more counselor, and I was asked to go. Marianne stayed at home. During the 3 weeks we were apart, it seemed every second of my spare time was consumed with thinking I had to do something about my life.

When I came back, I just said, "I can't go on with this." She was also feeling other difficulties. She had been an active, involved, independent person who had become dependent in our relationship. While I was working two jobs she wasn't working at all. She was not a housewife type and yet couldn't muster up energy to pursue her own career. The situation was not good for her either. We had our tears and stuff and I told her I was leaving. "It's because I'm gay and I have to deal with this."

She was very good about it, very understanding. We vacillated for a while. I took an apartment down in the Village, and from that point on it was pretty clear that this was going to be the way it was going to be—that I must deal with being gay and get on with my life, get involved with the gay world, join some organizations, go to groups.

The whole idea of being a parent was sublimated. I still loved being around kids. When I saw other people with kids, there would be an ache as I thought, "You're gay; you can't be a parent." It was incongruous to me at that point. But then, after a few years, I became much more comfortable with myself. I accepted that I was not bisexual but gay, and I then had a few relationships.

Once I was in my relationship with Ben—about 4 years— my desire to be a parent really started to churn. I was in my early thirties and people around my age were starting to have children. Straight people who were my friends, people I worked with, my ex-wife—they were all having children. It brought thoughts up again, you know, that I would make a good parent, that it isn't incongruous and I'd like to do it.

Well, it threw Ben for a loop, because I'd never talked to him about kids. We struggled with the idea for a long time; we're still struggling, but things are much better now. He was clear. He didn't want a kid. As in any relationship, straight or gay, it's one of those issues that is not negotiable. You either have a kid or you don't. And I felt if I didn't pursue this, something was really going to be missing in my life. At the same time, I wanted to keep my relationship with Ben. I care about him deeply. For a time, it was very difficult for us.

We lived on the West Side in a one-bedroom apartment. We loved the apartment, loved the building, loved the area. It was great! In New York, because of the housing situation, you don't have to have a separate bedroom for an adopted child. You just have to have separate sleeping space, but we would have had to move out eventually, 'cause it certainly wasn't big enough for two men and a baby.

So we started looking for a two-bedroom apartment. Ben didn't like any of the apartments we saw. Finally, after finding a suitable one, I said, "Listen, you don't like the idea of *why* we're going to this apartment. This is what we can afford and we have to pick something." So we wound up taking an apartment near Riverside Church. I really liked it. Ben didn't.

I started pursuing an adoption agency. There was a gay fa-

thers' group in the neighborhood. I went hoping to meet a father who had adopted. There was one. All the other fathers
had children from a marriage which they had left, and were
dealing with their ex-wives who, for the most part, had custody and were giving them a hard time about being gay. So
there were visitation issues. This was a support group, a social type of thing.

I connected with the one guy there who had adopted. I also
contacted an international gay fathers group and they had
given me this same person's name as the New York contact.
Warren invited me out to Long Island to see his house and
meet his son. Freddie was 6½ years old when Warren adopted
him. Warren was having a lot of problems. His adoption
wound up being rescinded because the judge who had
granted the adoption found out he was gay and accused Warren of purposefully withholding that information from the
adoption agency. Warren fled to Amsterdam with his son.
Only through negotiations between his lawyer and the city's
lawyers was he able to come back. He still hasn't been able to
re-adopt Freddie, although Freddie is still with him.

After hearing Warren's story and a few others, I spoke to
the Council on Adoptable Children (COAC). They are an information referral resource for anyone interested in adoption issues. They invited me to a group orientation. They go over the
realities of adoption and what kinds of children are available—public, private, or international adoption. Then they
meet with you individually and go over your situation.

Basically, they said to steer away from Catholic or Jewish
agencies. They recommended two that might be more receptive to the gay male or gay couple adopting.

I think it's a law in every state that an unmarried couple,
including gays, cannot adopt as a couple. So Alicia is not
adopted by us. Alicia is adopted by me. The gist is that
straight people have the option to get legally married whereas
gays do not have that option. So it still winds up being discriminatory, even though the law is meant for any unmarried
couple.

COAC said, "It's up to you as far as how you represent yourself. You could, for the sake of the intake, have Ben not be there, not talk about him, and you could be looked on by the social worker as a single male pursuing adoption. People are doing that. It's one of the options."

In the past 10 years I've become adamant about living my life openly, and the hell with everybody else. If it's somebody's problem, it's somebody's problem. I don't think I'm inappropriate. I can certainly separate personal and professional matters, and I'm not going to hide behind anything.

Ben was in shock. I believe he thought I'd get it out of my system and maybe I'd forget about it. I wasn't sure what was going to happen. I just knew it was something I was going to do, however it worked out. I think Ben and I have a pretty solid relationship. On some level, maybe I was banking on the strength of it.

The first agency I contacted ultimately denied my application. They claimed they didn't do homestudies in New York City even though at the outset, before extensive questioning, I told them where I lived. I then tried Lutheran Community Services. I said to the woman who interviewed me, "I want you to know I'm a gay man."

"That's fine with us," she said, and assigned us a social worker. I couldn't tell what her (the social worker's) problem was. I didn't know if she was just very different than I was and maybe was put off, maybe was threatened by the fact that I was a social worker, or maybe was just a very uptight woman—person. I had no idea. Anyway, she was very formal, wouldn't touch anything we offered, not a drink of soda, never a grape, nothing. She wasn't like your old-fashioned type social worker. She was a young woman.

She met with Ben and me in our apartment. I didn't say the "g" word. I said, "Ben and I are interested in adopting. We've lived together for 5 years. Any child that comes into our household will be part of our lives." She saw the bedroom, the pictures, you know, whatever. Still, I decided not to say "gay" unless she asked me, 'cause I thought if she had to write down what I said, I'd have a better shot if I didn't use the word.

It was taking so long. She never called my references, and I felt uncomfortable calling to complain. Finally, I had my references call her 'cause she wasn't calling them. Every time she spoke to them she would ask for more information, repeatedly going over the circumstances of my divorce. Finally, I just said, "Listen, do you want to know whether I'm gay or not?"

"Yes."

"Then why didn't you ask me? I'm gay. Now I want to know why you are asking me. What does that have to do with anything?"

She said, "Well, it's who you are. It's your life."

I said, "I was told that you put in the homestudy how I report to you and what I say. I didn't think it would be advantageous for me in the first line of the homestudy to put, 'I'm a 33-year-old white, gay male, living with Ben Marks.'"

She said, "How do you want me to portray this in the homestudy?"

So I said, "I'm not a social worker in this field. You know more than I do. I mean I want to have a kid, so I don't mind it not being explicitly stated, but I also am not going to hide the fact that Ben and I are in a relationship, that we live together, that we care about each other, that we're committed to each other, and that the child is going to be part of our family, and you don't have to be an Einstein to figure out what that means. If that's going to make it easier for me to adopt, then that's what I'd like you to do." She was open to that.

Even so, the thing that amazed me about a homestudy, at least this homestudy, is that she hadn't confirmed any of the information. I told her about my mother, my father, my brothers, my sisters, my work. Ben told her about his parents. The only thing she did was to call my job and confirm my salary. There was no confirmation of any other materials. Nothing!

As a social worker, knowing a child is being placed in a home, she should have checked. I could have been Jack the

Ripper. You do have your fingerprints taken so they can send it to the Child Abuse Register in Albany and get cleared that way. But I could have told her a lot of misleading information. Ben and I were surprised by that.

Anyway, the report was done, and it was time to look into getting a child. Any child legally freed for adoption in New York is put in a book called *The Blue Book*. Each adoption agency has *The Blue Book*. Lutheran was my agency, but kids in *The Blue Book* are from every different agency in the state. Some from upstate, some from Long Island, whatever. There are like 25 of these thick blue books, page after page of children—individual children, and sibling groups, and handicapped children.

You need to look in these books. It was heart-wrenching. It's like looking for an apartment in Manhattan. You get to know what the words mean. If the ad says the apartment's cozy, you know it's a shoe box. If a child is described as one who would benefit from being in a home that could provide structure, the child is probably emotionally disturbed, needs limit-setting, and would require therapy.

When you start your homestudy they ask you what type of child you're open to. A lot of the kids of different races, non-white children and children with disabilities are considered hard-to-place children. Ben and I talked about this. We were open to a child preferably under 5, of any race, boy or girl. The child could have a slight physical disability, but we preferred not to have a mentally retarded one.

Over the course of 6 months I found about 17 different individual children whose page number I gave to our agency. They would then contact the agency for that child. Rejections were coming back, and these were for children who I can guarantee did not have people banging their doors down to get them. Our agency thought there was a good possibility this was discriminatory. The replies would state something like, "No, this family is not appropriate because this child needs an intact traditional family." Give me a break! I mean, how many intact traditional families are there? Never mind how many intact traditional families are going to adopt a special-needs child or a child of a different race!

A short while later, I got a call about twin boys, 7 months old. Ben and I decided it would be too much, since I would be the primary parent. I didn't know if I could handle two kids at the same time. We said, "No."

Soon after, the call came about Alicia. All I knew was that she was a 5-week-old baby girl, black. Her mother had two previous children, both of whom were in placement, and she had abandoned Alicia in the hospital. It looked like a situation where the mother would not be getting custody nor would she pursue getting custody. She said she did do drugs and had no prenatal care, but Alicia appeared to be very healthy and had no sign of any type of drug in her system.

We got the call on a Thursday, had to let them know on Friday and when we said, "Yes," we were told, "She'll be there Monday."

"Monday!" I said, "I don't know if I can do everything I want to do!" Usually, single men do not get female children placed with them. I was prepared to have a boy, but it was to be a little girl and she was an infant!

I geared up for Monday. Ben and I had what we call our "lost weekend." We went to our friends in Westchester, who came shopping with us at Caldors. One stayed with me while I went through the aisles pulling all this stuff. The other one stayed with Ben, consoling him. It was really going to happen! We bought everything we needed.

I told people at work, wrapped up all my cases, transferred them to another person, and Monday was my last day at work.

The only thing I was very afraid of initially was how to bathe her. I didn't know how. She was a very small baby—5 pounds when she was born, and 7 pounds 2 ounces when I got her. You know, 6 weeks of age. So my mother came over and showed me how to do it, and my sister brought over a crib.

I read Doctor Spock and one of the things he said was that

if you start heating up milk that's what the baby will get used to. Whatever the milk temperature is when you start, that's the temperature you'll be stuck with. I figured if I don't have to heat the milk, I'm not going to heat the milk. I started giving her little bottles of formula from the refrigerator. The first night I fed her she started shaking. I thought she was having some type of seizure, tremors. I was worried. It stopped. The next morning I took the bottle out of the refrigerator and gave it to Alicia. She started having tremors again. I said, "Ma, what is this?"

She said, "The milk's cold. You don't give her cold milk."

That was my introduction to Dr. Spock. I guess I didn't read him very well.

A colleague of mine knew someone else who was gay and had just adopted a little girl a few months prior to my getting Alicia. We decided to get together and, including Warren from suburbia, organize a little informal support group for ourselves. The three of us then sent out word to people that we know announcing a picnic in Central Park. This was September of 1988. We thought maybe three or four other people would be there. Lo and behold, about 40 people showed up—gay men and gay women, all of whom were parents. Some of the women had given birth by alternative insemination. Most of the men were parents through adoption. Some creative couples, a gay man and a gay woman, had a baby together.

Well, then we held monthly socials. The group was primarily white and primarily female. Every month it grew. The gay community sponsored us as a sub-group. We're now a major part of the gay community center with a mailing list of about 700 that includes some from all parts of the United States. We run all types of seminars now for people considering parenthood, people considering adoption, people considering alternative insemination, workshops on the psychology of gay parenting from all points of view. Our resources have been primarily gay, or at least people that we feel are sensitive to some of the nuances. Until recently, the idea of children being incorporated into gay activities was nonexistent. We're sensitizing our own community to the idea of children being a part of their lives. For the most part I think we're well received. We had a lot of controversy with the transracial issues.

I'm having to desensitize myself to the high visibility we have as a family wherever we go. I underestimated the impact. It's taken a bit of getting used to for me because I like anonymity. I like going about my business and not having people notice, or whatever. I think I'm doing pretty well with it now.

The most important thing for a child is having a good foundation. For us, particularly, I think it's important to recognize that she's black. That's very significant. We need to insure that we connect with a diverse group of people. We've really made an effort. With the childcare situation, the one we chose is not the closest center and not the most convenient nor the cheapest, but it's the one both of us thought was wonderful as far as being multi-racial and multi-ethnic. The teachers are primarily black women, and they were very receptive to our family. And we have black friends—not many, but some.

Generally, the reaction has been mixed, whether black or white. I have black people say to me, "We just don't think it's a good idea." One reason is their feeling that most agencies are white and have not done outreach to the black community in a way which would insure that black children get placed with black families. In Chicago, there were many more black children needing placement than there were places. A group was given a grant to do outreach and now, in that part of Chicago, there is a waiting list to get children. So it shows that if you do creative stuff and recognize that blacks know how to do outreach to blacks, there can be a positive result.

Another issue is that as a white person I can never understand what it's like to be black and cannot adequately prepare Alicia for what she's going to have to deal with as a black woman in the world.

Another reason has to do with offering her cultural experi-

ences related to black history and her background, stuff like
that, general concerns. I'm not expecting it to be an easy time
at certain periods of her development. I'm going to show videos of everything.

First of all, every teenager rebels. Teenagers hate their parents, and whether you hate your parents because they happen
to have gray hair or are overweight or have an accent or whatever, they go through this. Certainly, this situation is significantly different. My guess is that the racial issue will be the
primary one, not the gay issue. I'm hoping that by keeping
communication open we'll have the solidity and the emotional
strength to be able to support each other through that. I expect it to happen. I just hope we give her enough to get her
through in as positive a way as possible with Alicia feeling
okay about us and still caring about us.

The other thing I've done is to get in touch with her half-
brother's and half-sister's families. I know where they are.
Even though I don't want to have contact with them right
now, I've asked if they would let me know where to reach
them so that when Alicia starts asking, when she wants to
have contact, I'll initiate it. I don't think it's realistic for me to
assume that she's going to feel that my father is her grandfather. If she feels my family is her family, that's wonderful; but
I think that most likely there's going to be a very strong feeling of wanting to know her biological family. There's no mention of her father, so I don't know what the father's scoop is,
but I have her mother's name and date of birth and a half-
brother's as well.

In the best of all possible worlds, it probably would be better or easier for children to be placed with parents of the
same race or culture. Given the reality of the situation, I think
the most important thing is to give the child a sense of security and a good sense of self. Whatever they have to deal with,
these children are fortified knowing they're loved and are
worthy. The bottom line is love.

Ben and I needed to be in counseling together. The underlying issues were presenting themselves at different times and were not resolved: his feeling that "You chose a child over me," and my feeling that "If you really cared about me you would put more energy into doing this." We're in a much better place now than we were 6 months ago, and I am thrilled with having done it. I would certainly do it again. I think I've learned a hell of a lot.

One of the things we've been told is to try to really deal with the basic issue of having a child in our life right now. The therapist kept saying, "The issues that you're talking about and struggling with are issues related to any couple with a kid."

If it were a 50–50 deal, if Ben felt differently, I would certainly think of adopting another child. But I don't think I could be the primary parent to two children. I don't think I have the stamina to do it. It's been more than I ever thought it would be.

I think professionally it's certainly helped me in terms of working with parents. I don't think you can understand what it's like being a parent until you've been there on a day-to-day basis, the daily responsibility. I mean, I thought I had a pretty good handle on what everything was like, having always been around kids and being pretty involved taking care of my brothers and sisters.

Also, working full-time, balancing professional life with the personal, and making sure I put the energy towards my relationship with Ben, it's been a challenge. But to me the positive certainly outweighs the drawbacks, and, from my perspective, my relationship with Ben has been strengthened by this. There was very little prior to Alicia that tested our relationship. It was very stress-free. So it validated the relationship because I still had the commitment to be in it. I was the type of person who worked 40, 50, 60 hours in doing whatever I had to do. I now have to be very clear that I work 35 hours a week. It's been a real help to me in recognizing what's most important in life. Relationships. My work is important but comes second.

Does your family consider Alicia family?

That's a hard question. I don't know. My mother recently died. There was my mother, my father, my two brothers, and two sisters. A brother and a sister are married, and I certainly am the odd duck of the family. To begin with, I'm viewed as the odd duck. I've always had a more distant relationship with my parents than my brothers and sisters have had.

My father said to my brother, "Why did he have to get a black baby?" The black issue was another struggle for them. From the beginning, my mother was fine with it and was always warm and wonderful. Both my parents are Archie Bunker types in that they always say things about groups of people. They'd come out with these ignorant, generalized statements—a standard bigoted response.

But growing up, I had all different types of friends. Everyone was always welcome in our house. We were taught that people should be treated equally no matter what religion they were, no matter what color.

There was this incongruity. . . .

PART V

Grandparents as Parents

In the natural sequence of events, parents have children and those children have children and thus is established that special relationship that exists between grandparents and grandchildren. Traditionally, this has usually been a pleasure trip with the elders bearing only occasional responsibilities, chiefly babysitting. The accents are on the delights of belonging to this third generation, bringing or sending presents on birthdays and holidays, eagerly exchanging hugs and kisses with little or no reprimands from grandma and grandpa to spoil the fun—a win-win situation with lots of snapshots to show for proud documentation.

This scenario still obtains. There are, of course, many instances where grandparents have had to take over the care of their children's children for various reasons, including illness, job dislocations, incompetency, imprisonment, death, and other major complications. During the sixties, there were 930,000 children living with grandparents with no parents present (U.S. Bureau of the Census, 1960). This number had increased to well over 1 million by 1993, representing 30% of almost 3.5 million children who live with grandparents with or without parents present (U.S. Bureau of the Census, 1993).

In recent years, drug and alcohol addiction and AIDS among parents have in many cases victimized both the children and the grandparents as well. In such cases it often is the grandparents who then become the full-time parents. More than 1 million of the 4.2 million parents on the rolls of Aid to Families with Dependent Children (AFDC) in 1991 were alcohol and drug abusers or addicts. Among the youngest parents on AFDC, the rate of addiction and abuse is 37% (Center on Addiction and Substance Abuse, 1994; Sisco & Pearson, 1994).

While the incidence of children raised by grandparents is not new in human history, the numbers of this particular family composition have substantially increased. There are an estimated half-million Americans age 45 or older who are caring for a grandchild without the help of a parent (American Association of Retired Persons, 1994).

The voices of today's grandparents tell of how the forces and pressures of modern times result in changes in family life.

The Flanagans

15

Well-tended landscaping frames the Flanagan's house in a Minneapolis suburb. The greenery continues inside the house, which is full of plants and morning sunlight. Their living room is carpeted wall-to-wall. A large oriental rug lies over the carpeting. The room has a variety of period furniture and finely upholstered pieces. A baby grand piano is laden with many music books and also supports assorted family photographs.

Jean is a pretty woman in her 60s, whose red hair and green eyes augment her delicate appearance. Her husband, Ted, has a full head of white hair and a rosy complexion. His humor and good nature play in his facial expressions. From the outset, they seem to have a prickly, yet loving relationship.

Ted says he has an errand to do and will be back. We sit down on the sofa and begin the interview with Jean, who speaks in a soft, clear voice.

Dick, our son, was a student in Moscow State University Law School and there he met a beautiful young Russian woman. She was his age at that time, 31. They fell in love and married. In May, we went over to meet her and her family. You had to be part of a tour then—all very much arranged. You knew you were being taped in the hotels, and you knew that they knew you knew. We visited her family more or less on the QT although we knew we were being followed. Even the family said, "Don't say who you saw here when you get back to your hotel." It was an unusual experience.

Not 'til we arrived in Russia did Dick tell us that Anna had a 5-year-old by a previous marriage. It was quite a surprise. We met him, a darling little boy.

Our son was given an extension on his scholarship and stayed on an extra month, since Anna would be allowed to leave in June. So she and Dick came back to the United States together. Her little boy, Dimitri, stayed in Russia for a year with his grandmother.

Dick had a grant with an institute in Washington and while they waited for it to start up and to find a place in Maryland, he and Anna lived with us for a few months. We got to know her very well. She says I taught her English.

In the summer, Dimitri came to the United States. He was 6 then, and spoke no English except the two words he knew, "MacDonalds" and "ginger ale." We went to Maryland to see him and took him to a toy store. I was sure his eyes would pop out just looking at all the things that were available. It was so different from what he knew although his mother was from a privileged family that had more than most Russians. I can re-member, too, how surprised she was when we took her into a supermarket here. She ran from one place to the other—the fresh vegetables, she couldn't believe it!—though she proba-bly would never admit that.

We all went to the lake. Dimitri, Anna, and Dick came with us. Afterward, Dimitri stayed with us for about 10 days before going back to Maryland to enter first grade. He was speaking only Russian, but by Thanksgiving he spoke English fluently. They say, at only 6 you can learn a foreign language without an accent, which he did. He has no accent. You would have thought he was born in this country.

Those first 3 years when he was going to school in Silver Spring, he came to be with us every vacation—at Christmas, at Thanksgiving, spring break, in the summers. He was with us so much because Anna was either going to school or work-ing, and so we got to know him well.

Our son was a wonderful father to Dimitri. He did much more than even Anna did for him, although Dimitri worshipped his mother. He would do anything she said. But she frightened him, too. That first summer he came here he said, "When Mama is mad and she starts driving extremely fast, I get in the back seat and cover my ears and eyes because I'm frightened." She would just be so out of control. As far as I know, she was never ever violent with him. She never did anything to indicate she was punishing him in excess, not physically. Now, verbally, she might have.

Toward the end of third grade for Dimitri, Anna started a job in an engineering company. It became difficult for her to take Dimitri to school in the early morning before work and pick him up later at after-school care.

We decided to bring him here that summer and also to consider keeping him here. We went to visit one of the schools in Silver Spring and were not impressed. We thought he would do just as well, if not better, here. We made arrangements to have temporary legal custody so he could enroll here in fourth grade. Dimitri could walk to school just two blocks away, and when he came home in the afternoons I was always here, because I tutor quite a few students.

In retrospect, we realized it was a traumatic experience for Dimitri—more than we anticipated. He seemed to feel so at home with us and never seemed to mind his parents leaving him on vacations. But the day they left him here to stay to go to school, he stood at the window and tears ran down his face. For the first time ever he cried when they left. We felt bad about that. We thought, "Should we have taken him? Should he have stayed with them? Maybe then they could have worked things out."

Anna says, no, they couldn't have, even though Dick had done so much for him—washed his clothes, fed him, shopped for him, cooked his meals, took him to his boy scout meetings, took him places Anna couldn't be bothered with because she had her career to think about. She's a self-centered person. While she loves Dimitri, she thinks of herself first before anyone else.

Dimitri started here in fourth grade. It was an agreement

we worked out semester by semester. He always agreed to staying because he'd made friends. He felt at home here. He considers himself part of this household. He has his bedroom and he has the den. One day he said, "Three or four of these rooms are mine in this house, you know." He'd go for visits to Maryland, but he's lived with us all this time. He's 13 now. He considers this his home.

He never wanted us to say, "This is our little Russian grandson," or that he was from Russia. Even his Russian name upset him. When his report card had his Russian name added to Flanagan, he would be in tears. We went to City Hall and had it changed legally. Dick had not adopted Dimitri and actually Dimitri calls him Dick; but to other children, Dimitri calls Dick his dad. "My dad," he says, because it makes him feel good to think that he has a dad.

I thought many times of his father in Russia who had not seen him in so long, and who had married again and who had two more children. I felt sad for that man, but Anna had gotten permission from him for full custody. She always said if anything happened to her, she wanted us to have Dimitri. She didn't want him to go back to Russia.

Anna had problems from the beginning of her arrival here. At times she could be charming, but then other times she was temperamental or angry. She could be very rude to our guests. It became a problem. That was one of the things that influenced our keeping Dimitri.

Eventually, Dick had Anna seek psychiatric care. She was given medication and also counseling, which did help. Since she's been on medication, she has learned not to be so selfish. Their marriage was having difficulty, but she would not agree to marriage counseling. We kept hoping things would work out. She is smart, very intelligent, and could be lovely, but these problems seemed insurmountable. I think now she wants Dimitri before he grows up.

Dimitri had a tendency to react many times much like his mother, and we were trying to control that as much as possible. He, too, is very intelligent, very smart, but without the drive in school that we hoped he would have. He could make very good grades; however, it depended on whether he had the desire. Many times he didn't, particularly after he became acquainted with Nintendo. We noticed a change in his not keeping a journal, not doing things his teachers were asking. So we curtailed his use of Nintendo.

What is it like to bring up a child at this stage of your life?

I felt very much like he was my youngest child over again in certain ways, and yet I never tried to take his mother's place. So I treated him differently. I think you treat each child differently anyway. I'm sure I was easier on him than my own children, but I don't think we spoiled him. He already was very spoiled, very willful, when he arrived. I would try to temper that to some degree. But it was very difficult because he is a strong personality.

We tried to see that he got a certain amount of discipline, but I was never as . . . I never spanked him like I did my own children. I can't say I never spanked him. I remember two times when I did. But he was extremely stubborn, and we had to really work on handling him when he was displaying those stubborn attitudes. Nevertheless, we felt he did well considering his background and the changes he had to face. We felt he was remarkably normal.

I would go to school with him, and go to the PTA functions. Yet, I knew that since I was older than the other mothers, it embarrassed him. It took him a while to get used to our coming to things where younger mothers and fathers were. Although he called me by my first name, he would refer to me as "my grandmother" and my husband as his grandfather. So did Anna. She didn't try to say, "They're not your grandparents." But Dimitri said, "Well, it is a little strange." So we knew that it embarrassed him for us to show up for certain things. We tried not to embarrass him. I'm sure he would have preferred his mother being there. I'm sure he would have felt better had he had a normal family, a mother and father.

I do want to say one thing. Anna had lived with her grandmother until she was 12, and so to her it was normal for a grandmother to keep a child. However, she always had great resentment and animosity toward her mother and not gotten along well with her at all. Zorina is a very strong personality who had an important job in Russia and was used to telling people what to do. So Anna resented her mother for lots of reasons. And I wondered if that might not be part of it, that she had been raised by her grandmother and resented not being with her mother. But she wouldn't admit that. Anyway, I thought that was interesting—that background and her willingness for Dimitri to come and be with us.

But then her husband also had spent a lot of time with his grandparents, because his father died right before he was born and his mother was working. Apparently, in Russia, that is much more traditional.

In the meantime, our son and daughter-in-law were divorced in December. Late in January, Dimitri told me that after Christmas he had joined a divorce group in school, which I did not know they had. He did it on his own. It has been a wonderful experience for him. There are a lot of children in there. You can imagine the number of children of divorced parents that are in that school!

It's made me feel sad for all the divorces in this country and all the children who don't have the traditional family that I felt our children had. And we've tried to make this as much a family for Dimitri as we could.

I would say 90% of the time being a parent at this age has been a good experience. There's a 10% of the time when I think, "Oh me, I have not gone to my poetry group." But I've continued a lot of my activities. I have continued tutoring and singing in the choral society.

Being a parent has also been very time-consuming. We've had to get babysitters, had to do the things that we had not done for quite a while, transport Dimitri to various activities, get him involved in sports and boy scouts, summer programs. It's been an interesting experience though. I really love children. I think if you didn't, it would be a real hardship. I will miss him. I will have another empty nest syndrome when he leaves—and he may next fall. (*Jean becomes tearful and leaves the room for a few minutes. When she returns, she's composed and continues.*)

My emotional investment has been strong, oh, very strong. I tried for a long time to hold off and not be completely caught up, because I certainly didn't want to take Anna's place and I don't think I have. I mean I haven't. And I've always insisted on "Ask your mother."

Ted, my husband, and I have talked with Anna frequently. We talk to her about any problems, and Dimitri talks to her on the phone several times a week, although, when she was involved with someone else, and Dimitri would call to speak to his mother, she wouldn't be there. Dick would have to say, "Well, she's at the store." She'd be with this other person. Dick would have to make excuses for Anna not being in touch with Dimitri. He would talk to Dimitri on the phone a lot then.

Anna's planning to take him when he enters eighth grade if she can find a place to live in a neighborhood that seems safe enough and is big enough for her and the man she's living with. They're not married. I have very strong reservations about Dimitri being an eighth-grader and on his own, because she'll be working. The person she lives with is a musician and his hours are not regular. He seems to be a nice person from a middle-class Delaware family, traditional. I don't think there is any problem with him as far as I know. I don't think he will ever take as much interest in Dimitri as our son did, but I think he will work out all right as a person for Dimitri to be around.

Do you have any regrets that you took Dimitri to live with you?

Only if it would have kept them together. I've wondered if they would have been able to work out their marriage and kept him and been good parents for him. We'll never know.

While Anna was interested in the same things Dick was, she was not supportive and was more or less destructive of his extra interests, which were Russian language and Russian culture. She didn't want to participate in that, although she would get very upset with people who criticized Russia's lifestyles. She was not a communist, she said, but she had been brought up under that regime, and she felt that people didn't understand.

She said, "Why do people think I can't leave? What do they think I am?" She felt hostile toward people who questioned her being here, her being able to leave. I would have been perfectly happy had it worked out for them as a couple. She's a smart person, can be very nice, can be very sweet. Dick is extremely bitter. He feels he lost 7 years of his life.

I mentioned that I felt as though Dimitri was a younger son, and yet I always knew differently. I've raised three boys, and Dimitri has integrated himself into our family. He's very fond of our other children. The other two are not married, but they are very fond of Dimitri and they were very fond of Anna. Now they feel estranged to a certain degree. Still, when she and they are here, they get along fine. There's no anger except from our son who divorced her and doesn't want to have communication with her. Anna feels upset that he doesn't, yet she admits she did not treat him very well. She now admits that.

Has there been any change in your relationship with your husband because you took Dimitri?

Well, he and I both enjoy Dimitri very much, but during a trip to Belgium, he had enjoyed just our being together and doing things together. It was hard for him to reintegrate someone else here and to accept my spending so much time with that person; and he's now retired. Ted has done an awful lot for Dimitri. He has paid the bills, has had to become the chauffeur since I teach, and he's felt quite a bit imposed upon, I think.

(*Ted comes into the room for his interview.*)

What are your feelings about being a parent at this point in your life?

Why does she get to listen to me when I didn't get to listen to her?

Would you prefer that she go out of the room? I'm sure she would.

I don't care. Well, having this child in our home has totally transformed what was my original idea of what retirement would be like. I thought when I retired there would just be the two of us and we'd be free as birds, and we could come and go when we wanted to and do whatever we wanted to, and wouldn't have to account to anybody. Having Dimitri in the house with us has totally transformed that conception, because we have to plan everything around him.

Generally speaking, I think I've accepted it pretty well, recognizing that this is a child who has been bounced from one place to another. He's a victim of circumstances as much as we are, and considering his situation, both Jean and I have been willing to do what we've done in order to help him. We haven't done it to help his mother, although it has had that effect. And we haven't done it to help our son. We did it to help him, Dimitri. So, by and large, I think Jean has accepted it better than I have, although I'd say almost all the time I accept it pretty well.

I don't have much use for his mother, frankly. She drinks more beer than I do. You just don't dump a kid. It's not his fault he's in the situation he's in. This is a human life that's in the process of maturing, and you just have to do what you think you ought to do.

There are times, particularly when he has been obstreperous or caused a problem, when the resentment over being thrust into this situation just boils over and I can't contain myself. So, I have to say, "Step back and look at it coolly and rationally." We've been, in a sense, victimized by circumstances—having to take this child on for this period of time. But in terms of day-to-day living—taking him wherever he has to be, getting him, financing all his projects and whatnot—we've gotten a certain amount of benefit and pleasure from that. Most of the time he's an interesting little boy and most of the time he's a pretty good kid. It's been a mixed bag. On net balance, I wouldn't want to judge which is greater, the pluses or minuses. It hasn't made me a bitter person, generally.

On the other hand, I haven't been able to develop a sustaining, close relationship with this child. He doesn't like my kind of music, and I despise his kind of music. He loves Nintendo and video, and I don't have any use for it. I love reading, and he's not much of a reader. I was highly motivated to do well in school, and he doesn't have great motivation to excel. I suppose if he were different or if I were different, we'd be closer than we are, which is not to say we're strangers. We get along pretty well together.

If you had it to do over again, if it was fourth grade, that first year, when you offered to. . . .

I think that was a mistake. I think the fact that we took him off of their hands, took some responsibility away from them, which, if they had had to exercise it, might have . . . I say *might* have prevented their separating and divorcing. They would have had to come to some kind of accommodation if not for each other, then for this child. Both of them, I think, have a good attitude toward Dimitri. I think if we had not taken him off of their hands, they might have been forced to live their lives a little differently and their marriage *might* have survived.

In many ways, he clearly has been better off here. There he

would have been living in sort of a huge apartment complex, surrounded by parking lots and . . . . Here he's had a more wholesome neighborhood to live in, and I think his school situation has been better than it would have been there.

I believe he's made friends here in a way that he might not have been able to there. Maybe my perception of what it's like there is wrong, I don't know. But here we can let him go out after school on his bicycle and not really worry about him because we think not much is going to happen to him up around the school grounds and wherever he goes with his friends. I have a perception that there the kids are more streetwise and street-oriented and the temptations for drugs and theft are greater in an urban area.

Purely as a matter of space, he's had his own room, his own bathroom. We've turned over the den to him, and he has all his video stuff down there. He wouldn't have had as much living room there in an apartment as he's had here. So I think, generally speaking, it's been a more wholesome way of living for him here.

On the other hand, he's been absolutely deprived of his mother for all these critical years, and she's been deprived of him. From that point of view I think a kid is better growing up with his own parents than he is with his grandparents. So you ask me if I think he's been better off in some very tangible, substantial ways. Yes, he has, but in another sense, I think he lost something.

Do you think you've had any influence on him?

I don't really know. I suspect Jean has had a lot more influence than I have.

Jean: I think he's had a great influence on him. Also, when Dimitri first came here, he was younger and Ted was not retired. Dimitri would get up in Ted's lap or lie down in the bed and read books or look at things with his grandfather, and they had a much closer relationship.

We would go walking, the three of us. We would walk around the blocks. In fact, that first summer and during the next vacations when Dimitri was here, we spent a lot of it walking around the blocks playing word games. That helped him with his English a lot. He learned words very quickly. I think with younger children you do have a much closer relationship. As they grow up and start playing outside more with their peers, they don't want to spend as much time with you; and he is reading more than he used to. I think that's been an influence on him. He reads every night.

Ted: I don't lecture him constantly as Jean does. I don't give him admonitions all the time. I do sometimes—not frequently—but I have tried from time to time to talk to him seriously, although not at length, about trying to be a good person and all that you might call the basic values, and responsibility, and so on. I try not to do it in a preachy way and I don't do it often. At the time when I do it, I have a feeling it may be registering, but whether it does or has in the long run, I don't really know. I think he looks on me mainly as a source of financing and transportation. I'm not a role model for him in other words. I know that.

Jean: Yes, you are.

Ted: No, I'm confident I'm not a role model for him. Jean spends a lot more time with him, and she does a lot more for him. He feels closer to her than he does to me. He would be a lot more willing to talk to her about some things that are important to him. He would never come to me and say, "Ted, sit down and talk to me." but I think he would with her. He calls me Ted, (*Ted turns to his wife*) and he calls you Jean. But speaks of us as his grandparents.

Jean mentioned that it's possible his mother will take him come eighth grade.

I'll believe it when it happens.

How do you think you'd feel if he wasn't living with you?

I'd have to admit that since he's been here for 4 years and we are as attached to him as we are, well, we'd miss him. On the other hand, I think missing him would be outweighed by the new freedom we would have. If he goes back with her, why, we don't expect to just cut him out of our lives. I don't think they expect that either. We would expect him to come and visit us, and we would expect to go see him or try to keep in touch with him as he gets older.

So far as I can tell, Dick has distanced himself. There's the divorce. Naturally it had some effect on Dick's relationship with Dimitri, because when he and Anna were living together they would all do things together. Once they got divorced, Dick doesn't have the same incentive to keep in touch with Dimitri regularly. And now he's living in Kentucky. I don't really know whether Dick has any real desire to keep a sustained relationship with Dimitri. Jean thinks he does, but I'm not convinced of it.

Jean: I think Dick is going through a very bitter feeling towards Anna, and he's trying to cut himself off from contact. He has called Anna's mother who is in this country now, and he's talked to her. And while he says he wants to cut himself off, he also was with Dimitri at the lake, was wonderful with him, and they had a wonderful time together last August. And he's planning for Dimitri to come visit him in Kentucky as soon as school is out. He's suddenly met someone who has occupied a lot of his time in the last 8 or 9 months. This woman has two children— two little boys.

Ted: You asked, a while ago, if we had any influence on him. One thing that makes me wonder is that this child has a propensity to be rude and discourteous to adults, including our friends when they come in this home. If he were to come right now and we'd introduce him to you,

he might say or do something extremely rude. We have
spoken to him, I don't know how many times, about being
polite, not just to adults, not just to our friends, but to
everybody, and it apparently has not had that much effect on him. If he feels the least bit inconvenienced or put
upon, he'll just be rude as he can be in front of everybody, and we haven't been able to eradicate that charac-
teristic in this kid. So, you ask me if we've had any influence on him. We're bound to have had some influence
just by his being with us, but influence him to be the kind
of person he should, and act the way we think he should
. . . no!

Jean: I think he's better than he was, and we took him, finally, to a therapist this past year. The therapist worked
with him for a while. The therapist told his mother that
the reason he acted rude was because he felt rejected. I
don't know. I think it's inherited from having seen his
mother do the same thing so many times that he can't
help himself sometimes. It depends on their mood. They
can both be very pleasant and very charming; but they
can be the opposite.

Ted: Casually, we asked if he was looking forward to moving to Maryland to be with his Mama. He said, "Well,
part of me is and part of me isn't."

Jean: I think he's mixed up. He's not been sleeping well
at night. He's been so restless. I think he is really torn with
the idea of moving there, and yet he wants to be with her.

Ted: He's going to have to give up everything he's got in
this house, and the neighborhood, and his friends.

Jean: And she has told him that he has got to learn to take
care of himself. He's got to do his own preparation of his
clothes, help cook, help in everything 'cause Anna is not
going to spend time doing those things for him. It'll probably be good training for him, and he's willing to do it.

Ted: He says he is. Wait 'til he's confronted with it.

He has indicated a couple of times that he may decide
not to go. We told him—just to try to give him some peace

of mind and make him feel wanted—we've told him, "Dimitri, you'll always be welcome in this house. You know that, don't you?" We don't want him to get the feeling that we're trying to get rid of him by sending him back to his mother. We want him to feel that it's his choice and her choice. As far as we're concerned, he can stay here.

Jean: I was close to my grandparents. But I had three sets. My mother died when I was a year old, so I had her parents. Then my father remarried when I was 4 and I had her parents. So I always said to my friends, "Oh, I've got three sets of grandparents." But they never had the responsibility of care of me.

I've told Anna I'm not sure that eighth grade is a good time to make the change, but I don't know when it is a good time.

Ted: One thing that has helped me accept the situation as well as I have is that when I was a child, I didn't have a father. My father died 6 weeks before I was born. When I was growing up, my mother was working hard to try to support three sons and also her parents. I spent an awful lot of my time with my grandparents. My grandfather was the closest thing to a father that I had. I'll never forget what my grandparents did for me when I was growing up. I think about that frequently in relation to Dimitri, and I believe that is one thing that has made it possible for me to accept this situation as well as I have.

The Caplers

16

Martha Capler, in her early 60s, lives just outside of Chicago. She is a large woman with short and curly, graying hair. Her friendly greeting, as she opened the door of her suburban condominium, didn't quite cancel out a look of expectancy and uncertainty behind her glasses. She led us past the living room, through the kitchen, and into the adjoining breakfast alcove where we seated ourselves. Her home is obviously a source of pride, amply furnished and with a profusion of photographs, mementos, and knicknacks covering all surfaces, including the wall of shelves that reaches the ceiling of this sunny, crisply curtained nook.

It is mid-morning, and Mrs. Capler's granddaughter, Deborah, is in school—junior high. Richard, Mrs. Capler's son and the father of Deborah, does not live here but is expected to join us later on. "Would you like some coffee?" asks this robust woman, bringing the fixings to the table. During the brief preliminaries to the interview, she pours coffee into a couple of mugs and sits down.

My son, Richard, had Hodgkins about 8 years ago, and after many treatments of chemo he was declared well. Everything went along fine with the medical thing until he developed a lump in his neck. They operated and found he had Hodgkins again. This is his second week of radiation. We don't want to hide anything from Deborah. So this is dramatic for her. But he's doing fine. Doctor looked at him yesterday and, hopefully, there'll only be another 2 weeks of treatment.

Richard met Henrietta when they were kids in high school.

She went after him—pursued him every way she could. About a year after they graduated high school, the two of them got married. A year after that, Deborah was born. Meantime, I had moved into this two-bedroom condominium that was supposed to be just for my husband and myself, but my son wasn't making a living at that time so we took them in—my son and the pregnant mother. We transformed the den downstairs into a bedroom to give them privacy.

Deborah was part of the family from the beginning. When Deborah was born, she came here from the hospital. Having a little girl after two sons, I don't have to tell you what went on.

My husband and I come from very loving families. Henrietta's parents, on the other hand, were so distant. They could match us in income, but they didn't do anything for her. They weren't interested. Anyhow, it was our gain to a point because we had Debby. She was very comfortable in this house. She grew up here.

Richard then started a little carpet-cleaning business, and we decided they ought to have their own place. They moved into an apartment and we subsidized them. Henrietta wasn't interested in housework. She got bored in the house. She was restless. She wanted guitar lessons. She wanted singing lessons. She wanted anything that she could do away from the home. Richard's hours were flexible, so he was able to come home and do the cooking and cleaning and take care of Deborah. He would take Deborah and the mother out for a ride or to a restaurant for lunch. He did everything.

Then, one day, Henrietta must have met some girls or something, and she started to play around with them.

What does that mean?

Well, every Wednesday I would go out there to take her grocery shopping and out for lunch or something. She would say, "Gee, look at all the people driving by, shining lights in my window."

So I would ask, "Aren't you afraid?"

She'd go, "No."

It seems she gave out the phone number. When the phone rang, if my son answered, they would hang up. He thought it was just a wrong number.

Henrietta is one of four children. She's different. The others are more stable. She can't stay with one thing too long, and that was the same with the marriage. When Deborah was about 2 weeks old, Henrietta said to me, "Here's the baby; here, take her." So I took her, you know, I was holding her. She said, "I don't want her anymore."

I looked at her and said, "What do you mean?"

She said, "I don't want her anymore. I want to do things with my life. She's in my way."

I said, "What are you talking about?" I couldn't conceive of what was happening. I said, "I can't believe what I'm hearing. She's your child. She's your responsibility, your problem, and you are going to take care of her and raise her, and you'll see what a joy she's going to be. And if you don't appreciate her now, you will as time goes by. She's going to be a friend to you, a pal, you're going to do things with her."

But she rejected the child. She was not good to the child. I don't mean physically. She used to leave her alone a lot. She would put her in her room and leave her there. I don't think she would walk out on her.

One night, Richard woke up about 3 o'clock in the morning and Henrietta wasn't there. He got up to look for her and couldn't find her in the house. He waited around and she came back all dressed up, and he says, "Where have you been?"

She says, "Oh, I just went out."

And he says, "Dressed like that? Something's going on."

A few days later, she picked herself up, took the child, and went away, moved to another part of town. Ohhh! My son called us. He was panicked.

"What's happened?"

"She took the baby. I don't know where they are." He called

her parents. They said she wasn't there. He didn't know what to do. He stayed here for a couple of days. When he went back to their apartment, all the furniture was gone. We found out her parents had done that, and they were hiding her.

My son confronted them and they said, "Yes, she's here."

He said, "Let me talk with her." She refused. She wouldn't talk with me either.

Three days later the grandmother calls. Her daughter ran away and left the child. "Please come and get this child. She's crying all day and all night."

Deborah was now about 2 years old. She hardly knew this grandmother, and she was scared, the child. Here she was, with these strangers.

My son picked up Deborah and brought her here. She was so happy to see her father. A few days later, the mother returned to her parents and said she wanted the child back. That whole family didn't seem to know whether they wanted the child or not. They didn't know then how to get that child back. And the father is an attorney!

Next, Henrietta called the police saying that we took the child out of the house, that we kidnapped her. The police came that night to get the child. We were stunned. This was a frightening thing for people who have been quiet people. Do you know what I'm saying? It's a whole different world. We never had anything like this happen to us. To think we would kidnap the child or take the child and do something!

I said to the police, "We didn't take the child. The child lives here." My son took them upstairs to Deborah's bedroom. When the police saw her sleeping, and how beautiful she looked, and how she had a gorgeous crib, and how she looked like she must have been well-cared for, they wouldn't touch her.

Henrietta's father was the attorney for the divorce and, of course, put my son into a bad light, so they could get custody. They said Richard molested her. None of it was true. Oh, I'll tell you it was horrible!

They were divorced. Visitation rights were granted to Richard and me—both of us. Deborah was only 2 1/2 years old. She was emotionally disturbed, confused. But when the judge saw her love for me, how she ran to me, how she uplifted herself, how she kissed me—it was a woman judge, and it broke her heart. And the judge said it was better to have the both of us there to take care of her. I'm the one who . . . I'm the mother. You know what I mean?

I was allowed to pick up Debby on Friday, so she could stay with us over the weekend. My son was living with me here at the time, and we would take her back Sunday evening. This went on every single weekend. We couldn't go out or have any plans because Deborah was the important thing.

One Friday, I went to pick up Deborah, and they wouldn't let me in. We went back to court. The judge said, "Henrietta, this woman is a very important part of this child's life, besides her father. Don't you ever refuse this grandmother permission to see this child." So, we had Deborah every weekend.

My son was not financially well off at the time, and he was immature. Maybe to some points he was grown up because of all that happened, but in another way he wasn't. He was not an irresponsible person. He wasn't a wild person. He didn't go to bars and run around. He was quiet, and all of this was a very dramatic thing for him.

By the time Deborah got to be 3 or 4, Henrietta took somebody in to live with her and she became pregnant.

On the weekends, Deborah would say to me, "I don't want to go home. I don't want to go back."

And I'd tell her, as little as she is, "Debby, you know you have to, darlin'. As bad as we feel about letting you go, you have to go back. Some day, when you're older, you can make your own decision and say, 'No, I don't want to go back,' and they will listen to you. But now you're too young. You'll have to wait."

And Debby would say, "I'm a big girl." She was about 3. As time went on, many different things happened. We used to get Debby for 3 weeks in the summer. My whole family would take a long vacation—Deborah, my husband, my son, and me.

She'd have a great time. She wouldn't want to go back to her mother. This went on until she was almost 6.

Deborah was living with her mother and her little half-sister at the time. Deborah never spoke about the half-sister—never mentioned her name. We would see her when we'd pick her up, and we would buy a little toy for her. She was a cute little girl. The two girls came here one weekend.

Just before Deborah was starting kindergarten. I said to my husband and Richard, "I'm worried about sending Deborah to the kindergarten up there. It's such a bad area." We talked it over and decided on a fine private school not far from where she lived.

We sent Deborah to this school once a week. We made arrangements with the bus to pick her up at her home and return her there. The bus would come for her in the morning, and the child would never be downstairs. They would call the mother, who was still sleeping. Or else she forgot it was the school day. There was always an excuse.

If Deborah did go that day, when they returned her to her mother's home—house—the mother wasn't there to greet the child. They couldn't leave the child off, so they would take her back to the school. Then they would call me, and I would have to go all the way there to see about her. Talk about traumatic, I mean, this is something else! I sat home with the phone most of the time because I never knew what was going to be. They didn't call the other grandmother, who lived closer by. If I wasn't home, who was going to take care of her?

Anyhow, Deborah was here one weekend, and Deborah was very nervous—scared—and I said, "Deborah, what sweetheart? What's wrong?"

She said, "Bubbie,"—she calls me Bubbie—"I don't want to go home."

I said, "Why sweetie?" 'cause she was older so we could talk more. "Now tell me, why don't you want to go home?"

"I'm afraid."

"Why?"

"Because at night my Mommy leaves me alone with my sister. She locks us in the house and goes away."

I heard that and almost died just thinking of what could happen. So when I returned with Deborah, I questioned the mother. She said, "Oh no I don't!"

I said, "Why would the child make that up?"

She says, "I'll do as I please."

I says, "Oh no, you will not—not when it comes to this child."

We went back to court, and that's how we have Deborah. Deborah is with us since she's 6 years old. She's lived in this house; she's a part of the house. She's everything. She's the king and the queen and the everything of this house, and she feels this is where she belongs. I mean, she never asks about . . . . She hasn't seen her mother in almost 8 years.

The court stipulated that Henrietta could call or write Deborah and could have her on the weekend if Debby's not left alone. At the beginning, Henrietta used to write her once in a while. She had her a couple of times for a weekend, and that was all. Deborah had become more of a problem for her. Deborah was already to the point where she could say, "My mommy left me alone. My mommy did this. My mommy did that." Henrietta didn't want that. So now she was willing to give the child up. She didn't ask for anything special. Nothing. I hate to say that, but we decided if worse came to worst, we would offer her money—anything to get her out of the way, and she didn't even ask for it.

By then, the other grandmother realized what the daughter had done, and there was a complete turnabout, though the grandfather wouldn't concede that. As a matter of fact, we keep in good touch now, because it's a better situation for Deborah. I don't want Deborah to be raised thinking we're against her mother.

Henrietta gave up her other little girl, and the grandmother is raising that child. Meanwhile, Henrietta had married a black man and later left him, and was living with a drug addict for a couple of years. They never married, but she had two boys with him.

After a while she ran away—went out west. Social Services

took the older boy away from her. He's been in eight foster homes! Now Henrietta's whole family is against her. It's a whole story.

Just a couple of weeks ago, Henrietta, her mother and father, and the little half-sister flew out to Oregon to see this boy. They're trying to get him adopted by somebody in the family, so she has this younger boy, and she just gave birth to still another, living with somebody else. They're worried because she could have given away or sold that other boy. They don't know. And, of course, with the baby, she'll keep the baby until it gets old enough and gets in her way. That's what she does.

I saw pictures of one of the boys yesterday. Deborah did too. A very nice little boy, I mean, a lovely little boy, 7 years old. He's very troubled. He's the third child. Then there's the younger boy and then there's a baby. When Deborah and I saw these pictures, I said to her, "You know, it would be nice if you wrote a little letter and told him who you are."

Have you had counseling along the way?

When Deborah was in kindergarten, her mother would fight with the teachers. I was embarrassed with the way Henrietta acted. Something stirred her up all the time. Something was wrong. She was so restless. She made the child restless—made her a behavior problem. Deborah would say to the teachers, "My mother told me I don't have to listen to you."

They didn't know what to do about her at school. They suggested the psychological department of the local hospital to have her evaluated. A summary of the report stated that Deborah was incapable of learning. It was a big problem.

I started her in first grade here in our neighborhood. The school recommended counseling. Deborah has been seeing Jean now for all these years once a week, every week. I had Jean come at the beginning and again at the end of every school year to see Deborah's progress and for Jean to talk with the teachers about it. They know at school about me, and that when I say I'll fight for her, for her rights, for her ways, for her things—whatever it is she's entitled to, I will be there. They know that, which is important.

When Deborah was to enter junior high, they said they would have to send her to another school because the behavior problem was so bad. They couldn't even talk about her grades because the child did no work. They didn't know what she could do.

Jean and I spoke with her. We told her, "Now look, Deborah, if you don't care, if you feel that you can't overcome your problem, then we'll have to send you to another school."

She went to camp that summer. In the fall, when Deborah started eighth grade, she was a different child. She was the most well-behaved, the most well-liked child by the teachers. They loved her. She made such a turnaround last year in school.

Debby's mother doesn't know what she's missing. First of all, Deborah is a dancer. She just finished 8 years of dancing. She won excellence in her school competition for her singing voice. She's going out for cheerleading this year. She's all around.

But she has no friends. She can't keep friends. She hasn't got one friend. She knows a lot of girls, but they don't call her. We can't figure out what the reason is. It's always been like this with Deborah.

(Richard, Mrs. Capler's son and Deborah's father, arrives and joins us around the table. He is about 40, somewhat overweight, with thinning dark hair. His face is pale and he seems tired. He is mild-mannered and soft-spoken and enters the discussion at once.

Richard: Two weeks after Deborah was born, Henrietta wanted to give her up. She gave her to my mother, "Here, I don't want her anymore." It broke my mother's heart when she heard it. It broke my heart, too. She looks at this child and wants to give her up? Why?

Was the pregnancy an accident or was it something that was planned?

Richard: She wanted to have children because she was trying to copy her sister's footsteps. Okay? Now she outdid her sister. It's an embarrassing situation for Deborah to know that her mother has all these kids and who's the fathers to them? It's frightening.

It was a bad experience; it really affected Deborah a great deal. I'm a lot happier that I'm not with Henrietta, even though I'm a single parent. I would like to do a lot more for Debby than I can at this time. If it wasn't for my wonderful parents who help me out, I wouldn't know what to do. I'd be in a bind. I'd do anything for Debby. I want Deborah to have more than what I have, and I have a hell of a lot—my parents!

I try not to stress Debby about my illness. It's going to be difficult for her to get through everything, although, so far, the prognosis for me is pretty good. I don't want to hurt her 'cause I know she has a lot of other problems. I just tell her I'm not feeling well and it's alright. Life goes on, pick up the pieces. It's the best thing, you know. I'm really happy because I've got a good job now, and I'm always happy with Debby. We spend a lot of time together.

Martha: I want to show you something. It's a Certificate of Recognition from the middle school, presented to Deborah (*Mrs. Capler reads*) ". . . in recognition of her accomplishments demonstrated in the following areas: task commitment, academic growth, school service, extra-curricular participation, talent, and personal growth." It's signed by the principal and it's dated June 1991.

Considering when the child was 6 years old, they said

she could never learn, you see what a long way she's come. Still, I say it's a handicap that she's growing up without a mother; but Jean has reassured me all through the years that nothing is worse than a bad mother. We're her parents, you know what I mean?—the three of us— my son, my husband, and me. Jean has helped me so much to come through this.

When Deborah was younger and would get a letter from her mother, I didn't know how to handle it. Do I show it to her or not? I had no experience. I didn't know other people went through the same thing. So when I'd speak with Jean, she'd set me straight. She'd guide me and help me and all that has come up to this (*Mrs. Capler pushes the Certificate of Recognition toward the tape recorder on the table*).

As soon as I got this, I sent it to Jean. You can see someone every week and talk to her regularly on the phone, but I wanted to give something from myself. I thanked her in a letter for all that she has done for Deborah. I think she appreciated it. Without her, I don't know if I could have gone through this.

My husband, Harry, had open heart surgery 8 years ago. We've been through a lot. Deborah's been through a lot of sickness, and has seen a lot of things that normally you don't see when you have young parents, but she's coped with it. She was very good when I had my operations last year.

The doctors told me I had lost the sight in this right eye—after three operations. To this day they don't know why. Maybe it was stress or strain or maybe there was a weakness there or what it could have been. Anyhow, to get back. . . .

Mrs. Capler, how old are you and your husband?

I am 66 years old and Harry's 71, but we're pretty active people. I mean, we go and we do. We're going away this weekend. We've got a *bas mitzvah* to go to in Madison, Wisconsin and we're taking Deborah and Richard with us. After his radiation, Richard is going on a nice trip by himself.

Rich: I'm going to Disney World for 5 days.

Martha: Sometimes I feel bad if she says she wants to do something and we say, "We're tired," or "It's too much," or something like that. If she had a mother and father that could take her and do something, it would be ... don't get me wrong, Richard does take her. He takes her to the Splish-Splash.

Rich: I take her to flea markets; she likes that. She likes Splish-Splash, an amusement park. Movies, she loves. Sometimes concerts. I see her almost every day. Every weekend we do a lot of things together. During the week, I get home around 8 o'clock in the evening. Sometimes I'll come over and see her for a couple of hours. Sometimes I'm tired.

I work at the hospital now—crazy hours—sometimes 6:00 A.M. to 2 in the afternoon, maybe 7 to 3, or 12 to 8.

Aside from these major problems you've had to face, what are some day-to-day difficult aspects of raising your granddaughter?

Martha: First of all, I raised two sons. I had a nanny for the children. I was always there but physically she did all the—she bathed them, she washed their hair, she fed them, she took care—I do all this now. Not that I object, but I'm doing things that I never did before. Then again, I'm dealing with a moody little girl.

A girl is a lot different to raise than boys. I raised two sons and, bless them, they were not moody. They were even-tempered, easy to get along with.

Deborah, on the other hand, maybe because she feels almost like—alone—an only child in the house .... I have to say we did spoil her. If I say, "Let's go to the mall," she thinks for her, to buy her something, not me, and I'll say, "Well, Deborah, we're looking this time for me."

"I know, but I saw this and I like this." She's selfish to that point because the attention has always been drawn to Deborah.

Do you feel resentful?

Oh no, I'm not resentful. It's irritating and I get angry.

It's also difficult now that my husband is home. He's retired, but he does picture-framing at home. I do very little driving because in my good eye I have glaucoma and a cataract. Being I have only one eye, I'm a little hesitant about having the cataract operation. Until it gets to the point where I have to have the operation, I hardly drive at all. That means my husband has to drive us around. If we want to go shopping or want to do something, he has to go. He's nice about it, but how much can I let him sit in the car and wait?

When she's with her father, my husband and I have a chance to look at each other. We go out to dinner with friends or go play canasta, or something. Deborah doesn't bother us. Even when Deborah's home she doesn't bother us. She'll go with us to eat, but when we come back to play cards or something she'll go up in her room. She's really not a problem. When she was younger, she was underfoot more. But now she's got her own things to do. I can never say that we resent her.

My husband would like to move to Florida. Richard wants to stay here. We don't want to take her away from her father so we adjust. We stay here.

What about Deborah's lack of friends?

Just 2 weeks ago we went to the mall. All of a sudden, we hear, "Deborah, darling!" It was a school teacher who gave her a big hug and a kiss and, "Oh, I'm so happy to see you!" And Deborah was happy to see her. It's always with adults, not with children. Jean and I have tried to work on that. Now she's started school. Yesterday she asked, "Can I invite a couple girls to go swimming here today?" And I said, "Yes, you can."

And she was happy. She brought a map to school to show them how to get here. It's a terrible thing to say, but I don't think they're going to come. I'd be very surprised if they do. She reaches out all the time, doesn't she, Richard?

Richard: All the time.

Martha: All of this has to take its toll someplace. I noticed one thing. When she talks with her grandmother on the phone and I'm on the other line, her grandmother talks about her mother. Deborah's quiet. Later, I see Deborah getting upset. Something must stir her up inside. Either she doesn't want to hear it, or she resents hearing it, maybe. I tried talking to her about it, and she throws it off. My husband has noticed the same thing.

Deborah had a little "2-year-old bicycle" and we brought it to the sister yesterday. The grandmother was talking about the little boy in the foster home and about not knowing where the mother is. After we got home, Deborah was being difficult.

Richard: Every time Debby visits at that house, she always shows a mean streak. Always! That's why she doesn't sleep over there. It would take about a week before she would get back to herself.

Martha: I don't know. Maybe it's too much. You don't know what's behind these kids. How do you know? You just try to do the best you can for them.

Richard, do you want to add anything?

Not really.

PART VI

Parents and AIDS

AIDS is a plague that has swept across America with devastating effect, destroying relationships, cutting into families, and robbing the public of some of its most gifted and creative personalities. It is indiscriminate in its choice of victims. Some, who succumbed, bear some responsibility for their fate—others do not. The most innocent are the babies born with the HIV virus.

At the end of 1993, the cumulative number of AIDS cases for infants under five years at diagnosis was over 4,200. Also, at the end of 1993, HIV-infected cases of children 5 years of age at diagnosis was 582. The cumulative figure at the end of 1993 for those under age 15 who died since the beginning of the AIDS epidemic was over 2,800 (Centers for Disease Control and Prevention, 1994). It should be noted that the data are under-reported because only 26 states allow anonymous testing.

More than one-third of HIV infected women intend to become pregnant. The transmission rate of HIV from mother to fetus during pregnancy is approximately 35% (ACT UP, 1990). Some of the HIV positive mothers will be able to parent for a time, and they must contend with the worry of whether their children have escaped the disease. New recommendations for treatment are expected to reduce this rate (Centers for Disease Control and Prevention, 1994).

A great number of HIV parents run away, abandoning their

children one way or another. Some babies are left in public places, some are given to relatives, some are put up for adoption.

In many cities, these infants are abandoned in the hospital soon after birth and have become known as "boarder babies" (Child Welfare League of America, 1992). These are infants who can no longer be placed in foster care because the system has become overloaded. They remain in hospitals until homes are found or adoption can be made.

There are individuals who knowingly adopt these babies regardless of the circumstance.

Denise

17

We touched the intercom buzzer at the front entrance to a building in a densely populated neighborhood of New York City. After identifying ourselves, we were immediately let in and rang for the elevator—a slow one. Upon exiting, we walked down a clean, undecorated hallway and rang the bell at apartment 5J. Denise, a middle-aged woman of medium build opened the door. Her soft hair, short and shiny, framed a full and pretty face. She was holding the hand of a young child whose creme de cafe complexion was somewhat lighter than Denise's.

Chantelle, the little girl, stayed close to Denise, watching us with an open, unguarded expression. We were invited to sit around the oval-shaped wood dining table just inside the door. The living room was beyond, and the kitchen and hall to the bedrooms were all in view. Denise brought out a pitcher of iced tea and cookies, and sat down across from us. Chantelle stood beside her, her arms just reaching the table top, and began using the crayons and paper Denise had put out for her daughter.

How come I decided to adopt is because this is my second marriage. My first marriage lasted 21 years.

My first husband, he passed in March of '79. We weren't together at the time anyway. But we had one child. My son is 21.

I remarried—met my second husband in the post office. He came from Charleston, South Carolina. We started dating and got married in '81.

I was about 39, and decided to have my IUD taken out. I

went to the doctor to have myself examined. I wondered why I couldn't get pregnant. They did a sonogram to see what was wrong. My tubes were blocked. He told me I would have to have minor surgery to get it repaired, and that's not a guarantee I could get pregnant. So I made my decision right there in the office. I said, "I'm not going to take that chance and have nobody cut on me to repair anything. Since I'm up in age and it's 50–50 chance, I know what to do. I'll adopt."

I never thought about adoption before. I talked to my husband about it. He was disappointed, but I told him, "With my age, I don't want to take that chance of having an operation and it doesn't work."

"Okay," he said, "just do what you want."

First we went to a Catholic agency. They sent someone out to investigate us. It seemed like the process—the investigation and all this stuff—is slow.

When I say this process is slow, they want your whole history. They want your rent receipt; they want your pay; they want what you make at the post office, your salary, your income, your family background, your mother, your father, your sisters and brothers. They want to know how many in your family and in his family and whether if you've discussed it with the family.

The homestudy, that's the thing, the homestudy, and the paperwork—it was dragging. I think we started in '84. I never got finished. The person we had to investigate us said how we were acting it seemed like we weren't interested. That's when I changed over.

I came to Lutheran through the black social workers after I spoke to them about the slowness. I called and made an appointment, and they sent somebody out. The young lady came, sat right here where you're sitting, and investigated me. I got my girlfriend and my next door neighbor to write a letter stating the type of person I was. Then the person came from Lutheran and did the homestudy on us. I got in touch with them maybe in '85 and in no time—in '86—we got Felitia.

I wanted a little girl anywhere from infant to 3 or 4.

(Denise pauses and settles back in her chair.)

I came from a large family. My mother had seven children—four brothers and three sisters. One died stillborn. My husband's mother had the same many children, six or seven, but she had lost a lot of children—miscarriages. So she only raised four children, two boys and two girls.

My father was a farmer, and that's how we made our living—selling vegetables and taking it to market, picking cotton, picking beans, tomato, anything he'd plant, and that's what he does.

I came up here in '61. Then everybody was leaving my home town because jobs were not plentiful for young people at that time in North Carolina. We were getting out of school. If you didn't go to college, there were really no jobs, unless you worked domestic or going to school for a teacher or for nursing. When everybody around my age was leaving home, there was nobody there to be with. I didn't really want to come up here. I was so homesick I didn't know what to do.

I said, "This is a big city. That's what this is all about," but eventually I got used to it. They sent me on jobs, and I didn't even know the city. They gave me the address. They just told me where to go, and I got lost. Many times, going through Grand Central and shuttling over to the east side, I went looking for jobs. I had no experience.

First thing I got was a factory job. I said, "Oh no, I can't make no money like this. This is piece work." I stayed there for a while, and then got a job at Woolworth on 125th Street. I stayed there about 3 years. Then I went to nurses aide. They gave you training at the hospital, and I stayed there about 3 years. Then the post office. My aunt says, "The post office is giving tests, exams. Take the test." I took the test for two, three turns. The third time I passed. I got into the post office in '66.

No one in my family except my sister went to college. I'm very close with my sister. She came up first to live with my Aunt Rose. She lives in New York in the Bronx.

I met my first husband at a dance. He went into the service right after we got married in '68. While he was away, I stayed with my sister. After he came out of the service he automatically had a job 'cause he had passed the civil service test. Meanwhile, I resigned from the post office when my son was born.

I left my husband in '72. We were having problems. He went to the Vietnam War so he had nightmares and stuff like that. He got to drinking pretty heavy. We went for therapy because he had an alcohol problem. I found out that I was going and he wasn't going. Then I found out he started drinking again. He would get into arguments about the money, and then he would want to fight. I took it for a while, and then I said, "Oh, ohhh, I can't stay here where we're getting into arguments. I don't think it would be any good for my son." He was 2 1/2. I moved in with my sister in '72, and that's when we went through the divorce.

I was reinstated in my job at the post office. In '78, I met my second husband.

One day, I got a telephone call. I says to my supervisor, the station manager, "Oh, I got something exciting to tell you. They want to know right away can I have some time off 'cause they have a baby for me."

He says, "You have a good record. Why not?" I got so excited, and he says, "I'm happy for you."

And I says, "Oh, wow! They want to know if I can take off the next day. They are going to bring the baby down the next day. I need the time right away."

He says, "Put in the slip." He gave me a month and 2 weeks, right away. I stayed home 6 weeks with her. I couldn't wait to tell my sister. I run and called my husband on the switchboard to let him know they were bringing this baby, and I took off the next day and waited here until they came up and rang my doorbell. Baby straight from the hospital. I said, "Oh wow!"

When they were ready to go, I laid her on the couch and let them out of the house. Then I came back and I whooped and hollered. I was excited. I looked at her arm and I said, "This babe was just born. She's not even quite 2 weeks old. This is the 22nd and she was born on the 9th of August—an infant!" I said, "She's mine. This is my baby. Straight from the hospital!" Oh, I whooped and hollered.

I know a little bit about her background. My husband met the father. I met the grandmother. She had never seen Felitia. The grandmother could not take the infant because she already had a 4-year-old from her baby daughter, and had just started a new job with the court. She was sad 'cause she couldn't take the child. She said they never really gave up any children for adoption in their family. She wanted to meet us, because she wanted to know what type of people we were.

Lutheran set up an appointment at the center. We took along just pictures of Felitia, and the grandmother said, "She looks just like my daughter." I met one of her other daughters, Felitia's aunt. I think she was a cop, and she was saying the youngest daughter was still in the streets, and she had no control over her.

The agency had told me, "If you want an infant, you have to take the high risk—'legal risk adoption'—taking a child that's not legally abandoned, and hope the parents eventually find out they abandoned their child."

At first I didn't want to do it. I asked my husband, "Do you think that's a chance we should take?"

He said, "Well, you want an infant, so why not?" We took the high risk.

We sent letters to the mother. We sent a letter to the grandmother's house for the daughter. But the daughter never stayed in one place, just would come and visit off and on. She never answered any of the letters.

It was a whole year before they could really say that the mother abandoned the child. We never got any release from her, but the father signed papers releasing the child. We went to court and everything. Felitia became legally ours in '89. I took the high risk and it paid off.

Nothing is wrong. They said the mother did use drugs, but by the time they released her, they said there was nothing in her system. Not at all.

I went back to work. My husband worked nights. Babysitting was no problem 'cause I waited until he comes home in the morning, and then I go off to work and he watches her in the afternoon.

My son is here. He's going to school. He helps every now and then. He said, "I don't mind." I don't know if he was very enthused, but he said it didn't bother him. He was like 15 or 16. He wasn't arrogant or anything. He did babysit Felitia a lot.

Then, out of the blue, the agency just called me. I was at work. They said, "Look, we have a little baby boy." I got so excited. I said, "Oh, a little boy!" I had to get permission to get some more time off, so I couldn't give them an answer right away over the phone. I have no idea why they called me. I never even thought about it. I just got excited when they did. By the time I got back to them the next day, somebody already had took the little boy. But they said, "We have two little girls. Would you be interested?"

I said, "Wait a minute; let me think about it," 'cause I was all torn up for the little boy. I spoke to my husband and I said, "What do you think about that?"

He said, "What do you want to do?"

I said, "I'm not so excited about the post office job anyway. The only thing you can do is move up to supervisor, and I don't want to be nobody's supervisor. You got to do a lot of dirty work."

I told somebody on the job when I left, "I'm taking a leave of absence from my job. There's something rewarding that I want to do in my life—something really nice that I think would be rewarding to be doing before I leave this side of this earth— something meaningful."

And he said, "Alright, sounds good. If you're going to do it, why not do it?"

I got back to the agency. They told me the babies were fine but had a low birth weight. One had a little problem. I had to decide which one. I told them I would take the other. I think she was younger, only 6 weeks old. They told me she was fine. No problem.

When the social worker came, she told me the mother did use drugs, but you couldn't really test the baby at that age, because the child would be carrying the mother's antibodies. We found out later that the mother was a heavy drug user. We didn't find out anything about her until Chantelle really got sick, and that was in September of '88.

Right after we got her, she started getting a cold and it seemed like she had got asthma also. Whatever the doctor gave her, she never got rid of the cold. He gave her medicine for asthma since she was wheezing. Later on she developed a breathing problem. The doctor kept insisting he needs more medical history on her.

I said, "I don't know anything."

So he said, "Tell Lutheran to send me her medical history." Lutheran said they didn't know anything other than the mother did use drugs. He still insists that they send something. He became suspicious.

I felt funny. I spoke to the social worker. I said, "The doctor I'm taking her to is in my health center, and he is requesting medical history on her."

He (the social worker) said, "Look, this is all we have. We knew that the mother was a drug user."

I said to the doctor that she looks like she's not gaining weight. That's when he said he had an idea that maybe something else was wrong with her, because babies who were not gaining no weight . . . he had an idea that she might be. . . . I got real scared. I got real shaky. I didn't want to really believe what he was saying. I called Lutheran, and they kept saying they didn't know anything on the baby.

We always go home for Christmas. I took her home. She was very, very sick. She wasn't keeping the food. She was having diarrhea, and she had this wheezing on her chest. We took her to emergency down in South Carolina. I didn't tell them anything about the drugs the mother was on. When I came back from the South, they gave me some asthma medication. That helped her breathe better. She was so sick.

I called Lutheran. I said, "Look, I don't particularly care for the doctor I'm taking her to. You're going to have to give me a doctor to take her to, because I don't like the way he don't really want to treat. I don't like the feeling I'm getting. So you all are going to have to give me a doctor that can help me to find out what's wrong with her."

That's when Lutheran gave me Dr. M. He referred me to Bronx Lebanon Hospital. At the clinic there, there was a doctor that worked with children that the mother used drugs, and he figured out something that maybe was wrong. He examined Chantelle real good and says, "I think that she is HIV. . . ."

I didn't want to believe it. We were so upset. I was just like devastated really. This was before she was a year old.

The doctor needed permission to draw blood. I couldn't sign any papers 'cause I was not yet legally the mother. I said, "You'll have to call Lutheran and get the Okay."

He called them up and got permission over the phone. He said, "I can't wait. You got to get it to me now. I want to check her out and get the bloodwork done and examine her and everything." And that's when they found out that . . . you know, 'cause he took and examined her.

He said her spleen was enlarged, her liver was enlarged, and she had a lot of those lymph nodes all over her. She was having diarrhea. She wasn't gaining the weight she was supposed to.

In February she had pneumonia. She stayed for almost 2 weeks in the hospital. They were pumping antibiotics in her. She had the tent over her for breathing. I mean my heart was . . . I was sick, I was so sick. I would spend 8 hours a day at the hospital until a certain nurse came and then I would go home. I mean she was so frail. You would see her and her little face; she was pitiful. And that's when he said that this is what she is. And I was hoping and praying that when she would get a certain age that . . . . They said sometimes when they get to 2. . . . He said if she's positive now most likely she'll remain positive.

We went to some meetings at Lutheran. They even asked me if I wanted to give her back. I said, "Give her back?"

The director said, "Some people, when they find out that the child is HIV positive, they can't handle it. It's devastating to the mother."

I thought about it and I said, "Hold it. I have a child. If something is wrong with her, I cannot give her back."

And I said, "What would you do? Stick her in the hospital and she'd be a boarder baby? And who would take care of her? What kind of nonsense is that? How could anyone give a child back they done loved and nurtured? How could anyone be so cruel? No, I couldn't do that."

But they called us down and told us that's our option if we didn't want to keep her 'cause some people are afraid of the disease because they don't know anything about it. They think they can catch it, or if they have other children in the family, they can catch it. So they gave us some reading on it and what could happen if you want to take care of her. They tell you the risks. They tell you that it's a disease, and you can only get it if the blood spills into something you have.

So I said, "We're going to keep her." Eventually they told us the mother died with an overdose. We don't know anything about the father. Nothing.

Did you ever think that the agency knew but didn't tell you?

Well, from the time the social worker started coming out, it seemed like they didn't know. I didn't question to find out whether there was something they knew and didn't tell us. I asked the social worker at the time, did they check her out, blood work, while she was in the hospital. They said at that stage of the game she was probably carrying her mother's antibodies. They said, if we wanted, we could have her tested after she got 6 months. We didn't want to. We didn't want to know. We had the feeling. We figured that she might not be and she might and we would put a stigma on her and her record. But we didn't know anything when we first took her.

How does your decision for her to stay feel to you today?

It feels great 'cause she's doing great. I wouldn't give her back for no price in China. She's been a mild-tempered child. She's really sweet. My sister said she's got a different temperament than Felitia 'cause Felitia's spicy, and Chantelle is like. . . .

And, you know, when she was in the hospital, she got real attached to me 'cause I would be there every day. So she was clinging to me.

She was back in the hospital for chicken pox. Last year. I didn't know that a child with her low tolerance would need something right away. The doctor didn't tell me that. So when I did tell them later on that my 3-year-old has chicken pox, he called all around to find out the special dose of medication so Chantelle won't get it, but by the time we got the shot in her, she still got it anyway.

They wouldn't take no chances in letting her be here in the house. They don't want her to get real sick, 'cause they know what could happen to her. My son quit work and stayed here with Felitia while I went to the hospital. I stayed with her every day. She was there 4 days.

Moneywise, Lutheran will high-rate children that have HIV and get them a Medicaid card. But whatever her bill was, the agency has a form they mail you. When I take her to the doctor he fills out the form. I mail it back to Lutheran and they reimburse the medical center, or hospital, or clinic. Chantelle has a small paper card, and the doctor or hospital that sees her has to write that number on it and fill out that form and send it back to Lutheran, and they pay, even the medicine.

Lutheran holds parent support group meetings, but I couldn't be there. They had an HIV meeting which I attended at a hotel. I think I went to one or two.

I told my youngest sister and she was like, "You what? What are you going to do?"

I said, "I should have never told you anything, you're gonna get upset like this?"

"She's what?! She's what?!"

"She's HIV positive."

"What you mean; what you mean?"

I said, "AIDS."

"Oh, oh!" She got excited and I felt so bad. I wanted to cry after I got off the phone with telling her. I got so upset, 'cause she was saying, "Are you going to tell the family?"

I said, "What family? I don't have to tell ... I shouldn't have told you if I knew you were going to react like this."

They told us at the center that it's our option who we want to tell. We don't have to tell nobody. I said, "I'm not going to tell my whole family anything 'cause look how you react. Just imagine if I tell everybody in the family and they don't want to touch her or don't want to kiss on her or nothing like that. I told you and you got an education. You went to college and acting like this?"

And then she told her kids and they said, "Oh, we know about that." They're kids at school, and they read up on it and her son told her, "Mom, what you getting excited about? They told us about that in school." And then she calmed down a little bit.

She knows a guy that went to high school with her and he's teaching medical in Georgia, and she called him up and spoke to him. He said, "I sure would like to meet your sister. She's smart. She's brave." And he sent her some information on it. She read up on it and she calmed down a lot.

I was thinking not to tell my oldest sister 'cause she's real nervous and she would get upset, but she didn't get like that. I said, "I don't know who to tell anything." But she understands about the HIV and diseases and she feels better about it.

Does it cross your mind that these are adopted children?

I know they are. I'm trying to mention it to Felitia that she is. One time she asked me did I carry her in my tummy. I told her no, she was adopted. She didn't ask me anything else. I don't think she fully understands what it means yet. All my family knows except for my father's sister. I haven't told my aunt 'cause she keeps saying, "Now who does she look like?" I don't answer. My cousin said, "Must be look like the father.'

I said, "Right." I still haven't told them who she look like. So let them decide, and then if anyone says, "They don't look like you," I don't answer.

We got Chantelle in '88, and she was legally ours in '90— February 7th. The mother was deceased, and they have no whereabouts of the father.

My husband died in April of '90. He had a weight problem, and then he had high blood pressure, and he wasn't taking the medication. I don't know whether he got disgusted or what. For some reason, he got off the diet, and started eating a lot of stuff he shouldn't be eating. He was six foot five, and he was about 400 pounds, but he was the sweetest person you ever met. It's just that he had a bad eating problem.

I think it was nerves. There was probably a lot of stuff he didn't talk about. He didn't really open up and tell me his feeling. I told him, "I think you are maybe a little bit insecure about certain things that you are supposed to be macho about." He was really sensitive. He was the type that would do anything for you, go out of his way and leave himself hanging and not get the proper rest. He was 48 when he died.

Between my son and my husband, I think they were trying to drive me crazy. My son was ripping around, and the type of people he was hanging out with. . . . He had got money from his father when his father passed. I was a surrogate over the money. The bulk of it I tied up in CD. It's still in CD, but when he turned 18, I had to turn the rest over into his name.

That's when the trouble begun. He started listening to people on the street and with the money I turned over to him he bought a bum junk car, and don't even have a license. He's really a nice person, but just the people that he picked was just. . . .

I said, "The street will swallow you up. You're no good for the street." The type of people he was with was fast-talking people and they'd talk him into buying some junk car. Now I'm a grandma. Beautiful child, and the young lady went back to work. She works at Bloomingdale's. We just celebrated the baby's birthday, a year old.

You said you like doing something meaningful . . .

Rewarding.

. . . is there any more to that than the fact that you obviously love being a mother?

My sister said, "You didn't seem that happy when you stayed home with your own child. You had no patience."

Well, I didn't know nothing about no children then, and I wanted to get back to work. I said, "I got to get back to work. I can't be no housewife," but as I got older . . . .(*Chantelle interrupts briefly.*) After you be home a while, you get to do things and it becomes easier.

I prayed for a lot of patience and understanding, and hoping that I be making the right decision or doing the right thing. I do a lot of praying. In the morning, I get up early and run my bath before they get up, and stretch out in the hot tub of water and do my little praying, meditating. That keeps me going.

What's the downside of having Chantelle?

When I found out she was like that and seeing her in the hospital ... makes you feel helpless, but I still don't regret that I have her. I made up in my mind, you can do anything if you put your mind to it.

But when I have to see her in the hospital and they're sticking her, taking blood, that's something you don't never get used to. When she sees them, she cries, "I don't like that."

I say, "I don't like it either." But they have to check her blood and see how the count is. At the clinic I have seen other children that's worse than her. One child couldn't even hold her head up. Chantelle was never limp. When she got so sick, I had to suction her with a machine. This stuff has to come out, all the mucus out of her nose and her chest. To see her like that, you know, depressing. She's not getting any sicker. She's taking AZT on an experimental program right now. She's taking the high dose.

They say they don't have a long life, but I'm saying I really want to see them grow up and go to school and be able to do for themselves. I pray a lot. I go to church. And my sister says she's praying and the one that I spoke to in Georgia. (*Chantelle and Denise talk for a moment.*) I pray every day that I can live a long life, that I can see them go through school and be able to do for themselves. She doesn't show anything of helplessness. I'm pretty sure she will live a long life. It might not be like I wanted . . . .

PART VII

Parents by Technology

Adults who want children and have been unable to conceive now live in an age where the previously impossible or unthinkable *is* possible. Research and technology in the sciences that deal with the intricacies of the human organism have made astonishing advances in recent decades and continue to make advances.

Various technologies and remedies can now be applied to achieve pregnancy when nature is thwarted. Hormone prescriptions, artificial insemination, and in vitro fertilization are all part of the present day help afforded to the hopeful, sometimes desperate, prospective parents. The human race is able to procreate with equipment that runs the gamut from a turkey-baster to high tech's cutting edge.

In vitro (Latin for "in glass") fertilization involves removing eggs from the female ovary, placing one in a petri dish, and introducing the male sperm. When the two gametes unite and form a single cell, the resulting zygote is implanted in the uterus where it develops into an embryo. The first successful in vitro fertilization occurred in England in 1978. Research in the causes of infertility had at last shown that it was possible to create human life outside the human body.

Variations on the in vitro technique have been developed. They include the transfer of both egg and sperm from the glass dish into the fallopian tube for fertilization to take place in that site, or the insertion of the already fertilized egg (zygote) into the fallopian tube. In either case, the fertilized egg can descend on its own to the uterus. These technological feats approximate, as nearly as possible, nature's course. Ironically, things as cold and clinical as pills or a petri dish, the antithesis of love and passion, may in some instances be the medium by which the loving, passionate desire for a family can be achieved.

Couples who select in vitro procedure are among the fortunate few who can afford it. Not all such procedures are successful. Measured by live births, the success rate for infertility treatment through 1992 is about 17% (Mosher & Pratt, 1990).

The growth of infertility care in this country within the last 16 years has produced over 20,000 babies and has generated a $2 billion industry (Mosher & Pratt, 1990; Gingerich, 1993). The perception of increasing infertility and impaired fecundity for women is not supported in the research, but is seen as being related to delayed child-bearing, new drugs and techniques for treating infertility, an increase in the number of physicians specializing in infertility, and an increase in the numbers of visits to physicians for fertility (Mosher & Pratt, 1990; Stewart, 1995).

As the technology becomes more sophisticated and intricate, ethical and moral questions arise. For the present, there is much pondering over the complexities of being able to perform miracles, and to what extent they should be allowed. There are many expert opinions, and no easy solutions.

There are few regulations so far except with regard to the frozen leftover eggs in the course of in vitro fertilizations. What should be the cut-off age for giving birth? Whose eggs and whose sperm will be the starting cells that result in another human being? Who are the rightful parents if controversy arises? Questions that pit human desire and technological capabilities against moral constraints are wrenching and difficult. These debates entail high stakes.

The Martins

18

The Martins' house on the staid, tree-lined street in one of Houston's older residential sections offers no clue on the outside to the overall ambiance within. Their home is furnished traditionally and is awash in sunny decorator colors, light, bright hues—yellows and oranges, blues and greens—which complement the original art on the walls.

Annabelle and Reid Martin are in their late twenties, trim, attractive parents of two beautiful boys, ages 3 1/2 years and 18 months. Annabelle is fashionably outfitted, which minimizes the third trimester of her pregnancy. She and Reid, with obvious pride, introduce us to their children and the babysitter who will care for them for the next couple of hours. They kiss the boys, tell them to stay with the sitter, and lead us into the long, narrow kitchen to sit at a table in the corner.

As Reid pours fruit drinks to go around, this married couple's pattern of conversation becomes evident. They look and talk at one another and finish each other's sentences. It is a pattern that is reflected throughout the interview.

Annabelle: Reid and I met in the fall of '84 and began dating. After about a year or so, we had some medical problems. It was diagnosed as endometriosis, and I ended up having exploratory surgery. They found out it was a mess in there. After surgery, the doctor told us how much stuff he had to take out, how he had to remove one ovary, and tried to save the other one. He said it was the worst he'd seen, but he hoped there would be no fertility problem.

We hadn't talked about getting married at that point, but I sure was thinking it.

Reid: We were fearful it was cancer so, in a sense, we were relieved. But it wasn't like everything was okay. We weren't sure we could talk in front of the doctor and, while he's a great friend of ours now, he wasn't sure whether he should talk openly in front of me and your mother, because we were not married.

Annabelle: I had never heard of endometriosis. Mother said she had had it, but hers was no problem. Then Reid read all about it and told us what it was. Soon afterward, we got married.

Reid: The doctor was very hopeful and kept saying, "There's no reason to expect problems. You've still got one ovary and that's enough. Don't worry about it." But we did worry—at least I did.

Annabelle: I kept thinking about it. Each month I wondered, "Will we get pregnant?" It was on our minds since the big surgery. We tried for a whole year.

Reid: We tried pretty much from the time we got married. We intended to have a family. Family means a lot to both of us and there wasn't any doubt that we wanted children. That's what we both envisioned for our marriage.

Annabelle: But it just wouldn't work.

Reid: You just wouldn't get pregnant. You didn't have any other symptoms, did you?

Annabelle: Nhnn, nhnnn. Then we went back to Dr. Johnson, my OB/GYN. He referred us to Dr. Borne, a fertility specialist with a group of doctors in private practice—a sophisticated fertility practice in Houston. At that time they had maybe the only such office. Three doctors. It was unbelievable. You ought to see, you ought to go out there. It would be educational for you to sit in their lobby and just watch the folks come in and out of there.

They see a lot of patients in their fertility practice. But in their in vitro, they must do six or more cycles per person a year, and they run a hundred plus women through

their cycles every time. They had to turn cases down
'cause it's too many. Dr. Borne started us with a series of
tests. More endometriosis had developed, and the scar tissue was causing blockage.

Reid: He did a laparoscopy and then a dye test to see whether the laparoscopy had been successful and whether the
fallopian tube was clear.

Annabelle: They put dye in your tube to see if it will go through.

Reid: They have a screen and we both saw that the dye went
nowhere, and the doctor said, "This is not working. Everything's off." That was a big blow.

Annabelle: Yeah, that was the worst. And now I'm sitting up,
and we said "What's next?"

"Well," he said, "you're not going to be able to conceive
naturally, on your own." That hadn't occurred to us.

I remember talking to friends—Sara, remember?—and
she was talking about in vitro, and I thought, "I'm sorry
for you." It never occurred to me that would be me. When
he said, "You're not going to be able to do this," I just remember the tears. We couldn't believe it.

Then, 2 seconds later, we both said, "What can we do?"
We had to do something fast. It didn't occur to me not to
do anything.

Reid: And the doctor said, "We have this new thing now called in vitro fertilization. You're welcome to try that."

Annabelle: And I said, "Well, let's hurry and sign up now, fast."
I mean, we were still in the room, robe on, and everything.

Did you know what in vitro was at that point?

Annabelle: Barely. Just hearing about it from friends. And the
doctor said, "Now calm down. We've a lot of stuff you can
read. It's a big deal thing, and I want to talk to you about it."

I just said, "Well, if that's our only option, we have to
do it."

Reid: She had already decided. Her next menstrual cycle
was about to start and she was ready to go. She didn't

want to hear anything much. She just said, "That's it. That's what we'll do."

Annabelle: Yeah, ready to go.

Reid: I was struck by her reaction 'cause it's her body and her life. You know, she was a bigger player in this than I was. I figured that's the conclusion we're getting to but I guess, because I'd read about it, I was more cautious. I would have let it soak in—probably waited 3 months before starting.

Annabelle: As far as I was concerned, the point was we wanted children and there's no reason to sulk about it. Let's try to do something. So we did, and we were so lucky that it worked.

Reid: That's easy to say now.

Annabelle: I know. The first time was bad. We ended up in the hospital—hyperstimulation. You're given medicine to make you produce a lot of eggs, and they gave me too much medicine.

Within what period of time does all this take place? What's the cycle?

Annabelle: Usually 14 to 16 days after the start of your period you ovulate.

Reid: You get those shots of . . .

Annabelle: . . . a hormone to make you ovulate. Every 2 hours, you have to urinate and save it. You can't like run somewhere and use the bathroom at work. You have to put it in this thing and then pour it in these little tubes, and then you've got to write on it how much you did, and the time you did it, and its, it's . . .

Reid: . . . it's a real pain in the neck.

Annabelle: We had to bring the urine samples once a day.

Reid: It was about 25 miles, round trip.

Annabelle: When the urine indicates that ovulation is about to take place, you go to the doctor two or three times a day and they check the levels in your blood, and then do an ultrasound and measure the eggs, every day. When the eggs get to a certain size and correlate with the blood level, they figure it's time to take them out. They call that mining. Hopefully, it's not too early. They do this in the operating room . . .

Reid: . . . out-patient.

Annabelle: They use the natural passageways. They go up vaginally and get 'em out. You're half asleep, half awake.

That first time we did all this was probably not so bad, 'cause we were kind of geared up for it, and we did everything right 'cause we were anxious. I was nervous. I was afraid I was going to not do it right and mess up; and if you mess up, you get thrown out of the cycle, because they can't assume anything. So if you lose track then you're gone.

Reid: It costs a bunch of money, too.

Annabelle: Yeah, it costs a whole lot.

Reid: But they work with you to try to convince your insurance company to pay. We had insurance and, in fact, it was all covered, but it costs. Like seven to eight thousand. But that was 5 years ago when it started. So it's probably around ten thousand now.

Reid: With that first cycle I had the worst night of my life—(*looking at Annabelle*) your life, certainly. I mean, I wasn't doing anything but watching.

They gave you that booster shot the night before they took the eggs. You're hoping for a whole bunch of eggs, and they're counting the whole time and . . .

Annabelle: . . . you're hoping for like, you know, six. That would be great! And they write on your hand, 'cause you're groggy, how many you got. There were 18!

Reid: I mean, that's like a world record.

Annabelle: They're in the lab behind me, and we could hear them talk. One will hand it to someone else in the lab 'cause, I guess, they've got to keep it in something, and they'll say "Egg!," or they'll say, "Nothing," or they'll have a word for when it's not an egg. So I kept hearing "Egg!", and "We got another one!", and one of the nurses said something like, "The Easter Bunny's here!" They were laughing. I could hear it.

So I asked, "So we're doing okay?"

The nurse said, "Yeah, you got a lot."

And I thought, "Great, we can get a family, 18 eggs! We've got to get two children out of that."

And we go home, so excited, 'cause it had worked so well and we had 18 eggs and how wonderful that is! When I got home I started getting sick. My stomach swelled— looked like it does right now—I mean, just huge. I was nauseated. I couldn't get up. I couldn't get comfortable. I couldn't go to the bathroom.

Reid: It was terrible.

Annabelle: We kept calling the doctor and, basically, they said we just had to make it through the night.

Reid: There was nausea—terrible nausea—and there was pain. I mean, she couldn't even walk. I remember that. We called all night. She spent the whole night in the bathtub, 'cause they told her to take a bath. Maybe that would help her feel better.

Annabelle: I don't think we realized how serious it was at the time.

Reid: No. Somewhere in the fine print it does say there's a danger of hyper-stimulation but it's 1%, and nobody had ever said anything to us about it.

What happens is your system goes crazy. Her ovary became as big as a grapefruit.

Annabelle: The medicine keeps working and makes your ovary grow and grow and grow. When we got to the doctor the next morning, I couldn't lay still when they went to put the eggs back in. Do you remember?

Reid: Mmmmmhmmmm.

Annabelle: I mean, I couldn't sit still, and you're supposed to lay there on your back while they go put the eggs back up in and I was supposed to lay there, still. (*Lots of laughter.*) We were trying this new thing and, hopefully, it would work. Then it was just the two of us. Now we've got a lot of running around and responsibilities. We were freer then, and that's all we thought.

Reid: She's always very positive. I wasn't as hopeful as she was.

Annabelle: I figured if you didn't think it was going to work, then why do it? So you may as well think it's going to work, and if it doesn't, then it doesn't.

Reid: Annabelle, being young, that helps, too. (*Reid turns to Annabelle.*) I think you were a prime candidate 'cause you've got strong hormones. I think what happened with that strong cycle the first time was that you didn't need all those hormone boosters for producing a lot of eggs to give you the best chance.

Annabelle: I got real sick.

Reid: I think you would have done fine without them or with a much lower dose. . .

Annabelle: . . . which they did in the next cycles.

Reid: They took five of the eggs and fertilized them. Now we had these embryos.

Annabelle: Some of the embryos are really healthy and look like they're going to make it. Others don't look very healthy. Any that are to be frozen really have to be very healthy to stand the freezing and then to be thawed.

Reid: She is back there, and they place the embryos in the womb. That's the next part of the procedure. It's then that they give you this booster shot that is designed to make the lining of the uterus receptive to the embryos and give them a better chance to implant and take. That's the thing that set her off.

Annabelle: After they placed these back in, your natural reaction is to lie absolutely still and don't do anything that would jostle that little embryo so as to give it every chance to implant. They say it actually doesn't make much difference if you ride a bicycle.

Reid: In Europe, I understand, in France, when they do this, you go back to work after this procedure but the doctors here said, "Lie down for 24 hours, stay on your back for 24 hours." She couldn't do that, she was retching. She was in the bathtub. It was terrible, and I was worried about her,

I was also mad as the dickens 'cause I knew that there wasn't any way that this could have possibly taken 'cause she had had such a violent night. I just felt confident she wasn't pregnant. We'd gone through all of this and here she was feeling terrible and certainly not pregnant.

Again, we called several times through the night—the doctor's office. We got the nursing service and answering service and told them what was happening and they kept saying, "Well a little bit of nausea is not unusual, and there may be a little pain." They weren't on the ball; they didn't diagnose it. Finally we said, "We're coming in in the morning." We arrived in the morning and saw another doctor who was there. He knew at once what it was, and admitted her to the hospital immediately. There was a risk of clotting and circulatory problems, and so they put these vibrators on her legs. All of a sudden the whole thing had gotten very, very serious and marginally life-threatening. So she was in the hospital for a few days. That was the low point of the whole works. Oh, it was just terrible. At any rate, that cycle was over.

I think they implanted five for the first time.

Annabelle: Four. We had 18 and nine of them fertilized. So they did four, and then that happened, and none of them worked.

Reid: Their whole notion is to get us pregnant. We finally said, "Whatever you think is right, do it." But I remember being worried that implanting four was silly.

Annabelle: And we were so new at it. We thought, "Well, four? Two would certainly work, wouldn't they?" I mean, so you could have twins anyway. Why waste 'em all, and why risk multiple birth? We could have had quadruplets, and we worried about that.

Reid: But then we just realized that we had wasted four embryos because of this mistake they'd made.

Annabelle: We were angry that it didn't work. When you hyperstimulate, your body is just working overtime to act like you are pregnant. So far as those embryos were concerned, it's a perfect place for them. I mean they have everything just the way it ought to be. Your uterus is all lush and perfect for accepting the embryo. So, yeah, we were upset. I was kind of shot, 'cause you're up so high thinking, "Eighteen eggs and nine fertilized and, to be sure, we're going to at least get one, probably two children!" Then that didn't work, and we were kind of more sad then mad—and scared.

Reid: Felt stupid in a way, explaining to people we were in the hospital because we were trying to get pregnant.

Annabelle: Just disgusted.

Reid: Good golly, nobody was here with us at the hospital. It was just us. I was thinking how they've got these vibrating things on your legs to try to keep the blood from clotting, and there you are all alone, and I am going to work and coming out there and . . . it was bad.

Annabelle: Then it kind of hit home. We both went, "Wait a minute! We still have frozen embryos."

Reid: Yeah, we had all those embryos in the bank.

Annabelle: We were thankful. A lot of people have to go through the whole thing again . . .

Reid: . . . or can't even. A lot of them have a problem where they can't ovulate and can't even produce the eggs so they can fertilize, and that's the difficult part of the process. We knew that all of that would work for us. I think if you can produce eggs and can produce healthy embryos, then you're about 90% there, in in vitro. Sometimes the sperm count's fine, and the eggs are fine, but there's some other problem.

Annabelle: Or if the sperm is a problem, I think that's almost harder to fix. I can't believe that was me going through all that.

Reid: It was terrible. We cried about it, I mean the two of us together. (*Reid looks at Annabelle.*) You cried a lot more than I did. And when you cried, it made me cry and I wasn't sure we'd get pregnant. And I hated that you had to go through all that stuff.

How did you feel about your role in producing the sperm?

Reid: Well, there was some anxiety about that.

Annabelle: (*Annabelle turns to Reid and smiles.*) You seemed fine to me. 'Cause you have to produce it at a certain time, they would let you do it either at the doctor's office and give it to 'em, or at home and take it over there. And we always did it at home and took it, and we'd have to keep it warm and I'd have it right near me. I'd hold on to it . . .

Reid: . . . driving through red lights trying to get it there in time.

Annabelle: Because if it gets a little bit cold, then some of them will die. We'd get 'em in a little jar and speed to the doctor and, you know, say, "Here they are!" They were always fine. They'd call him and say what a great thing and then he'd get all excited 'cause he'd had such a great, you know—performance.

Did you feel you couldn't ever go through this again?

Annabelle: No.

Reid: She got right back into it as soon as they would allow her to do it. We talked to the doctor about altering the drug regimen. He assured us that wouldn't be a problem. It was a great relief.

Annabelle: The next time we already had the eggs. We were able to use the frozen lot. All they do is just monitor you to find out when you ovulate, which is when your regular egg would be coming out. I think there's like 3 days, 72 hours that you can get pregnant. So they try to put that fertilized embryo back in at the time when you would have gotten pregnant normally and when your body is at the proper stage to receive it. So all I had to do the next time was the urine and the blood and the ultrasounds, and just go back and forth to the doctor.

And then, maybe, there's a booster shot at the end once they put them back in, a level of progesterone or something, to make sure it stays in.

There were five frozen eggs left. They call you and they say, "Okay, now we're thawing two," and we call back the next day to see if they survived the thaw. It's almost like they're already children 'cause you're calling to check on 'em to see how they're doing and did they make it. I remember we went there and walked in . . .

Reid: . . . that was a downer . . .

Annabelle: . . . and they said, "Well, only one survived," and we were like, "What?!"

We both got upset because I remember thinking they put four in last time, nothing worked, they're going to put one in this time. We've done all this—one is going in, you know, *one!* But then again, it only takes one. So there's that little bit of hope that you gotta hang on to. Maybe this is the one. So we started hanging on to that, and it didn't work.

I remember feeling . . . I basically started my period and I'd have to have the pregnancy test and I'd be crying, thinking, "I'm not pregnant. We don't need to do a test because I'm spotting."

But they have to do it, to confirm you're not pregnant, and let you know before they can send you out—just going in for a pregnancy test when you've started your period after you've been so up, thinking, "I know it's going to work. I know it is." And trying to be positive and then it doesn't work, you know it doesn't work, and you just go completely down to the bottom because you gotta go in and have them do a pregnancy test and they call you and tell you, "No, you're not" and you're having this big old period. I *know* I'm not, you know!

You'd probably get a little mad if you could; I mean, it's nobody's fault. It just didn't work. I remember I would cry a lot when it wouldn't work. But then you'd think so hard and then you'd kind of imagine that you're pregnant.

You know, people will say, "Well, if you feel this way and if you have this. . . ." I'd have all those things and I'm probably making 'em up. You know, "I'm kind of tired, maybe I *am* pregnant." And then it wouldn't work.

But we still had some more frozen. At this point, the family of nine from the 18 eggs was just dwindling. We waited our time and went back through the cycle, back to the urine, back to the blood, back to the shot, and all that.

Reid: And now it's all getting old—and we're losing faith.

Annabelle: Right. Well, this is scary because if these don't work this is it. They thawed them, and we went in, and they put 'em in. It was three. And then, you wait your time.

But this time it did work; I remember I didn't have any of that spotting. I started thinking, "Maybe it could be," and then we went in for the test. You go home and the doctors' office calls you between four and whatever, and you're sitting by the phone and you're all nervous. (*Annabelle turns to Reid.*) Where were you when they called me?

Reid: I don't remember. But I do remember thinking we were hopeful 'cause you felt a little bit different. And our mothers would check in.

Annabelle: Everybody knew the days. It was kind of a problem. I kind of wished everybody hadn't known, 'cause when it didn't work, it's not much fun telling 25 people that call up, "No, it didn't work."

This time the doctor's office called and said, yes, I was pregnant. I remember touching my stomach, just thinking, "I'm pregnant," you know, "Me, I'm pregnant." I just couldn't believe it, and then all the family called, and we told everybody it worked.

Reid: We didn't believe it until we went in and had an ultrasound and saw the heart beating. And at that point they tell you it's like any other pregnancy.

Annabelle: Ninety percent chance of nothing happening.

Reid: Ninety-eight percent to have a normal delivery and they chalk it up on their statistics as a successful pregnancy. I would say almost a year from the start of it all.

We always felt we were fortunate 'cause we'd go in that waiting room and all manner of 40-year-old women were trying hard, and no telling how long they'd been trying.

Annabelle: They'd say, "How old are you?"

And I'd say, "27."

And they'd kind of glare, like, "Please, I am 40 and can't even make one egg and you're worried. . . ." Most of 'em were 35 and older. I think most people go through years of trying, then go to the doctor, have to go through all this process of medicines and stuff, and they get burned out.

When did you make the decision to have another child and go through this again?

Reid: We knew we wanted to have sibling companions—pretty close together. We were encouraged 'cause we knew it would work since it had worked once.

Annabelle: Right. So it was a whole different feeling the second time. I was almost cocky by then. I'd walk in there and if it didn't work, it's okay. I have a precious little boy at home.

Reid: We'd take Neil with us to the doctor.

Annabelle: Yeah, and they were all so sweet and they'd love to see him. We'd send 'em pictures.

Reid: And we'd tell all the people in the waiting room that he was an in vitro baby. . .

Annabelle: . . . and they'd get excited and like, "Tell us how it happened!" We'd tell them our whole story and they're like, "Oh see, it can work!" And the husbands would be there, and the husbands would be kind of watching Reid, and I'd think, "It'll work if you just stick with it." But I guess it doesn't for everybody.

Our boys are 2 years apart. We tried two times for Ned.

Reid: We started when Neil was about a year 'cause we knew it might take a while.

Annabelle: We went through it all at a whole different level. We only made six eggs. That was a shock—only one had

worked from 18 and now there were just six! But most
people make about that many.

Reid: But we had Neil at that point so it wasn't . . .

Annabelle: . . . so desperate. He kept our minds off of it. He's
wanting juice and gotta go outside and all this kind of
stuff and we're going to the park, playing. Life was a lot
better now. We have a little boy, and if we never have another one it's okay. I was just a whole different person.
Before I'd kind of tip-toe into the doctors' office, look
around, shy and scared, and this time—"Hey!" They put
the last three back in the second time, and one worked.

Reid was at work and I remember writing this little
note, this little poem. It was like Neil talking, "Daddy,
we're going to have a little brother or sister."

Reid: Yeah, I still got it somewhere. Gosh, that was a thrill! I
remember being even more surprised that time 'cause I
assumed it wouldn't work, and that would be the end. And
the other happy ending that we would have no more embryos . . .

Annabelle: . . . to have to worry about what to do with . . .

Reid: . . . to go through that concern. We've got friends
or we know people who have . . .

Annabelle: . . . she had twins from the in vitro, and she has
like five frozen, and she doesn't' want to use them all . . .

Reid: . . . and she's worried about what to do with 'em.
I don't know how much that would have bothered us, but
we don't have to worry about it.

Were there any ethical or moral issues that you struggled with?

Annabelle: A little bit. I remember in the reading that they
gave you before you do it. They talked about all that. And
you have to sign . . .

Reid: . . . a release or waiver where you each agree that
you have no rights to the embryos without the partner's

consent. So if we had disagreed about how to use the embryos at some point, then they weren't obligated to give them to either one of us. If you have them left over, the options are to use them, or to allow them to use them for science experiments, or to destroy them.

Annabelle: Or to give them to other people to use them. It's a form of adoption. If we had had embryos left over, we would have had to pay a fee every year to keep them in cryopreservation.

Reid: Whenever I read in the paper about 60-year-old women being impregnated in Europe, or about partners arguing over 'em, that gets out there on the edge of ethical dilemmas for me. I have absolutely no ethical problems with basic in vitro fertilization for a married couple where we're not trying to engineer sex. I do see concerns with where the technology and the science goes. I worry that because of ethical dilemmas there might end up being some restrictions . . .

Annabelle: . . . for people who are just trying to have a child . . .

Reid: . . . for folks like us. Lord knows, our lives are wonderful. We'd have adapted to whatever we had to. We might have adopted and that might have been a great thing for us. We can't quite feature ourselves not having children.

Annabelle: We would have done something.

Reid: But the point is it made a huge difference in our lives, and it's just unbelievable to think that 15 years ago the first one of these babies was born. There's a woman who works in our office, a good friend, who never had children and she was probably in our exact situation. I'm not sure she was ever diagnosed. Around holidays I can see her get sad. I can see the emptiness, in a way, as she listens to other people, her contemporaries, talking about their kids getting married and all that.

Annabelle: Could have been us.

Reid: Yeah, at another place, another time, it could have been. So it would be a lousy thing. I once worked with a lady who couldn't have children.

Annabelle: We made her an appointment and she went.

Reid: You referred her to Dr. Borne . . .

Annabelle: . . . but she couldn't afford it . . .

Reid: . . . the tragedy of that! We were lucky. We could afford it.

Annabelle: It was about the same amount of time, a little over a year later, that I got pregnant. I still can't believe that. We've never had birth control. I never had to take the pill or any of that kind of stuff.

All of a sudden my period didn't come ,and I thought, "What in the world!" It didn't occur to me I might be pregnant. It just couldn't happen. I mean, after all this. I started feeling kind of funny and then I'd forget it and 3 more days would go by and then my breasts would get tender and I thought, "Now that happened when I was pregnant."

That was the first thing that made me think something. I was feeling tired and I thought, "It's been 2 weeks and my period should have been, and it hasn't."

Reid: We thought . . .

Annabelle: . . . we were happily finished with our family.

Reid: We rationalized that two was a good number, and who in the world would have three anyway?

Annabelle: Oh, I know it! I snuck to the drugstore and bought one of those pregnancy tests and didn't tell Reid. I remember paying the lady, the woman. My face was blood red. I'm like, "I'm so embarrassed I am doing this." I shoved it in my pocketbook as fast as I could, got home, hid it in my drawer, still embarrassed I had done that. My period still didn't come and I thought, "Well, I bought it. I've got it. I'm just doing it."

About 3 o'clock in the morning, I woke up and I thought, "Well, now I could go do it. Nobody would know I was doing it and think I'm crazy for doing this." So I went in the bathroom and did the little test. It had a little chart on it, and it says that if it's kind of this color—pale blue—you might be pregnant. I mean, it was navy blue!

And I just went, "Oh, my gosh," and burst into tears. I couldn't believe it.

I went into the bedroom and I was like, "Are you asleep?"

He's like, "Yeah, it's 3 o'clock, what are you doing?"

And I said, "Well, I need to tell you something, you need to sit up."

And he's like, "What?"

And I said, "Well, you know those tests you can go buy that tell you if you're pregnant?" I felt like I needed to tell him a little bit before I said, "We're pregnant." 'Cause he didn't even know the first thing about this.

I said, "Well, I went to the drugstore the other day and I bought one; and I just did it in the bathroom and it said 'yes.'" (*Annabelle turns to Reid.*) You were just like, "Hold on, hold on." You sat up and you were like, "What are you talking about? What's going on?" So then I told him the whole thing about how I felt funny and all that, and I was all excited thinking, "I'm pregnant."

And he's more rational and said, "It's probably in your tube or somewhere that it's not supposed to be, because of all the mess down there. I mean they've already done the dye test, nothing can get through there." He immediately got us all alarmed.

So we went to the doctor the next day and he said, "I agree with Reid. You're probably not pregnant, Annabelle, so just calm down. We'll find out where it is and we'll take care of it." It was too early to really figure it out, so we had to wait a few days. I didn't know what to think, get excited 'cause I'm pregnant or worry about having to have an operation to get this tube out or.... We just didn't know what to think.

We waited our time and they did the ultrasound and there it was, right in the middle of my uterus where it was supposed to be. I still just can't believe it.

Reid: The doctor couldn't believe it.

Annabelle: It occurred to me I could have gotten pregnant on my own the second time.

Reid: This will always bring the specter of whether we ever had to do in vitro in the first place.

Annabelle: The first time I think we did.

Reid: Goodness knows the doctors are perplexed by it. They can't believe it.

Annabelle: Yeah, I mean, Dr. Borne couldn't understand how that happened, and I still can't, after seeing the dye not going anywhere. But I think pregnancy's the best thing for endometriosis. It stops it.

Reid: Well, she had a C-section with each baby, and each time a doctor who assisted in the C-section and didn't know her case history—each time just looked in there and said, "Whoohooo, how'd *you* get pregnant? This is a mess in here."

Annabelle: And jokingly I said, "Clean some of it out if you can." And one of them drained a bunch of fluid, and maybe they did a little bit, or just got the right scar tissue out of the way.

Earlier, Reid said, "Family means a lot to us." Could you talk a bit more about that?

Reid: Well, Annabelle just has one sister and I've got two sisters, but we both grew up in very traditional households. Neither of our mothers worked while we were at home. They were full-time moms to each of us, and I guess what we envisioned was what everybody envisions—to some extent something like what they knew growing up.

Annabelle: I thought, after you get married it was just the next step.

Reid: Neither one of us had a passion. What I do for a living, my professional work, is important to me, but it's below family on my priority list. We couldn't have derived enough satisfaction without kids. Neither one of us could imagine life without that focus. (*Reid turns to Annabelle.*) You like what you do, graphic design, but you weren't driven or motivated to make that a total career.

Annabelle: If we had tried forever and none of this worked, we would have adopted. I mean we just wouldn't go through life without children. I know that for both of us. We were going to get them one way or another.

How did your parents feel about what you were doing?

Annabelle: They were real supportive, worried to death we would not be able to have children, and both our mothers read everything. The doctors gave us this big packet, huge, to read about it, and our moms both read it so they could know what we were doing.

Now, our grandparents are another story. I think they thought . . . I'm not sure they still know . . . they think the whole thing is weird.

Reid: Well, they're thrilled about it.

Annabelle: They're so grateful we have the children.

Reid: Your grandfather loves to tell people, "Let me tell you something about these two," but I don't think he even knows what he's talking about. Matter of fact, I think he thinks it's even more fantastic than it is. I think he thinks maybe the baby grew 9 months in a test tube or something.

Annabelle: Yeah, and you try to tell him, but it's so foreign to them, and my grandmother, she knows something went on. I think for a while they thought we used other people's sperm and other people's eggs, and so they weren't sure. They're the funniest ones.

If somebody came to you and said, "I'm in your situation, what would you tell me to do?'

Annabelle: To do in vitro or not? I would say, "Try everything you can." My sister is at that point. She has an ethical problem with it, I think.

Reid: Religious.

Annabelle: Yeah. To her I say, "Why not? The help is out there. Go get it, and just try." She's done the medicines and all that, but not in vitro. She feels God is telling her to not do that right now. My sister doesn't have endometriosis, and they don't really know why she hasn't gotten pregnant. Nobody's told her she can't conceive on her own, and maybe she can. So she's holding on to that right now.

Will you tell your children that they were conceived through in vitro fertilization?

Reid: Sure.

Annabelle: I'd rather they did not know.

Reid: But it's so commonplace now. It's not a big deal.

Annabelle: I don't want him to think he's different. I don't want his friends to say anything.

Reid: I used to worry about that. Neil had a medical problem when he was 5 or 6 weeks old, totally unrelated, and he had to have surgery. The doctors explained that it had absolutely nothing to do with in vitro. Although I knew intellectually that it didn't, I felt sure other people who knew thought, "Uhnhunh, they had one of those funny babies."

I worried there might be some stigma because all our friends knew. But now, 4 years later, I don't worry about any of that stuff. I used to also worry that he was so precious to us. I felt sure more precious to us than any other child born out there 'cause we'd been through so much, and I worried that I'd never even let him go out in the front yard without being worried he'd run in the street, and I'd be overly protective. At this point, I treat him just like any other parent who loves their children. Both of us do.

Annabelle: Several people have called me who are having to go through it. I'm happy to tell them the whole thing, step by step. I remember that I called a stranger. I didn't even know her. I called her on the phone and asked her about it right before we did it. I said, "I'm Annabelle Martin. We're about to do in vitro and they're getting ready to take my eggs out tomorrow and I'm a nervous wreck." I didn't know if it was going to hurt, or what it was going to feel like. She went through the whole thing, explained it all to me, and was so nice. I remember appreciating that so much. So, yeah, if anybody ever calls to talk about it, I'm more than happy to.

Reid: Our family is so normal now, absolutely indistinguishable from any other family.

Conclusion

As far back as we can know, family life has been the most efficient and satisfying design for human living. If it is to survive as the most viable system for maintaining the individual in harmonious balance with society, it must respond appropriately to the external forces impinging on its fundamental character.

The twentieth century has been marked by the intensity of its wars, nuclear threats, violent social movements, and an attenuation of values and structure.

Seemingly unrelated factors pervade and impact on our lives. Many are caught in the tenacious and venal grip of the drug business. At the same time, advances in technology and all the sciences, communication and transportation capabilities, and multicultural exposure leading to an ever-expanding global view, are among the significant movements and powerful forces which continue to mold the thinking of individuals and alter the tenets of society. Much of what we heard from our interviewees reflects this change and turmoil.

The roles attributed to males and females in the past have become less distinct as the sexual revolution and issues of feminism, gay and lesbian rights, and the daily involvement of fathers in the lives of their children more assuredly move toward center stage. Changes in the world occur with stunning swiftness. Alliances dissolve while others form which were unimaginable before the latter half of this century. The basic unit of human relations, the family, is altered.

Sean finds that, as a gay man, he and his partner experience difficulties and frustration trying to adopt a child. He describes how many times he was rejected by agencies with the explanation, ". . . this child needs an intact traditional family." At this point, Sean exclaims, "Give me a break! How many intact traditional families are there?"

It is a valid point. Although there are no data about traditional family intactness, it is hardly a secret that in America a two-parent traditional household in no way guarantees that the children of such families are being raised in a healthy or even compassionate environment.

Rearing children, nurturing the young, providing them with a solid start in life is a formidable job. The numbers of psychiatrists, psychologists, counselors, social workers and clergy who are engaged in family and child therapy and who deal with incidences of domestic violence, and emotional and sexual abuses, all sound a warning. Structure without appropriate content is manifestly unsatisfactory, and frequently catastrophic when it comes to family, and is, consequently, of major concern to society.

The apathy, neglect, substance abuse, and street violence that occurs at an earlier and earlier age is rampant in our country. This suggests that the family, whatever its constituency, needs help in dealing with the enormous pressures of today's world.

Governments can and do provide programs that are more or less helpful depending on the philosophy of the party in power. Local communities, activist groups, and the private individuals who create mechanisms and environments which will ensure necessary supports for child and family, however, are closer to answering basic needs. Many of the interviews reflect the voluntary involvement of one individual in helping another. Many more are attempting to create their version of a family today, when the traditional family is evidencing cracks in its structure.

While these people want to make a difference, they are usually focused on the children in their lives for primarily personal reasons. But in the broader sense, the hope of future societies, indeed of the civilized world, rests with just such individual commitment—to give children the opportunities they deserve from the start, so that one day these children will be proud citizens and make their own contributions to our civilization.

The importance of tradition cannot be dismissed. Certain traditions are so much a part of our lives that we don't even think about them as such. Most human beings need to know that some things will not change. Some traditions will gradually be let go by some segments of the population to be replaced by new ones. Basically, what is at work is the human need to express one's individuality in a highly complex and competitive world and still be part of that larger entity which is the human race.

The safest, surest, most constant place for one's beliefs and dreams to reside is in one's family. There is an overriding conviction that if that place is not there, it should be.

For many, it's not there.

When this occurs and the need to realize one's dreams and actualize one's beliefs prevail, an outlet to express it is sought and the boundaries of our culture are stretched. Those who persevere are the pioneers who point to another way. The stories presented here afford a closer encounter between the reader and individuals who are redefining family.

Franklin asks the question, "What right do any of us have to bring a child into the world in a family that is not going to be traditional?" The answer may be hidden in a series of questions: How can we take a measure of the worth of the new lifestyles as compared with the tried traditional except by asking if there is less dysfunction in the family unit and its members. Is there more harmony, better education, less violence, more personal productivity, less substance abuse, sexual abuses, and so on, comparing and assessing the extent of the ills and their root causes that plague so many in modern times?

The oral accounts in this book pose questions of decency and respectability, of ethics and morality, and of the reciprocal effects that new configurations in human relationships will have on family and society. What determines the sanctity of the family? What might violate the integrity of the individual members? Most of all, what about the children?

The answers, of course, await the maturation of the next generation. A freer composition in the structure of family life is being implemented in various ways and will eventually and inevitably change our mores. It is too early to know just how society will deal with and accept or reject some of the more radical experiments being tried in family life throughout the country.

Nevertheless, what society calls untraditional or "alternative" is gradually entering the consciousness of more and more Americans, affecting a significant number and altering their way of life. Clearly, the emergence of new traditions is what we are seeing. It is part of the historical continuum in the evolution of family life.

The reasons for the decision to be a parent and the meaning and ramifications of such a choice are the unifying threads that tie the diverse personalities presented here together and, in effect, tie them to the rest of humanity. What remains unknown for the present is whether the child born of this decision and his or her family will have been served appropriately and advantageously. Time will tell. The ways in which the rest of society thinks about and adjusts to all of this requires an expansion of understanding and broader acceptance of human behavior.

Like the metaphorical willow tree in the hurricane, a seemingly fragile entity subjected to elemental forces, the family is strongest when it is flexible and is able to bend with the winds of change without being uprooted—a difficult challenge in these complicated and shifting times.

References

ACT UP. (Eds.) (1990). *Womens' AIDS and activism*. Boston: South End Press.

American Association of Retired Persons. (1994, September 8). *Grandparent-headed households and their grandchildren*. Washington, DC: Grandparent Information Center.

Bartholet, E. (1990). *Family bonds, adoption and the politics of parenting*. New York: Houghton Mifflin.

Center on Addiction and Substance Abuse. (1994, June). *Substance Abuse and Women on Welfare*. New York: Columbia University.

Centers for Disease Control and Prevention. (1994). *Recommendations of the U.S. public health service task force on the use of zidovudine to reduce perinatal transmission of human immunodeficiency virus*. (Morbidity and Mortality Weekly Report; 43, no. RR-11). Washington, DC: Government Printing Office.

Centers for Disease Control and Prevention. (1994). *The HIV/AIDS surveillance report, U.S. HIV and AIDS cases*. (Year End Edition, 6, no. 2). Washington, DC: Government Printing Office.

Chesler, P. (1994). *Patriarchy*. Monroe, ME: Common Courage Press.

Child Welfare League of America. (1992). *The youngest of the homeless 11. A survey of boarder babies in selected hospitals in the United States*. Washington, DC: National Association of Public Hospitals.

Gingerich, J. (1993, Fall). Engineering embryos. *Smith Alumnae Quarterly, LXXXIV, no. 3*, pp. 10–14. Northampton, MA.

Gonsiorek, J.C. & Weinrich, J.D. (1991). *Homosexuality, research implications for public policy*. Newbury Park, CA: Sage Publications, Inc.

Johnson, D. (1993, August 31). More and more the single parent is dad. *The New York Times*, pp. 1,15.

Mosher, W.D., & Pratt, W.F. (1990). *Fecundity and infertility in the United States, 1965–88*. (Advance data. Vital and Health Statistics; no. 192). Hyattsville, MD : National Center for Health Statistics.

National Center for Health Statistics. (1994). *Births to unmarried women: 1970–1991*. (Vital Statistics of the United States, annual; Monthly Vital Statistics Report; and unpublished data). Washington, DC: U.S. Government Printing Office.

Rix, S.E. (Ed.) (1990). *The American woman 1990–91*. New York: W.W. Norton.

Sisco, C.B., & Pearson, C.L. (1994) Prevalence of alcoholism and drug abuse among female AFDC recipients. *Health and Social Work, 19* (1). 75–77.

Stewart, B. (1995, January 8). Tough choices: In vitro vs. adoption. *The New York Times*. Sec. 13, p. 1.

Tauber, C. (Ed.) (1991). *Statistical handbook on women in America*. New York: Oryx Press.

U.S. Bureau of the Census. (1930). *1930 census of population, social and economic characteristics*. Washington, DC: U. S. Government Printing Office.

U.S. Bureau of the Census. (1960). *U. S. census of population 1960*. (Special Reports: Families). Washington, DC: U. S. Government Printing Office.

U.S. Bureau of the Census. (1960). *1960 statistical abstracts*. Washington, DC: U. S. Government Printing Office.

U. S. Bureau of the Census. (1990). *1990 census of population, social and economic characteristics*. Washington, DC: U. S. Government Printing Office.

U. S. Bureau of the Census. (1993). *Fertility of American women: June 1992*. (Current Population Reports, Series P-20, no. 470). Washington, DC: U. S. Government Printing Office.

U.S. Bureau of the Census. (1993). *The national data book, statistical abstracts of the United States*. Washington, DC: U. S. Government Printing Office.

U. S. Bureau of the Census. (1994). *The national data book, statistical abstracts of the United States*. Washington, DC: U. S. Government Printing Office.

Womens Action Coalition. (Eds.). (1993). *The facts about women*. New York: The New Press.

INDEX

Index

S *Springer Publishing Company*

ANNUAL REVIEW OF GERONTOLOGY AND GERIATRICS, *Volume 13*

Kinship, Aging, and Social Change

George L. Maddox, PhD, and M. Powell Lawton, PhD, Editors

This volume examines the demographic and socioeconomic changes of the past few decades and their effects on the aging population and the family unit. The expert contributors address topics ranging from the latest theory and research findings to the changing balance of work and families, as well as patterns of kinship.

Contents:

1993   280pp   0-8261-6495-1   hardcover

536 Broadway, New York, NY 10012-3955 • (212) 431-4370 • Fax (212) 941-7842

§P *Springer Publishing Company*

ADULT INTERGENERATIONAL RELATIONS
Effects of Societal Change

Vern L. Bengtson, PhD, **K. Warner Schaie,** PhD, and **Linda Burton,** PhD

Drs. Bengtson, Schaie, and Burton have assembled impressive contributions from specialists in aging research to examine the impact of social change on intergenerational relationships across the adult lifespan. As a special feature, each chapter is followed by expert commentaries which offer different perspectives on each topic. For academics, students, researchers, and other professionals concerned with social gerontology and family studies.

Contents:

- The Demography of Changing Intergenerational Relationships, *J. Farkas and D.P. Hogan*
- Intergenerational Continuity and Change in Rural America, *G.H. Elder, Jr., L. Rudkin, and Rand D. Conger*
- Intergenerational Patterns of Providing Care in African-American Families with Teenage Childbearers: Emergent Patterns in an Ethnographic Study, *L.M. Burton*
- Kinship and Individuation: Cross-Cultural Perspectives on Intergenerational Relations, *C.L. Fry*
- Perceived Family Environments Across Generations, *K.W. Schaie and S.L. Willis*
- The "Intergenerational Stake" Hypothesis Revisited: Parent-Child Differences in Perceptions of Relationships 20 Years Later, *R. Giarrusso, N.M. Stallings, and V.L. Bengtson*

1994   328pp   0-8261-8560-6   hardcover

536 Broadway, New York, NY 10012-3955 • (212) 431-4370 • Fax (212) 941-7842

S *Springer Publishing Company*

HOMICIDE IN FAMILIES AND OTHER SPECIAL POPULATIONS
Ann Goetting, PhD

"The public health perspective that Professor Goetting describes in this book and to which her research is directly applicable represents a new vision of how Americans can work together to prevent violence...This volume provides the proper knowledge about patterns of primary homicide and clues to the actions needed to prevent this problem. As the demand for action to prevent violence in our society increases, this book will become an increasingly valuable resource for researchers, policy-makers, public health workers, students, and, in fact, for everyone concerned with the problem of violence."
— **James A. Mercy,** PhD
Centers for Disease Control and Prevention

Partial Contents:

I: Female Victims. Introduction • Female Victims of Homicide: A Portrait of Their Killers and Circumstances of Their Death • Men Who Kill Their Mates: A Profile

II: Homicidal Women. Patterns of Homicide Among Women

III: Females as Victims and Offenders. Patterns of Marital Homicide: A Comparison of Husbands and Wives • When Females Kill One Another: The Exceptional Case

IV: Child Victims. Child Victims of Homicide: A Portrait of Their Killers and the Circumstances of Their Deaths • When Parents Kill Their Young Children: Detroit 1982–1986

V: Homicidal Children. Patterns of Homicide Among Children

VI: The Elderly Offender. Patterns of Homicide Among the Elderly • In Conclusion: Some Preventive Considerations
1995 232pp 0-8261-8770-6 hardcover

536 Broadway, New York, NY 10012-3955 • (212) 431-4370 • Fax (212) 941-7842

§P *Springer Publishing Company*

INTERGENERATIONAL LINKAGES
Hidden Connections in American Society

Vern L. Bengtson, PhD,
Robert A. Harootyan, MS, MA, Editors

Published in cooperation with the American Association of Retired Persons (AARP), this volume contains the results of a national study intended to better our understanding of the many linkages between generations in American society. This study, undertaken by eminent researchers in gerontology, unveiled a complex set of attitudes and behaviors — hidden connections — between different age groups in our society, including relations and conflicts between parents and their children, and between entire families and their communities.

Contents:

1994   352pp   0-8261-8670-X   hardcover

536 Broadway, New York, NY 10012-3955 • (212) 431-4370 • Fax (212) 941-7842